The Power of Sacrifice

IAN BRADLEY

DARTON·LONGMAN+TODD

First published in 1995 by
Darton, Longman & Todd Ltd,
1 Spencer Court,
140–142 Wandsworth High Street,
London SW18 4JJ

ISBN 0–232–52057–7

A catalogue record for this book is available from the
British Library

Phototypeset in Postscript Garamond
by Intype, London

Printed and bound in Great Britain by
Page Bros, Norwich

Contents

iii

Preface

I am very grateful to several friends and colleagues who have helped me in my reading and thinking around a vast and difficult topic. David Burgess gave me valuable insights into Hindu thought on sacrifice and made helpful comments on a draft of Chapter 2. Another Aberdeen colleague, Howard Marshall, helped me sharpen my ideas on the approach to sacrifice in the New Testament, not least by letting me loose on one of his honours classes. A very early draft of Chapter 8 formed a paper that I read to a meeting of the Green Theology Group at the University of Leeds in May 1993. I am grateful to Jacqui Stewart for inviting me to address the group and to those members who offered constructive criticism of what I had to say, notably Ben De La Mere and Jonathan Clatworthy. I also benefited considerably from more detailed comments from Dennis Richards.

I first floated some of the ideas that are central to this book in a sermon which I preached at St Columba's Church of Scotland in London in March 1993. I must thank the minister there, John McIndoe, both for inviting me to occupy the pulpit and for his kind comments about what I had to say.

Iain Torrance, Michael Hare-Duke, Ruth Gipps and John Winckler have directed me to particular books and I have benefited from talking with James Gray, Charles Sherlock, James Bradby, David Young and Geoffrey Rowell. Gregory Morris nobly assisted me with the translation of some particularly difficult passages of Hebrew. I also owe a particular debt of gratitude to William Storrar, a fellow 'enthusiast' for sacrifice (there aren't many of us around!) and much-valued soul friend during our time as new boys in the academic world.

The Research Committee of the Faculty of Arts and Divinity at the University of Aberdeen kindly awarded me a grant which enabled the timely completion of this book. I have received consistent support for the project from the head of the Department of Divinity with Religious Studies, Professor David Fergusson. I must also record my thanks to Lawson Brown, minister of St Leonard's Church, St Andrews, and to the kirk session for their kindness in letting me reproduce details from the window 'Our Lord and Three Apostles' by Alec Walker on the front cover.

As always, the staff at Darton, Longman & Todd have been extremely helpful and pleasant to work with in the preparation of this book. It began life as the 'baby' of Mary Jean Pritchard before she acquired a more demanding and, I am sure, far more rewarding one in the person of Anna. It was then taken over by Jane Williams. To both these midwives, and to all the other long-suffering folk at DLT whom I have badgered and bothered during its gestation and birth, my sincere thanks.

For permission to reproduce copyright material I am grateful to Bishop John V. Taylor (the prayer beginning 'Father, if the hour has come'); Nicol Blount (extracts from his privately published booklet, *The Eucharist – Not a Static Concept*); Janet Martin Soskice (extracts from her unpublished paper, 'Blood and defilement'); John Moses (extracts from *The Sacrifice of God: A Holistic View of Atonement*); George Mackay Brown (extracts from *Magnus*) and Robin Gill (extract from his lecture 'Beyond self-interest').

The credo from Sheila Cassidy's book, *Sharing the Darkness: The Spirituality of Caring*, is reproduced by permission of the publishers, Darton, Longman & Todd. The words of 'Now the green blade riseth' by J. M. C. Crum are reprinted from the *Oxford Book of Carols* by permission of Oxford University Press and the two verses from Thomas Kinsella's 'Carol' from *The Deer's Cry* by permission of the Four Courts Press, Dublin.

As far as I am aware, all my other quotations from copyright material fall within the limits for which permission is not required. If I have inadvertently quoted more than the permitted amount in any case, I can only apologise and promise to rectify my omission in any future edition.

Except where otherwise stated, all quotations from the Bible are from the Revised Standard Version (copyright: Division of Christian Education of the National Council of the Churches of Christ in the United States of America).

For various reasons this has not been an easy book to write. Nor, I imagine, will it prove an easy read. Its subject matter is uncongenial and more than a little forbidding. Both the idea and the reality of sacrifice disturb and discomfort us and I suspect that this study will have that effect on its readers, as it has on its author. Yet it is not without consolation and hope. I can only ask those who are accustomed to rather lighter and gentler musings from my pen (or rather from my aged and faithful Amstrad to which I also pay grateful tribute here) to bear with me as I wrestle with a darker side to the faith that we confess and the world in which we live.

Ian Bradley
St Andrews

Introduction

The love that dares not speak its name: the riddle of sacrifice

Sacrifice is at once the most inescapable, impenetrable and off-putting theme in Christianity. It is central to Jesus' own teaching and to the way that his life and death have traditionally been understood and given meaning by theologians. The word 'sacrifice', used both as a verb and as a noun, occurs 213 times in the Bible. It figures prominently in the eucharistic liturgies of virtually every church and recurs again and again in the familiar hymns which have been so important in shaping popular faith and theology and which now form the residual spiritual folk culture of our so-called post-Christian society.

Yet there is often something rather strange and forbidding about the references to sacrifice in these hymns which we still sing with such gusto. We are pulled up short, and if we pause to reflect on them surely also both discomforted and more than a little puzzled, when we come to the lines in Isaac Watts' 'When I survey the wondrous Cross':

> All the vain things that charm me most,
> I sacrifice them to his blood.

There is a similarly jarring effect when we come to the third verse of Henry Hart Milman's otherwise rather jaunty Palm Sunday hymn:

> Ride on! Ride on in majesty!
> The winged squadrons of the sky
> Look down with sad and wondering eyes
> To see the approaching sacrifice.

1

The first verse of Thomas Ken's bright morning hymn, 'Awake, my soul, and with the sun' also ends on a note that sounds strange and rather unattractive to modern ears:

> Shake off dull sloth, and joyful rise
> To pay thy morning sacrifice.

That very brief opening excursion into hymnody (and there will be more to follow) indicates, if nothing else, the wide variety of connotations that the word 'sacrifice' has had for Christians. It can refer to our own offerings of praise and thanksgiving to God (as in 'Awake my soul'), to a more specific surrender of selfish pleasures and distractions to Christ ('When I survey') or to Christ's own self-offering on the Cross ('Ride on! Ride on'). The application of sacrificial language to the events of the passion and crucifixion continues to be a marked feature of much contemporary hymn-writing. Graham Kendrick's 'Meekness and majesty' talks of Jesus 'suffering to give us life, conquering through sacrifice' while in 'The servant king' he uses the vivid image of 'the scars that speak of sacrifice'. Yet even the simple and straightforward language of these two justly popular modern worship songs raises questions about what we mean when we describe Jesus' death as a sacrifice, such as who exactly is making the sacrifice, to whom it is offered and just where its efficacy lies.

The theme of sacrifice is not, of course, peculiar to Christianity. It is fundamental to both the beliefs and the practices of most of the world's religions, especially the primal religions associated with so-called primitive societies. It seems to point to a disturbing and mysterious world of darkness and violence. We need to acknowledge and confront this side of our existence: indeed, much recent work by anthropologists has suggested that ritual sacrifice is an essential mechanism for channeling and neutralizing violence and disorder in society. Maybe, too, we should follow other religious traditions in accepting that sacrifice is a mystery which we can never fully comprehend. One of the most important books in the great collection of Hindu hymns, the *Rig Veda*, is enigmatically entitled *Asya Vāmasya*, or the *Riddle of the Sacrifice*.

Yet the theme of sacrifice is too fundamental in both our Scriptures and our faith for Christians to leave wholly unexplored and undiscussed. The trouble is that the consequences of trying to unpack its meaning have too often been bitter argument and division. The fundamental split between liberals and conservatives within the Church arises to a large extent from different interpretations of the doctrine of atonement and different understandings of the nature of the sacrifice of Christ. The historic division in Western Christendom between Catholics and Protestants has been perpetuated by continuing disagreement about the sacrificial nature of the Eucharist.

It is hardly surprising in view of all the dissension and dispute which it has provoked that several Christian theologians have suggested that the whole notion of sacrifice should be abandoned. They argue that it belongs to a particular era of human evolution and religious development which is now over and that it is an unhelpful and inappropriate concept for understanding or living the Christian gospel in the modern world. There are other very good reasons why many contemporary Christians are unhappy with the idea of sacrifice. It seems to take us back to an unappealing world of ritual slaughter and cultic blood-shedding to appease and pacify an angry deity. It is often bound up with notions of substitution and propitiation, which many people now find understandably repellent, and with a doctrine of atonement which portrays Jesus' death on the Cross in crude legalistic or commercial terms as a ransom paid to God for our sin. Its stress on denial and giving up seems inappropriate to the life-enhancing and affirming message of the gospel. As Frances Young comments at the beginning of her important book on the subject, 'Sacrifice does not appear at first sight to be a potential "growth point" for interpreting the gospel now. It conjures up memories of warm appeals to wash in the blood of the Lamb and cold requirements to give up meat for Lent'.[1]

3

My aim in this book is to recover and restate the centrality of sacrifice not just in the Christian *kerygma*, and therefore in the faith, life and worship of all who call themselves Christians, but also in the very constitution of the universe and the basic processes of life. Far from feeling that the concept of sacrifice is outmoded, I believe that it has never been more relevant than in our present age when science is revealing the extent to which all life is dependent on surrender and death, when the very survival of our species and our planet depends on human self-limitation and self-denial and when we are waking up to the enormity of the havoc that has been wreaked morally, socially and culturally over the last few decades by the widespread pursuit of individual gratification and indulgence and the illusory cults of independence and self-sufficiency.

Sacrifice, like death, is one of the great taboo subjects of the late twentieth century. It is certainly the love that dares not speak its name. The notion of a costly sharing in what T. S. Eliot called 'a lifetime's death in love' is wholly missing from the self-centred romanticized package of instant sexual gratification and conspicuous consumption which is presented to us daily as the essence of the 'good life' in popular magazines, television soap operas and advertising slogans. Our economy is ordered on the principle that any kind of sacrifice, any limitation, surrender or postponement of selfish pleasures, is not just undesirable but wrong. It is built on credit, on the 'live now, pay later' principle exemplified by the little plastic flexible friends who 'take the waiting out of wanting'. This has led to the emergence of what has been described as the 'I want and what I want I get generation'.[2] A similar approach underlies modern psychology and educational theory and the so-called 'New Age' religion. The stress is on self-fulfilment, self-realization, self-awareness – the very opposite of the ideas of limitation, surrender and denial expressed in the term sacrifice.

The absence of any notion of sacrifice is particularly apparent in the worlds of politics and economics. Politicians of all parties fall over themselves to condemn higher taxes, irrespective of the redistributive benefits or enhanced public services that these might bring, and to promise that they will bring greater prosperity to the individual. The most important commodity in the enterprise culture which we now inhabit is added value understood in purely monetary terms. The prime objective of nations, communities and individuals has thus come to be producing and consuming more and more, identifying new niche markets and turning wants into needs. If we stop consuming, the economy falters. The notion of holding back and limiting consumption in the interests of the physical environment, the poorer parts of the world, the good of the community or one's own moral and spiritual well-being is anathema and heresy.

Sacrifice, it would seem, has become as obsolete as the horse-drawn plough or the small corner shop. Indeed, the word has a distinctly archaic ring to it. In a perceptive article on the changes in British public life during the first forty years of the reign of Queen Elizabeth II, the journalist Anthony Howard focused particularly on the steady rise of materialism and selfishness on a national as much as a personal level:

> When Rab Butler predicted at the 1954 Conservative party conference that the standard of living would double in 25 years, he was delivering a message that was music to the public's ears; when, in more sententious mood some years later, he quoted a couplet in the House of Commons – *'This is the way great nations rise/By service and by sacrifice'* – he risked getting a raspberry even from his parliamentary colleagues.[3]

It is no coincidence that this growing sense of the obsolescence of sacrifice should have coincided with a substantial weakening in the influence of Christianity on the lives of both individuals and nations. There are still notable differences between Christian and non-Christian perceptions of what constitutes the good life. A recent survey found that while 43 per cent of those who never go to church agreed with the proposition that 'the main purpose of life is to fulfil yourself', only 19 per cent of regular churchgoers accepted it.[4] As the extent of Bible reading, churchgoing and Sunday School attendance has waned, it is not surprising that Jesus' words about denying self and taking up the Cross should have had less and less impact and appeal. The progressively weakening hold of Christianity has undoubtedly made it much easier for advertising copywriters, tabloid journalists and populist politicians to write sacrifice out of the script for living in the late twentieth century.

My main purpose in writing this book, however, is not to prescribe a large dose of sacrificial medicine as a cure for the ills of modern society. That would hardly constitute a work of theology, nor would it be very original. There are now plenty of pundits and columnists who, not before time, are urging on us both individually and collectively the virtues of self-denial, limitation and abstinence. I have what I dare to suggest is a more radical message which is aimed particularly at those who are Christians and for whom therefore the concept still has some meaning and force. It is that we need totally to rethink our attitude towards the whole subject of sacrifice, abandoning or reversing many of our most widely held preconceptions and beliefs, which are in fact the result of centuries of wrong thinking guided by the besetting human sin of anthropocentrism. In their place we need to develop a bolder, more comprehensive and more God-centred perspective which recognizes sacrifice as the principle which is eternally at the very heart and centre of the life of the Holy Trinity, the divine purpose and plan for creation and our response to our crucified and risen Saviour.

There has been a profound flaw, amounting I would say to a heresy, in the way that sacrifice has traditionally been presented in the teaching of most churches and understood by many Christians. It has been seen primarily as something that is done to God, either by us or by Christ on our behalf, with the object of pleasing him or appeasing his wrath. This view derives in considerable part, I think, from a fundamental misunderstanding of the nature and purpose of the sacrificial

6

rituals of primitive societies and the practices of the Israelite cult. These have been conceived as involving a one-way movement in which the initiative lies entirely with humans while God is simply the object or recipient of the sacrifice. This view has become widely established within mainstream Christian thought at the academic as much as at the popular level. A standard Roman Catholic work on the subject defines sacrifice as 'the movement or action by which we try to bring ourselves to God'.[5] In similar vein a dictionary of religions and beliefs published in 1992 states that 'the purpose of sacrifice is to establish or maintain good relations with the supernatural world'. It goes on to enumerate three specific purposes for which sacrifice may be practised: to bribe a deity, to give thanksgiving for what has already been received and to atone for breaches in the community's relationship with the divine. In this last form, the sin of the community is transferred to a scapegoat who is offered as a sacrifice in its place. The dictionary notes that 'the Christian doctrine of atonement can be understood as a sophisticated form of this type of sacrifice. For Christians Christ's death on the Cross constitutes the ultimate and perfect sacrifice that redeems humankind from its sins and makes redundant all other forms of sacrifice'.[6]

It is easy to see how this widely held understanding of sacrifice as essentially something offered by humans to please or placate God leads on to a view of Christ as the sacrificial victim or scapegoat slaughtered to make atonement for sin. It has, of course, led more specifically to ideas of propitiatory and substitutionary atonement. Calvin's chilling analysis of the nature and purpose of Christ's sacrifice still finds wide acceptance as an orthodox statement of belief among many Christians today:

God was the enemy of men until they were restored to favour by the death of Christ. They were cursed until their iniquity was expiated by the sacrifice of Christ.

Christ interposed, took the punishment upon himself and bore what by the just judgment of God was impending over sinners; with his own blood satisfied and duly propitiated God the Father, by this intercession appeased his anger.[7]

Many of our most popular Passiontide hymns carry this message of substitutionary atonement and portray Christ's death as a sacrifice made to God which achieved its effect by somehow satisfying his anger over human sin. The language of the counting house is often employed to suggest that some kind of financial transaction was accomplished on the Cross, as in Frances Alexander's 'There was no other good enough to pay the price of sin', Charles Wesley's 'And can it be that I should gain an interest in my Saviour's blood?' and Graham Kendrick's 'The price is paid':

> For every sin
> More than enough he gave
> And bought our freedom
> From each guilty stain.

There is to me, and I suspect to many Christians, something rather repellent about this kind of approach to the idea of sacrifice in general and to the sacrifice of Christ in particular. It smacks of a crude tit-for-tat transaction. What kind of a God is it who can be bought off by the payment of this terrible price in blood and suffering? Surely not the God whom Christians worship and who has uniquely incarnated himself in the form of a weak and vulnerable human being. No less monstrous is the notion that God engineers human salvation by means of the ritual slaughter of his own Son. Yet this is what so much of the Church's teaching, resting on ideas of substitutionary atonement and propitiary sacrifice, seems to say.

There are several flaws in this position but two in particular stand out. The first is that sacrifice is related narrowly and exclusively to sin and seen purely in terms of propitiation or expiation. That there is a clear relationship is undeniable (it is explored in Chapter 9). To suggest, however, that the whole purpose of sacrifice in the world is to make atonement for sin is hugely to confine and diminish its power and scope; it also gives a largely negative and reactive character to the purpose and character of God. Just as the coming of Jesus Christ into the world cannot simply be explained in terms of the need for a saviour to redeem humanity from the consequences of sin, so the centrality of the principle of sacrifice in the divine as well as in human life is not just a response to the negativity of evil. It points to a much more fundamental and positive impulse at the heart of the being of God – a self-giving which is incarnational as much as atoning.

I should make it clear that I am not in any way seeking in this book to diminish the importance of the theme of atonement in Christian doctrine. Living in an age which has witnessed such brutality and suffering as our own, even the most optimistic and liberally inclined Christian must surely concede the terrible reality and devastating consequences of evil forces and human sinfulness, the estrangement which exists between God and his creatures and the need for redemption and reconciliation. What I do want to escape from, though, are those still all-too-prevalent theories of atonement which suggest the settling of a debt or the completion of a commercial or legal transaction. Indeed, one of the main reasons why I want to champion a sacrificial interpretation of the life and death of Jesus is because I believe that it avoids these forensic and legalistic categories. It locates the tragedy of Calvary in the context of the cult rather than the counting house or the law court. This, as we shall see, is not without its problems and potential for distortion but at least it does not reduce the mystery of atonement to a crude and calculated transaction.

It is relevant here to make a brief comment on the origins of sacrificial rituals in primal religions. Many anthropologists, building on the pioneering work of the late nineteenth-century historian of religion, William Robertson Smith, believe that their original purpose was not propitiatory or placatory at all but rather sacramental. They seem to have been solemn feasts of communion with the gods rather than gift or sin offerings. Animals, and even humans, were not slaughtered in these rituals to be offered as a gift to the gods but rather to release the life-blood which had a unique and mysterious sacramental efficacy. It was only through the death of these victims that a holy bond could be established between the human participants in the ritual and the divinities who also took part in it. This understanding of the origins of sacrifice has very important implications for Christian worship and the centrality of the theme of communion within it. It is also very important in showing that from the first the gods were not conceived of as the objects of sacrifice but rather as participants in it. They were, indeed, the initiators of sacrifice, providing and establishing it as the holy meeting point between earth and heaven, the supreme occasion for human communication with the divine.[8]

This brings us to the second major flaw in a primarily propitiatory understanding of sacrifice. By viewing God as the object rather than the subject and thinking in terms of victims and scapegoats, it gets everything the wrong way round. Sacrifice is reduced to a largely passive and mechanical exercise performed by humans to please or appease the Deity. This is where the cultic origins of sacrifice, or rather our misunderstanding of them, have led to a serious distortion. We think of sacrifice in terms of the destruction and offering of some life other than our own rather than as a universal principle of self-limitation and self-surrender that emanates from the very being of God himself and involves us in constant and costly self-giving. This is hardly surprising: it lets us off the hook and is a much more convenient and comfortable concept. It is this notion that has made the whole idea of sacrifice, quite understandably, so unpopular among many sensitive and devout Christians. It seems always to involve sacrificing others and finding victims and scapegoats. It is an utter travesty of the true Christian understanding of God as the supreme self-giver and of the biblical image of Christ as the one who is priest as well as victim.

Here we come to what is perhaps the most important feature of all concerning sacrifice that we have lost and that we must regain. Twentieth-century theology has rightly made much of the doctrine of patripassianism, the idea of the suffering God; we need now to recover the idea of the sacrificing God. Indeed, I would go further and suggest that we need to see sacrifice, understood in terms of costly self-giving and the bringing about of life through the agency of death, as the most distinctive characteristic of both the being and the work of God. That surely is the clearest message of his unique revelation of himself to us in the person of Jesus Christ. The God who is revealed in Christ is continually sacrificing himself, as much in the activity of creation as in the work of redemption through his Son. He is the author of life through sacrifice. The Christian revelation points us to the truth that growth and progress are only possible through self-limitation and surrender and that sacrifice, understood as a two-way process of giving and responding, dying and rising again, lies at the heart of our relationship with our Creator and Redeemer.

When I was well advanced in this study I came across this passage on 'the divine self-emptying' written a hundred years ago by the great Congregationalist theologian P. T. Forsyth. Inspired by the well-known words in Philippians 2:5–8 which talk of Christ emptying himself, it exposes very clearly the fundamental flaw in the widespread heresy which sees God as the object rather than the author of sacrifice:

> The one thing which it is the business of Revelation to let us know about the depths of the eternal Godhead is this, that its Divinest power is the power to resign, to sacrifice, to descend, to obey, to save. The key to the prehistoric Godhead is the historic Jesus, and His historical obedience, even to the historic cross. And I could almost think that the deepest error which has blinded and lamed Christianity in the world, the root of every other perversion and failure is indicated here. It is in having conceived of God as a Being whose first and Divinest work was to *receive* sacrifice instead of offering it – one who demanded sacrifices He had never made. Deep into the fabric of Christian thought and habit has struck this pagan strain, that it is God's one royal work to accept sacrifice, and man's one saving duty to offer it. The Christian note is quite other. In the face of all

the paganisms, ancient and modern, civil or ecclesiastical, it is bold and original in the extreme. It not only carries into Godhead the power of sacrifice, but it declares this priestliness to be the very saving power of God, the root of all that is glorious in everlasting glory, or kingly in the King of Kings. God so loved that He *gave*.[9]

To argue, as Forsyth does, that sacrifice has its origin and source in God and that it is the power which saves, is to make a bold enough claim, given the unease which the whole subject provokes among so many Christians. To assert further, as I want to, that it is also the engine which drives the life of the world, is to court controversy and opposition. Arguing for a recognition of the centrality of the theme of sacrifice in the Christian faith is not, as I have discovered, a route to gaining popularity among many fellow believers. In fact, I believe it to be a profoundly ecumenical and eirenic enterprise. Evangelicals and Catholics are united in stressing the importance of the concept of sacrifice even if they differ in their understanding and interpretation of the term. There has been a long and honourable tradition of Anglican writing on the doctrine of atonement which has sought to find a *via media* between Protestants and Catholics on the basis of the sacrificial language used by both sides. As long ago as 1920 Laurence Grensted suggested that the retention of sacrificial language in Protestant theology 'formed a certain common Catholic basis for doctrinal statement, the value of which for mutual understanding has been very great, and may perhaps become greater still'.[10] Subsequent official consultations between Roman Catholics and Protestants have produced statements indicating a wide measure of agreement on the sacrificial nature of both Christ's death and the Eucharist. One of my aims in writing this book is simultaneously to affirm and bring together the evangelical insistence on the centrality of the Cross and the sacrifice of Christ (which is, of course, by no means confined to Protestants) and the catholic emphasis (which is equally not confined to Roman Catholics) on the eternal nature of that sacrifice.

It is among Christians of a broadly liberal theological persuasion that there is the greatest unease about the theme of sacrifice and the greatest desire to discard it from the vocabulary of contemporary Christianity. Of all the individuals and groups with whom I have shared my thoughts about the centrality and power of sacrifice, I have found least support and encouragement from those with whom in other contexts I find myself in close agreement, namely feminist and 'green' theologians, those actively engaged in interfaith dialogue and enthusiasts for process theology. Yet it seems to me that an understanding of God as the supreme self-giver who is the creator of a world built on sacrifice and the author of life through sacrifice is one that should have particularly strong resonances for both feminists and environmentalists. It also draws on truths and insights contained in other religious traditions, without detracting from the uniqueness of the Christian revelation, and squares with the understanding of the world that we have been given by modern science.

Liberal theologians in the past have, in fact, made a very significant contribution to constructing the kind of theology of sacrifice for which I am arguing in this book. I am thinking in particular of the work of F. D. Maurice, George Matheson and others in the nineteenth century, which is discussed in Chapter 6. Much of the kenotic Christology so characteristic of late Victorian Protestantism in Britain, and so fruitful as a basis for understanding the incarnation as much as the atonement in terms of sacrifice and self-giving on the part of God, was developed by liberal Christians who were often deeply committed to social and political reform and to such movements as Christian Socialism. I find it sad when their writings and work are dismissed, as they are by some contemporary liberal and feminist Christians, as no more than the expressions of a guilty conscience on the part of the privileged sons of an age of imperialism.

Much of the unease which contemporary liberal theologians feel about the concept of sacrifice undoubtedly arises because of the grotesquely distorted way in which it has so often been presented. In his book *The World to Come* Don

Cupitt sees sacrifice as intrinsically connected with the hierarchical nature of society – a gift to be offered so that favour may be obtained from a superior.[11] This, of course, is to fall into the heresy of narrowing sacrifice down to a mechanical cultic act with a propitiatory purpose. The objection of many feminists to a theology based on sacrifice is more fundamental and more understandable. It is powerfully stated by a women's group in India: 'The theology of sacrifice that is thrust on women is of no purpose. . . . Women are the scapegoats of this theology'.[12] What particularly ires feminists is the presentation of the crucified Jesus as a sacrificial victim and the way that this image has been used to excuse and justify the victimization and suffering of women. For the American theologian Ann Carr, 'images of Jesus as sacrificial victim and of his sacrificial love and self-surrender on the cross . . . [are] destructive for women and amongst the most difficult for feminist Christians', while the American Episcopal priest Carter Heyward has written, 'I cannot image Jesus' death as a "sacrifice" at all'.[13] A recent report from the World Council of Churches links the churches' generally unsympathetic attitude towards violence directed against women to their sacrificial Christology: ' "Christ suffered and died for you on the Cross. Can't you bear some suffering too?" is a question often addressed, in one form or another, to women when they appeal to the church for succour. Perhaps one of the most pernicious aspects of Christian teaching has been this imposed *theology of sacrifice and suffering*'.[14]

This feminist critique is extremely important in highlighting the danger that a theology based on the centrality of sacrifice can be turned into a justification of suffering, particularly the suffering which is caused by oppression and force. The relationship between sacrifice and suffering is an extremely delicate and complex subject which I will attempt to explore in Chapter 9. It is enough here to restate what I have, I hope, already made clear is one of the central messages of this book: that Christianity must rid itself once and for all of a propitiatory theory of sacrifice which portrays God as an angry and vengeful deity who can only be appeased by the slaughter of an innocent victim. Until that is done, we cannot escape this indictment:

> Christianity is an abusive theology that glorifies suffering. Is it any wonder that there is so much abuse in modern culture when the predominant image or theology of the culture is of 'divine child abuse' – God the Father demanding and carrying out the suffering and death of his own son? If Christianity is to be liberating for the oppressed, it must be liberated from this theology.[15]

A rather different objection from the feminist standpoint comes from Daphne Hampson in her seminal work *Theology and Feminism*:

> Feminist writers have often thought men to be oriented towards death in a way that women are not. Thought about death occupies a major place in male religion. Moreover, it is often death connected with sacrifice. Indeed there is a theme of death through sacrifice and rebirth. This paradigm is obviously built into Christianity. May it be that women are more interested in giving birth to life?[16]

I find this an interesting but not altogether convincing analysis of the difference between male and female approaches to the motif of 'through death to life' that is central to the concept of sacrifice. It may conceivably be true that the experience of killing or being killed in their traditional roles as hunters and warriors has given men more of an orientation towards death. It has almost certainly led them to put more of a premium on heroic death and giving up one's life for a cause – the kind of view of sacrifice which reached its apogee in the First World War. Yet it is not my experience that women, who on the whole lead much more sacrificial lives than men, are without the sense that life comes through death and creation through pain and suffering. The supremely and uniquely feminine experience of childbirth is surely profoundly sacrificial. Within the natural world it is almost always the female of the species who sacrifice themselves for the sake of their young (see pp. 233–5).

It is significant that at least one prominent contemporary feminist theologian has recently taken a much more affirmative view of the whole concept of sacrifice, and specifically of a sacrificial interpretation of Christ's crucifixion. In a fascinating paper delivered to the 1994 conference of the Society for the Study of Theology Janet Martin Soskice of Cambridge University draws on traditions of Christian symbolism which have portrayed the blood and water that flow from Christ's side on the Cross as emblematic of human birth. In this imagery, and in the linked eucharistic symbolism of the blood on which believers feed, she sees an identification of the crucified Christ with the female human body, both in giving birth and in feeding. A highly original exegesis of the story of Jesus' healing of the woman with the haemorrhage (Mark 5:21–43; Matthew 9:18–34; Luke 8:40–56) leads her to find a link between the flow of blood in menstruation and the passion of Christ: 'As the woman's flow of blood is stopped and turned from defilement to fertility, so Christ's flow of blood brings not dishonour but new life'.[17]

Dr Soskice avoids drawing any direct comparison with the action of shedding blood which was so central in the life-giving sacrificial rituals of primal religions. She is, however, emphatic that blood is a 'vital element [which] refers to women, fertility and the assurance of fecundation' and she goes on to acknowledge its deeply ambiguous sacrificial power as 'the propitious place for abjection where death and femininity, murder and procreation, cessation of life and vitality all come together'.[18] She is also at pains to underline the close link between birth and death as types of sacrificial giving. For her an understanding of the passion and death of Christ in terms of sacrifice does not automatically involve substitutionary and propitiatory theories of atonement: 'the symbolics of blood and the Cross are by no means restricted to punitive and penal readings'.[19] Her paper provides the basis for a positive and distinctively feminist theology of sacrifice.

I suspect that what lies at the root of much of the contemporary feminist objection to a theology centred on sacrifice is something which unites many women and men in the modern age – an unease about death. Daphne Hampson, for example, asserts at the end of the passage quoted above that life does not necessarily need to come out of death. Yet what modern science is telling us is that in all sorts of different ways death is indeed the foundation of life, whether on the macro-scale of evolution with its dependence on the disappearance and destruction of whole species or the micro-level of the individual cell where a programmed cycle of death and renewal is essential to healthy growth and development. To use the word 'sacrifice' about this constant process which is at work throughout nature is surely not inappropriate.

> The structures that are constantly being replaced are themselves living organisms. From their point of view the self-renewal of the larger system is their own cycle of birth and death. Birth and death, therefore, now appear as a central aspect of self-organisation, the very essence of life. Indeed, all living things around us renew themselves all the time. . . . For every organism that dies another is born. Death, then, is not the opposite of life but an essential aspect of it.[20]

This same motif of 'through life to death' is at the heart of the Christian understanding of the crucifixion and resurrection of Jesus. Christianity is unique among the world's great faiths in having death as its starting point. Its founding figure, central icon of holiness and great high priest, is a dead man on a cross. Of course it is specifically and crucially the risen Christ whom Christians acknowledge as lord. It is his resurrection appearances which convince his disciples that he is, indeed, the Son of God and which lead to the foundation of the Church that has borne his name ever since. The fact of resurrection, however, does not negate or diminish the fact of death. Indeed, the ultimate triumph is only possible because of the initial tragedy. The Christian religion does not preach that death is an illusion or that the human soul is immortal. Rather it acknowledges the reality of death, physical and spiritual, and points to the new life that comes out of and through it. This sacrificial principle of dying in order to live extends to an acceptance that we need to go through a whole series of lesser 'deaths' if we are to grow and develop before we make the final surrender at the end of our time on this earth. In the words of John Moses, 'sacrifice recognises intuitively the necessity of the *death* – the giving up, the offering, the handing-over, the destruction – that leads to *life*. The Christian understanding of atonement encapsulates this universal principle of life that Jesus embodied in His death and resurrection'.[21] Understood in these terms, there is nothing morbid or perverted about either a theology or a worldview based on the centrality of the theme of sacrifice. It affirms rather the very positive message that in the midst of death we are in life.

If unease about death is one dominant characteristic of our present age, then concern with self is another. I am thinking now not so much of our rampant selfishness and materialism but rather of the very proper concern that many counsellors and psychologists have with building up a sense of self-esteem among their clients. It is widely agreed that low self-worth is a major problem in modern society, particularly among young people, and that it is a major contributory factor to poor educational achievement and the drift into drugs, vandalism and crime. Preaching a sacrificial gospel of self-limitation and surrender hardly seems appropriate in such a situation. Where is the boundary between self-sacrifice and self-destruction? At a time when more and more people seem to hate themselves, should not Christians be aiming to affirm the value of individual human life rather than extolling the virtues of a sacrificial approach which could be seen as dangerously close to self-immolation?

It certainly needs to be stated very clearly that Christianity is at heart a life-affirming not a life-denying faith. One of the underlying themes of both the Old and New Testaments is the intrinsic importance in the sight of God of the life of each and every human being – and, indeed, of every other creature and plant on the earth. Jesus came into the world so that people might have life, and have it abundantly (John 10:10). He came eating and drinking with the result that he was taken to be a drunkard and a glutton, playing on the pipes in the hope that the people might dance (Matthew 11:17–19). Too much Christian writing and preaching has made Jesus into a puritanical killjoy and has not been faithful to the biblical portrayal of the lord of the dance and founder of the feast who turns the water into wine so that the wedding guests at Cana can enjoy themselves.

Yet at the same time we cannot avoid the centrality of the Cross and the themes of surrender and costly discipleship in the Christian gospel. We cannot flee from Jesus' command that those who would follow him must take up their crosses and lose their lives for his sake. The clue to reconciling these two apparently contradictory threads in Christianity, the life-affirming and the self-denying, surely lies in Jesus' assertion that it is precisely in the process of losing ourselves that we find ourselves. The truth of this paradox is affirmed by our modern understanding of the concept of alienation and the tyranny of self. We know only too well how the ego can become so dominant and controlling in some personalities that they are effectively enslaved and have no real freedom. The same can happen as a result of obsession or addiction. It is through losing ourselves in something or someone beyond and outside us that we find liberation and relief from that terrible and oppressive state of being curled in on ourselves, or *incurvatus in se*, which Luther rightly saw as the essence of sin. This is, of course, what makes being in love at once one of the most profoundly sacrificial and most fulfilling of all human experiences. It is a condition not to self-obsession but of self-giving. In the words of a song from the *Sound of Music*:

> A bell is no bell till you ring it,
> A song is no song till you sing it,
> And love in your heart wasn't put there to stay,
> Love isn't love till you give it away.[22]

19

This truth was also beautifully expressed by Catherine Bramwell Booth, granddaughter of the founder of the Salvation Army, in an interview shortly before her death at the age of 104 in 1987; 'Love is the secret of life. Those who have not learned to love someone better than they love themselves have not begun to live'.[23]

Sacrifice, then, is profoundly liberating. It is about the enhancement and communication of life. We need to recover the note of joyful celebration that was a feature of so many ancient rites and rid ourselves of the notion that sacrifice is something cramping and negative. We also need to be very clear that the whole concept of sacrifice is founded on the notion of individual self-worth. You cannot have self-limitation and surrender if there is not a self there in the first place to be given up and offered to another. Christianity begins by affirming the worth of the individual, particularly those who are frightened, broken and unsure of themselves. 'Do not be afraid, for I have redeemed you. I have called you by name, you are mine' (Isaiah 43:1). That is the starting point of all faith and growth. It is just the starting point, however. As the self grows and matures, it begins to follow the sacrificial way of giving itself up. This process is described with great clarity and simplicity by George Matheson, the blind nineteenth-century Church of Scotland minister who was so gripped by the power of sacrifice: 'There are four phases in the birth of the religious life: self-awakening, self-reflection, self-help and self-abandonment'.[24]

If sacrifice is liberating, then it is also profoundly costly. It is certainly not easy. It is not about self-punishment or self-abasement but it is about growing in our discipleship through self-denial and limitation. This is not a comfortable concept but then Christianity is not a comfortable faith to live by. In the words of John Wesley, 'in some things we may please Christ and please ourselves, in others we cannot please Christ except by denying ourselves'.[25] The essence of sacrifice is the surrender of what is precious and valuable, not just giving but giving up. This is as true of the rituals of primal religions as the apparently more spiritualized and ethical demands of

Christianity. The anthropologist E. E. Evans-Pritchard has observed with reference to the practices of the Nuer people of South Sudan that 'in sacrifice . . . some part of a man dies with the victim'.[26] Once again, we are reminded of the fact that in its cultic origins among so-called primitive societies the practice of sacrifice involved not just the ritual slaughter of some unfortunate victim but a participation in the experience of dying and self-surrender by all those taking part.

There is no getting away from the costliness of the sacrificial lives which Christians are so clearly called by Jesus to lead. In the Communion services of most churches worshippers ask to be made 'living sacrifices', taking up Paul's injunction in Romans 12:1. The plea trips readily off our tongues yet its implications are anything but attractive:

> To be a living sacrifice would be like being a permanent exile from home, living among people of another tradition whose ideas and customs one did not share, and accepting them as equals. This is what we ask to be: we ask to be those who have cut themselves off from their origins and background, even from their most prized religious convictions, to be free for one another in a new way, that makes groups, parties and movements completely out of place. This is being a living sacrifice, and it is not at all pleasant; it is not what we want.[27]

It may seem a rather futile exercise to be seeking to assert the primacy of sacrifice when it seems so unappealing and to fly in the face of so many modern nostrums. Yet there is a sense in which it is still a highly valued ideal in our society. The great Congregational theologian John Whale has argued that sacrifice is a dead and debased metaphor in the modern world. For him it has been stripped of its technical religious meaning as a cultic offering involving the shedding of blood, which people now find revolting, and has become a mere figure of speech.[28] I think this is to underestimate its continuing hold on the human imagination. The word 'sacrifice' does not seem to me to have become dead and debased. Certainly it is not used nowadays beyond academic circles with any connotation of ritual blood offerings but it does still carry a sense of costly self-giving in the interests of another or for the sake of some higher good. It is generally associated with altruistic behaviour in some form and it is more often applied as a term of approval than of condemnation.

I have before me a pile of recent newspaper cuttings in which the word is mentioned. An obituary of the Marxist historian and peace campaigner, E. P. Thompson, quotes the former CND chairman and Roman Catholic priest Bruce Kent as saying 'he sacrificed his academic and social influence for the causes in which he passionately believed'.[29] A profile of the former MP and once contender for the Labour Party leadership, Bryan Gould, reveals that his favourite film is *Shane*, 'not just a great western but also a moral story of individual sacrifice for the common good'.[30] A report of events arranged to commemorate the fiftieth anniversary of D-Day notes that they are designed to 'salute the heroism and sacrifice of the veterans' while a quotation from President Clinton's speech on the site of the Normandy landings begins, 'We are the children of your sacrifice'.[31] A letter in the *Church Times* calls for all Anglican clergy from archbishops to curates to be paid the same stipends so that 'the spirit of equality and sacrifice which bishops urge upon industrialists for the good of the nation would be demonstrated in the Church itself'.[32] A national newspaper columnist dares to question the prevailing wisdom that freedom is the only absolute human value and to suggest that 'it might sometimes be necessary, even desirable, for adults to *sacrifice* some of their own happiness (or sexual inclination, or professional ambition, or personal development) in the interests of others'.[33]

This diverse collection of contemporary references indicates that sacrifice is still widely regarded in favourable terms. It also shows a clear understanding of the element of cost and personal disadvantage. What is missing is any specifically religious connotation. As it is now commonly used and understood the word 'sacrifice' has lost its basic original meaning which comes from the two Latin words from which it is derived, *sacer* and *facere* – to make holy. This sense is crucial to the centrality and the power of sacrifice in so many religious traditions. Describing the rites of primal religions, the French scholars Henri Hubert and Marcel Mauss point out that 'in every sacrifice an object passes from the common into the religious domain; it is consecrated'.[34] In the Vedic scriptures of Hinduism sacrifice is conceived of as sacred action. In a *Simple Church Dictionary* it is defined first and foremost as 'a holy deed'.[35]

At first sight there is no obvious connection between the idea of giving something up and the idea of making something holy. We can agree that costly acts of altruism are commendable, even that there is something noble in individuals or communities surrendering their own interests or advantages for the sake of some higher cause, but that is not the same thing as saying that the process of sacrifice actually has the transformative power of making holy. This is to introduce a wholly different note – to move from this world to the next and to suggest that the surrender and loss which is inherent in any kind of sacrifice has a supernatural or metaphysical significance quite apart from and in addition to its value here and now. Yet this is the unavoidable implication of the word's derivation:

> The word sacrifice in our language means always losing something, being deprived of something. But in Latin, in Greek, in Hebrew, in Slavonic, in all the ancient languages, sacrifice comes from sacred – it means to make something sacred, make something holy and not to lose it. Indeed, when you bring a life to God or a gift to God, it becomes His, it is no longer yours in the greedy and possessive sense of the word. But it becomes holy with the holiness of God.[36]

The notion that in offering something to God we are somehow consecrating it and making it holy is, of course, at the root of Christian worship just as it was at the root of the sacrificial rituals of primitive societies. It is not just confined to the sphere of formal worship, however. All that we do and think can be made holy if it is offered up as a gift to God. It was this sacramental understanding of even the most mundane tasks that led our Celtic Christian ancestors to invoke God's presence and blessing as they kindled their peat fires and milked their cows. A similar attitude pervades the writings of that quintessentially Anglican Celt, George Herbert. In his poem 'The Elixir', better known to us now as the hymn 'Teach me my God and King in all things thee to see', he calls for the most menial job to be approached in the sacrificial spirit which makes it holy:

> A servant with this clause
> Makes drudgery divine;
> Who sweeps a room, as for thy laws,
> Makes that and the action fine.

> This is the famous stone
> That turneth all to gold;
> For that which God doth touch and own
> Cannot for less be sold.

It is more, much more, than an attitude of mind, though. There is an objective and universal link between our common understanding of sacrifice as costly giving and the original meaning of the word as making holy. It was well stated by one of the leading Anglican theologians of the early part of this century, Oscar Quick:

> The moral meaning of the term 'self-sacrifice' may seem to have as little connexion with the ritual sacrifices of antiquity as it has with the jargon of modern commerce which speaks of 'goods offered at sacrifice'. And yet the use of the same word in all cases is not a pure equivocation or a mere accident of speech. Everywhere 'sacrifice' expresses the notion of gain through loss, of the best won through the surrender of the good, or of life attained through death – it

24

is the characteristic term of that 'dialectic' which lies at the heart of the moral and spiritual experience of mankind.[37]

The key to integrating the common meaning of the word and its specific religious connotations lies in the realization that sacrifice is at once the power which animates and drives life throughout the physical world and the principle at the very heart of the being and purposes of God. Once this truth is grasped, we can see how acts of surrender and self-giving bring us in touch not just with the rhythms of nature and with our own deeper selves but with the profound holiness of the eternal Other. They are our means of communication with the One who is himself the supreme self-giver. They are also our means of salvation from the slavery of selfishness and alienation. As John Moses observes:

> It is sacrifice that makes the connection between the holiness of God, our search for wholeness, and the hope that God will be all in all. God manages His creation and His redemption in such a way that He puts Himself at risk. Creative and redemptive love involves sacrifice. To be made whole, to become holy with the holiness of God, presupposes the sacrifice in which the giver and the receiver – God and man, man and God – both participate in the gift. The origin of the word gives us the all-important insight into the meaning of sacrifice.[38]

We are brought back here to the primitive sense, so powerfully expressed in the bloody rites and cults of antiquity, that sacrifice involves a mutual communion between humans and gods and a sacred participation in life-giving energy. At the same time we are also in the midst of the modern search for wholeness in a world of alienation and fragmentation. Sacrifice provides the link between holiness and wholeness. It is the God-given power which transfigures and heals, turning the secular into the sacred and restoring our shattered souls. In the words of the Anglican theologian Cyril Richardson, 'Man is estranged from himself and from God until he can sacrifice every part of his self for the sake of a larger harmony. He must become Whole, that is, Holy'.[39]

We need to guard against falling back into the heresy that sacrifice is something that originates with us and that we do to God. It comes from God and it returns to God. He is the beginning and the end of sacrifice, its author and its ultimate recipient. Sacrifice can be seen as our destiny as his creatures. This teleological dimension is well expressed by the French Roman Catholic scholar Eugene Masure: 'Sacrifice is essentially the decisive effort and imploring prayer which is imposed on us if we would reach our end; it is the attitude of adhesion to God by which we deliberately ratify our destiny; above all, it is the attainment of the goal, when the creature makes the final act of casting itself into the Creator's arms, losing itself there in a complete abandonment'.[40]

This act of abandonment should not be understood in negative, masochistic terms: it is not the desperate surrender of a soul which hates itself and which is seeking escape through annihilation. It is rather a homecoming, an acknowledgement that we are not autonomous, self-sufficient entities but creatures who belong to God and can only find wholeness and completion by giving ourselves up to him. It is the recognition of the truth encapsulated in St Augustine's famous prayer: 'Almighty God, in whom we live and move and have our being, you have made us for yourself, so that our hearts are restless until they rest in you'. George Matheson expresses it beautifully in the opening verse of his deservedly popular hymn:

> O Love that wilt not let me go,
> I rest my weary soul in Thee;
> I give Thee back the life I owe,
> That in Thine ocean depths its flow
> May richer, fuller be.

So there is a real sense in which sacrifice, while undoubtedly costly, is also very natural. If we are, indeed, created in the image of a God whose own nature is to sacrifice, then it is not surprising that it should also be one of the most basic and widespread human instincts. In his classic study, *The Varieties of Religious Experience*, first published in 1902, William James noted that 'the impulse to sacrifice is a prominent, a universal phenomenon [which] lies deeper than any special creed'. He went on to define this impulse not in terms of cultic blood-lettings and ritual slaughter but as expressed in numerous acts of renunciation and self-giving. For him it was exemplified in the way in which Cotton Mather, the New England Puritan divine, gave up his dying wife to the Lord, 'simply expressing what seemed right at the time between the individual and his Maker'.[41] Towards the end of his great book on the Christian understanding of atonement, which first appeared in 1968, F. W. Dillistone remarked in similar terms that 'If there is one thing clear in the history of human thought and action it is that man will not abandon the idea of sacrifice'.[42]

I rather doubt if anyone would write in quite so certain a tone today. Is the impulse to sacrifice in danger of being lost along with so many other primitive human instincts in our increasingly sophisticated and dehumanized technological culture? It certainly often seems as if we lack the strong sense of both the centrality and the power of sacrifice that previous generations had. If we are to regain it, we will need to recover something of the understanding that lay behind the rites of our pre-Christian ancestors. We will need, too, to explore and to learn from other religious traditions, notably the great Vedic hymns which form the sacred texts of Hinduism and the Israelite cult which is so central to the Hebrew Bible. We will also need to draw on the writings of that long line of Christians who have understood the power of sacrifice. Above all, we must return to the Cross of Christ and to the supreme sacrifice made there by God's own Son. It is ultimately only *sub specie crucis* that we can begin to comprehend and to respond to the tragic and triumphant power of sacrifice which is at once at the heart of the being of God and central to the life of the world.

1

The pelican, the lamb and the burning bush: the relevance of sacrifice

The concept of sacrifice, understood not as something done by humans to appease or placate the gods but rather as a universal liberating principle of life through death and gain through loss, speaks to many of the most pressing concerns of our age. As we have already noted, it has a particular relevance to the contemporary search for wholeness and identity. It offers a way of integrating and affirming the findings of biologists that life quite literally depends on death. It may even provide the glimmerings of an explanation as to where God is as we search for a theodicy in the aftermath of the holocaust and genocide that has marked the twentieth century. It enables us, perhaps, to go beyond the statement that God is in the midst of the world's pain and suffering and to say that he is not just sharing it but in some profound and mysterious way giving himself up to it. Brutalized and cynical as we are, indeed perhaps precisely because that is our condition, we hunger and long for signs of real sacrificial spirit rising amidst the selfish pall of consumerism.

Let me just give two examples of this longing. Polls to determine the most admired figures in the world consistently put those who devote themselves selflessly to others near the top of the list. Theirs are lives which defy almost every maxim of the added-value, me-first enterprise culture. Yet they are admired not just for what they do for others but for their own integrity and vitality. In the words of Paul Fiddes, 'It is those who have given themselves away in the most spendthrift manner who stand out in history as the most vital personalities – from Francis of Assisi to Simone Weil and Mother Teresa of Calcutta. Above all this is the pattern of the cross and resurrection, which gives us the courage to believe that to give oneself away in forgiveness is to become more truly oneself'.[1]

Another remarkable sign of this longing is the huge popularity over the last decade of a musical which has as its theme the redemptive power of sacrificial love. *Les Misérables* has been justly described as 'the world's most popular musical'. By the spring of 1994 it had been seen by more than 30 million people in twenty-two different countries. More than three hours long and set amidst the poverty and political fervour of post-Revolutionary France, it has no glitzy chorus girls, no big production numbers and very few catchy tunes. Rather it presents a succession of episodes involving costly surrender and self-giving, most notably on the part of the hero, Jean Valjean, but also and almost more movingly by Fantine, the single mother who sells herself as a prostitute to pay for medicines for her daughter, and Eponine, the hapless innkeeper's daughter who sacrifices her own love for the student Marius to bring him closer to the girl he desires and who dies on the revolutionaries' barricades. Even the bishop who appears in the first scene is portrayed not as a timeserving ecclesiastical dignitary but as a saintly figure who forgives Valjean when he steals his silver and saves him by lying to the police. With its references to Calvary, communion, grace and sacrifice, the libretto seems to belong as much to the world of sacred oratorio as to that of musical theatre. I find it both fascinating and deeply moving that this of all shows should have captured the hearts of millions in the supposedly cynical and jaundiced 1990s.

It is not just theatre-goers who have testified to the relevance and power of the theme of sacrifice at the tail end of the twentieth century. The last few decades have also seen a significant revival of interest in the subject on the part of theologians. Some of their arguments will be dealt with in more detail in Chapter 6. In this chapter I want briefly to outline some of the most important recent studies, not just to underline the topicality of this whole subject but also to acknowledge my own debt to them.

I have already quoted from Frances Young's important book, *Sacrifice and the Death of Christ*, first published in 1967 and republished in 1983. It took issue with those who feel that the idea of sacrifice is now outmoded and argued for its recovery in both theology and liturgy to counter the prevailing modern heresy of self-sufficiency. Another book which has done much to put the theme of sacrifice at the heart of modern Christian thought is F. W. Dillistone's magisterial work, *The Christian Understanding of Atonement*, first published in 1968 and republished in 1984. While principally a study of different perspectives on the atonement, it is also a powerful apologia for the centrality of sacrifice. Dillistone warns against boiling down 'the full-orbed testimony of the Christian tradition' into the one proposition that sacrifice is the unifying principle of all knowledge and all experience – a timely admonition which I am conscious I could be accused of failing to heed in the writing of this book. Of all the many ways that Christians have tried to approach and understand the mystery of the Cross and the even deeper mystery of human existence, however, he finds it to be the most meaningful and suggestive concept:

In all its many forms sacrifice has involved some kind of deliberate offering which appears to deprive the original owner of some valued possession. In this sense it is a deliberate acceptance of a symbolic death. It is a renunciation, a surrender, a conscious recognition through a sacramental action that the ultimate principle of existence, the highest that we can conceive, is *through-death-to-life*. But is it possible to conceive such an activity taking place within the being of God Himself? . . . It is irrational, it is absurd.[2]

It has, of course, been precisely this irrational and absurd concept that has dominated late twentieth-century theology. The notion of patripassianism, the idea that God suffers and that the principles of surrender, limitation and self-giving are at the very heart of his being, has been a marked characteristic of recent writing across a broad spectrum of traditions. The

Jewish scholar Abraham Heschel has stressed the element of divine pathos found in the writings of the Hebrew prophets. Kazok Kitamori, a Japanese Lutheran, has developed a mystical understanding of the pain of God that we are called on to share. Miguel de Unamuno, a Spanish philosopher, has written movingly of the infinite sorrow of God. Perhaps most strikingly and originally, the great German reformed theologian Jürgen Moltmann has built on his hugely influential work, *The Crucified God*, first published in German in 1972 and in English two years later, to argue that God's eternal nature is best summed up in the phrase 'the self-sacrifice of love' and that the whole process of creation involves him in the sacrificial activity of withdrawal and self-limitation.[3]

Recent writings by British theologians pursue and develop these themes. In his two fine books, *The Creative Suffering of God* (1988) and *Past Event and Present Salvation* (1989, reprinted in 1993), Paul Fiddes has sought to construct 'a theology that embraces divine weakness at the centre' and to suggest that 'the sacrifice of God is woven into the whole painful story of human evolution'.[4] Professor Colin Gunton finds in *The Actuality of Atonement* (1988) that of all the metaphors which have been employed to describe the saving action of the Cross, 'sacrifice brings us closest not just to the historic action of God in Christ but to the heart of his very being'.[5] A series of essays by academics connected with Durham University, collected and edited by Stephen Sykes and published in 1991 under the title *Sacrifice and Redemption*, point to the possible ecumenical benefits of rooting both theology and worship in the concept of sacrifice and explore many interesting byways of this whole complex theme. More recently, John V. Taylor's impressive work, *The Christlike God* (1993), builds on St Augustine's exposition of the Trinity as a threefold relationship in love to suggest that God the Father can be seen as the self-giver eternally fulfilled in pure generosity, God the Son as the given self, fulfilled in dependence upon and obedience to the will and purpose of the giver, and God the Holy Spirit as the 'in-othered' self, fulfilled in the effect of that self-giving.

Faced with such an impressive and weighty catalogue of recent works on the subject, the reader might well wonder how there can possibly be room for yet another book on sacrifice. I have to confess that this was very nearly my reaction when, at a comparatively early stage of my research for this volume, I read John Moses' *The Sacrifice of God: A Holistic Theory of Atonement*, which was published in 1992. This book, little noticed and I rather fear therefore little read, is to my mind the most stimulating and significant of all the recent crop of works by British authors on the theme of sacrifice. Its particular originality lies in its attempt to construct a holistic theory of atonement appropriate to contemporary concern with the concepts of interdependence and interconnectedness both at the biological and ecological level and also in terms of human attitudes and society. Moses is struck by the fact that patterns of relationship, whether among humans or in the biological and physical world, 'are distinguished by a recurring motif of life and death and life. It is the element of sacrifice. It involves an infinite number of unseen deaths – a dying to patterns of independence and self-sufficiency as the part discovers a new identity within the larger purposes of the whole'.[6]

Like Dillistone, Moses is led from his observation of this universal process whereby the complex systems of life achieve their completeness and wholeness through some kind of death to ask whether this sacrificial principle is not also present in the life of the world's creator:

> The motif of life and death and life is found throughout the created order as the cycle of birth and growth and activity and decline and death occurs and repeats itself. Is it possible that this motif can be found within the being of God? Is the inescapable fact of death to be seen within the Godhead? Does sacrifice begin and end in God?[7]

Moses' answer to this question is a resounding yes. Like Moltmann, he finds the Cross of Jesus to be the sacrifice of God.

There is a necessity about the cross if God is to be consistent with His own determined pattern of creation. But the cross is about creation and redemption. In giving Himself to His creation, God gives Himself – hands Himself over – to the pattern of life and death and life. And why? Because it is only in this process that the essential life-giving principle of sacrifice is to be found.

If sacrifice is the way that leads from life through death to life then it must have its origin and purpose in the life and will of God and it must be demonstrated to be so located. This is not to suggest that the cross is merely a demonstration or a revelation of sacrifice. It is *because it is a sacrifice* that it is the means whereby redemption is secured.[8]

What is particularly impressive about Moses' argument is his insistence that the initiative always lies with God, who is the author of all sacrifice with its life-giving and life-enhancing power, coupled with his acknowledgement of the power and validity of the sacrificial rituals of primal religion and the ancient Israelite cult. Indeed, he sees the key stages of cultic or ritual offerings as mirroring the sacrificing activity of God:

It is possible to identify the distinguishing marks of the Christian sacrifice: God's activity in drawing near; God's participation in the human predicament to the point of total identification; God's engagement with evil, sin, suffering and death; God's crucifixion in the person of the Son; God's sacrificial love which absorbs and conquers and remains inviolable; God's invitation to participate in the divine life. And this leads to the final proposition which belongs to a holistic theory of atonement. The Christian sacrifice brings us from life through death to life. To possess and be possessed by God is to be born into a new relationship which has the promise of new life. This is the *intended*, the *desired*, the *God-given* relationship. Death and resurrection which form the distinguishing marks of

Christian experience are used in a metaphorical sense but they point in the light of Christ's dying and rising again to the Christian hope which goes beyond all metaphor and simile to the new life which is God's free gift.[9]

Much of what Moses writes in *The Sacrifice of God* so closely echoes and so clearly expresses my own thoughts that I did wonder when I read it about abandoning my own work on the subject. Yet on reflection I have felt it to be worth writing this book. While we share the same central conviction, which he expresses in the statement that 'the suffering love which gives itself in sacrifice is the principle of life, the power by which God acts to transform and make whole',[10] we come to it by rather different approaches and I hope those readers who tackle both books will agree that our work is complementary rather than duplicatory. I may say that reading John Moses' book has given me both a clearer direction and a title for mine. I had originally intended calling it 'The Centrality of Sacrifice' and then toyed with 'The Necessity for Sacrifice'. After reading *The Sacrifice of God* and the helpful review in the *Church Times* by Tom Baker which alerted me to its publication, I was in no doubt that my focus should be on the power of sacrifice about which Moses writes so eloquently:

Sacrifice is about power. The power that is displayed *and released* in the sacrifice of the cross is the power of the divine love. This is the power in which the divine life has been lived from before the foundation of the world. This is the power in which the divine life gives itself to the world. This is the power which loves its own and loves to the end. This is the power by which the Son lays down His life for us. This is the power by which we pass from death to life. This is the power from which nothing in all creation will be able to separate us. But man is called to share in this sacrifice of the divine love. It is part of the challenge of the cross in Christian experience that it makes explicit the truth of our condition and invites a response. It is by entering ever more deeply into the pattern of life and death and life – the pattern of the incarnate and crucified and risen Lord – that men and women find their identity, meaning, wholeness, participation in God.[11]

There is, I think, a danger that we can lose a proper sense of the power of sacrifice in our keenness to distance ourselves from its cultic, ritual origins and to see it in entirely spiritual or metaphorical terms. This is a tendency of some of the modern treatments of the theme. Colin Gunton, for example, is very keen always to talk about the 'metaphor of sacrifice' in a way which I feel rather diminishes its objective reality and force. Others have followed Robert Daly, the American Jesuit scholar who has done so much to uncover the early origins of the doctrine of sacrifice, in stressing the way it is 'spiritualized' in the Christian tradition.[12] This is, of course, to some extent true. In common with other advanced religions, Christianity does put much more premium on the inner sacrifice of a broken and contrite heart than the mere outward performance of a cultic act. The sacrifice of Christ on the Cross has a physical as much as a spiritual dimension, however. It involves the shedding of blood as well as the offering up of a willing heart. Jettisoning the notion of sacrifice as a form of propitiation or bribery, which we must, does not mean giving up a sense of its objective power or its awesome mystery, which we must not.

It is a power which is deeply paradoxical, binding and bringing together what is broken and fragmented through a process which itself involves surrender and suffering. Nowhere is this shown more clearly than on the Cross where Christ's body is dismembered and broken for the world, to be re-membered at each celebration of the Eucharist and in all our work for reconciliation and forgiveness. Sacrifice is the supreme *opus Dei*, the working out of God's power to make holy and to make whole. At the same time it is also the work to which we are continually called as his creatures. Its full life-giving and life-restoring energy is released when divine and human come together. This was the insight that led our primal ancestors to see the sacrificial altar as the source of sacred energy which kept life going, the meeting place between earth and heaven. To quote Robert Daly, sacrifice was 'the centre of a dynamic process in which the divine and human came into contact'.[13]

The word 'dynamic' is very important here. When we talk about the power of sacrifice, it is the Greek word δυναμις that is appropriate rather than the Latin *potestas*. Sacrifice is not static; it is a form of communication and a form of energy. It is about movement and it is, as we have seen, a two-way process. Its power is that of a poem – the power to evoke a response. It achieves its work by yielding and giving up rather than by forcing and imposing. Its strength is its weakness.

This, of course, is the power that is at the heart of the Christian gospel. It is the love that suffers which is the love that saves, the wounded healer who alone can heal, the servant of all who is the lord of all. The power of sacrifice is the wholeness that comes from self-emptying, the secureness that comes from self-giving, the majesty of meekness. At its heart is the paradox so beautifully expressed in the third verse of Sebastian Temple's reworking of the prayer traditionally attributed to St Francis:

> Make me a channel of your peace,
> It is in pardoning that we are pardoned,
> In giving to all men that we receive;
> And in dying that we're born to eternal life.

There are two particular areas of contemporary life where I am struck by the power of sacrifice, in one case potential and in the other actual. The first is the environmental crisis. It is becoming increasingly clear that our planet is only going to survive as a living system if human beings, and more particularly those human beings who live in the richer parts of the world, lead much more sacrificial lives. I do not think that I made nearly enough of this point in *God is Green*, the book that I wrote in 1990 about Christianity and the environment.

I was struck by a review of it in the Quaker journal, *The Friend* which concluded:

> I'm disappointed that the message isn't rammed home and readers will feel free to carry on shopping. In a world of finite resources, unrestrained economic growth spells doom. The chance is missed of bringing out the imperative of the Christian message of not laying up treasures on earth: that we need, as far as possible every one of us, to steer ourselves away from material wealth. In short, we must orient our lives more towards spiritual values. If we do not, life on earth will perish.[14]

The whole environmental crisis has brought an unprecedented urgency to the 2,000-year-old call to Christians to be living sacrifices. We need to give up the convenience of travelling everywhere by car, the luxury of eating strawberries in winter and the excitement of constantly buying new gadgets and appliances for our homes. It is within our power to save the world if we apply the principles of limitation, moderation and restraint to our appetites and our desires. If we fail to harness these sacrificial powers, it is equally within our power to destroy life as we know it.

There is another way in which the current environmental crisis underlines the power and the necessity of sacrifice. It has been largely caused by the fact that we see the world in instrumental terms, as an object which exists to satisfy our greed and which we can dominate and control. We have lost any sense of awe and wonder: we have desacralized the world and in the process we have desacralized ourselves. This is the antithesis of the sacrificial approach. In his useful study, *Sacrifice: Its Nature and Purpose*, yet another of the volumes on the subject which have appeared in the last few years, Godfrey Ashby notes that sacrifice is 'the language of communication used from time immemorial by men when they have approached the supernatural, the unseen. This language makes use of material gifts which belong to the normal life of the offerers, and the offering of sacrifice is seen either as a divine command prescribed by the supernatural powers, or at least as a holy custom long since used in intercourse with the ancestors or the gods'.[15] At the heart of this traditional understanding is the idea of sacramentality, a recognition of the holiness of the mundane, the spirituality of the physical, the transcendence of matter. This insight which was so fundamental to the faith and practice of our Celtic Christian ancestors has been largely lost in modern times, despite finding significant twentieth-century exponents in such figures as Pierre Teilhard de Chardin and George Macleod. We badly need to recover it, not just so that we can live in harmony with the rest of nature, but so that we can live at peace with ourselves. In short, we need to view the world through the lens of sacrifice which shows that the destiny of things is to be offered up and made holy before God rather than to be exploited and used for our gratification and pleasure.

The other area I want to mention shows the power of sacrifice in actual rather than potential terms. It is in the field of care which involves that huge army of parents, children, partners, relatives, neighbours, friends and volunteers who help those who are in need and who often exhibit the most extraordinary level of selfless devotion and costly attention to others. We can all think of examples from our own family, our own congregation, our own neighbourhood: the elderly man who tirelessly looks after his wife smitten with Alzheimer's disease; the young wife who lavishes care on her husband crippled with multiple sclerosis; children who have given up both job and marriage prospects to stay at home with ailing parents. There is nothing new about such examples of costly self-giving, of course, but over recent years the whole concept of community care has had a much higher profile, and the need has arisen for a much greater body of carers, partly as a result of the significantly higher proportion of elderly people in the population and also because of a conscious policy of closing long-stay hospitals and other institutions which previously housed many of the more frail and vulnerable members of our society. Community care can only work if there is a substantial reservoir of altruism and compassion in society:

it depends on the persistence of the sacrificial spirit. The remarkable webs and networks of care that exist even in our increasingly fragmented and atomized society surely demonstrate that those who see human beings as selfish gene machines and who suggest that people are motivated primarily by self-interest are wrong. The power of sacrifice, costly, self-limiting and at the same time liberating and healing, is manifestly at work here more clearly than in any other area of contemporary life.

The widespread incidence and persistence of human altruism is both a wonder and a mystery greater, perhaps, even than the mystery of suffering with which it is so often and so intimately linked. Not infrequently, indeed, it is those who suffer most themselves who show the deepest compassion and most selfless devotion to others. I am thinking, for instance, of sufferers from AIDS who often show an extraordinary level of concern and regard for one another (see p. 252). I suppose the classic example of altruistic behaviour in modern Britain, at least in its institutionalized form, is the blood donor system celebrated in Richard Titmuss' seminal book, *The Gift Relationship*. The most vital commodity for saving and preserving lives is provided freely by volunteers and not, as in so many other countries, bought and sold. It is perhaps not altogether fanciful to see this as a contemporary demonstration, albeit secularized and directed humanwards rather than heavenwards, of that same sacrificial impulse which led our ancestors to pour out the blood of pigeons and lambs on their altars. Professor Robin Gill has recently pointed to the paradox that in a society apparently dominated by self-interest altruism still flourishes. He goes on to argue powerfully that self-regarding interest, with its attendant values of autonomy, entitlement and rights, is an inadequate basis either for moral behaviour or for living in a community. Altruism, conceive in terms of concern for others and a sense of duty and 'other-directedness' is a requirement not just of moral behaviour but of human living. 'Fortunately', he observes, 'most people seem to recognize this in practice, even if they currently tend to deny it in theory.'[16]

So much for illustrations of the continuing need for and the enduring power of sacrifice today. I want to end this chapter on a more personal note by describing some of the symbols that have helped me to approach the mystery of sacrifice and to understand some of its many levels of meaning. Symbols are immensely important in all religions – symbols of sacrifice perhaps particularly so. 'Sacrifice and symbol belong together and cannot be eliminated. It is an impoverished society that has lost all awareness of the power of symbols. A discovery of the signs of the mystery of atonement will involve a rediscovery of the symbols by which we live. The symbol system of the Christian religion is inseparable from sacrifice.'[17]

Sacrificial symbols are among the most prominent features in the architecture and decoration of churches. It is as much through meditating on them as through theological reading and reflection that I have become more and more convinced of the power, depth and rich mystery of sacrifice. The simplest and starkest of these symbols is, of course, the Cross which is the focal point of virtually every place of Christian worship. It can be simple or elaborate, standing at the level of the worshippers or raised up high in glory, exhibiting the agony and passion of the dying Christ or empty to symbolize resurrection and victory. It is at once both an emblem of suffering and shame and a pointer to transfiguration and glory. More than anything else, however, it speaks of the power of sacrifice in all its mysterious complexity: the life that comes from the midst of death, the holiness of costly self-giving, the victoriousness of surrender and the wholeness of abandonment. 'In a mysterious way', writes Dillistone, 'the Man upon the Cross retains His place in the human imagination as the timeless symbol of reconciliation through sacrifice'. John Moses puts it even more directly: 'The cross is the element of uncompromising and inescapable sacrifice at the centre of the Christian faith'.[18]

In the parish church where I have worshipped for the last five years, as in many in the Church of Scotland, the cross is fixed on the wall of the east end. Below it, on top of a wooden chair which sits behind the communion table from where the minister presides at the celebration of the sacrament of the Lord's Supper, is another sacrificial symbol in the form of a carved figure of a pelican apparently pecking its breast. Initially I was puzzled as to why this particular image should have such a prominent place in the sanctuary. It was only when I saw this bird similarly depicted in carvings and windows in other churches that I began to realize that it must hold some special significance. There is a particularly fine example at Bradford Cathedral in the south chancel window which was largely designed by William Morris. Beneath a centre light representing Jesus as the Saviour of the World a picture by Morris' great friend Philip Webb depicts a pelican feeding its young.

So why does the pelican feature so prominently in Christian art? The answer lies in the belief which seems to have arisen in early medieval times, if not before, that the mother bird pecked her breast to feed her young with her own blood. The influential *Aviarium* of Hugh de Folieto stated that as young fledgling pelicans grow, they often attack their parents who sometimes come near to killing their offspring in self-defence. Filled with remorse, the mother pelicans pierce their breasts and revive the young with their own blood. This self-sacrificial act was taken as a metaphor and symbol of the redemption of humanity by the atoning blood of Christ. It ties in with medieval images of Jesus as a mother nurturing his followers with a mixture of the blood and milk that was seen to flow from his breast. St Thomas Aquinas' great hymn in adoration of the Blessed Sacrament, translated into English in the mid-seventeenth century by Richard Crawshaw, addressed Christ as '*Pie pelicane*':

> O soft self-wounding Pelican!
> Whose breast weeps Balm for wounded man.
> Ah this way bend thy benign floud
> To a bleeding Heart that gaspes for blood.[19]

Biologists whom I have consulted on this matter are unanimous in their view that there is no truth whatsoever in the idea that the mother pelican feeds its young with its own blood. They surmise that the myth may have arisen because of the bird's habit of resting its long, pouched bill on its breast and manipulating the oil gland which is located there. Pious fiction though the legend of the sacrificial pelican may be, however, there are plenty of genuine examples from the animal world of altruistic behaviour. Octopuses and sea-lice might not be as easy or attractive to depict in carvings and stained-glass windows but, as we will discover, they are among several species whose behaviour is characterized by a quite extraordinary level of costly self-giving. The prevalence of altruistic behaviour in the world of nature is one of the most significant pointers to the existence of a universal law and principle of sacrifice working throughout creation. If the symbol of the pelican can point us towards the creative and redemptive power of self-giving, universally experienced and uniquely focused and realized in the person of Jesus Christ, then let us not consign it to the demythologizers' and post-modernists' dustbin but rather rejoice in the rich prescience of the medieval imagination.

There is another sacrificial symbol from the animal world which is found in many churches. This is the *Agnus Dei* or Lamb of God often depicted on a banner or pennant in stained-glass windows, carved on pulpits and communion tables or embroidered on vestments and altar-cloths. Thomas Aquinas' other great eucharistic hymn, *Lauda Sion Salvatorem*, again translated by Crawshaw, makes use of this image to underline its sacrificial theme:

> Lo, the full, finall, SACRIFICE
> On which all figures fix't their eyes.
> The ransom'd ISACK, and his ramme;
> The MANNA, and the PASCHAL Lamb.[20]

The idea of Jesus as the sacrificial lamb that takes away the sins of the world, with its clear echoes of the Jewish Passover tradition, is expressed particularly strongly in St. John's Gospel. It is an image that has appealed to many hymnwriters, ancient and modern. J. M. Neale's translation of a sixth-century hymn, *Pange, lingua*, includes the couplet 'On the Cross the Lamb is lifted/There the sacrifice to be'. A hymn written by Michael Saward in 1968 begins 'O sacrifice of Calvary,/O Lamb whose sacred blood was shed' and one of Graham Kendrick's finest songs about the passion starts with the words 'Led like a lamb to the slaughter'. At a rather cruder level a whole host of gospel songs and revivalist choruses has exhorted us to wash in the blood of the lamb.

For me even more significant and striking than the words in the Fourth Gospel about the Lamb of God that takes away the sins of the world is the description of 'the Lamb slain from the foundation of the world' (Revelation 13:8). It presents the sacrifice of Christ as an event which has been ordained from the beginning of time and not as an emergency rescue operation which God had to mount to deal with the unforeseen consequences of human sin and disobedience. This text has had a very powerful influence on sensitive Christian souls like George Matheson and Nikolai Berdiaev who have seen it as stressing the eternal quality of the sacrifice of Christ.

There is another New Testament text which draws on the world of nature to illustrate the theme of sacrifice that has come to haunt me more than any other passage in the Bible. I have had plenty of opportunity to ponder its meaning since it is engraved on the stained-glass window beneath which our family nearly always sits on Sunday mornings. The window, part of which is reproduced on the cover of this book, commemorates Lieutenant John Alexander Hay Smith of the Royal Scots who was killed in action at the age of 24 in August 1915. The central section shows Jesus talking to his disciples. At the top is a depiction of the crucifixion and other sacrificial scenes. Towards the bottom, above two roundels portraying a farmer scattering grain and a harvest scene, is a scroll with the words recorded in John 12:24: 'Verily, verily, I say unto you, except a corn of wheat fall into the ground and die, it abideth alone: but if it die, it bringeth forth much fruit'.

The more I have meditated on these words, the more richly suggestive and widely applicable I find them. They proclaim the tragic yet triumphant truth that death is necessary for birth and growth, beautifully expressed by the early twentieth-century French philosopher of religion, Alfred Loisy, in his classic essay on sacrifice: 'to die is but to live again; life issues from death, and death is the condition and means of life'.[21] Jesus' words strike a chord at many different levels. They are, of course, manifestly true about the growing of plants and crops as every farmer and gardener knows. The dependence of life on death here is not just seen in the need to bury grains and bulbs in the ground but in a whole host of other ways, some of which are indicated in this meditation by Mervyn Wilson, small farmer and Anglican country parson:

> The fruit farmer kills the aphis and the larva of the codling moth. The gardener does his best to destroy the hosts of the scale insects and potato-boring wireworm and the leaf-killing red spider. Thorn hedges are cut and laid to keep in livestock. Trees are felled for the carpenter and for fire-wood. The ground is scarred for building materials. The gardener plants shrubs close together; one he must uproot if the other is to thrive.[22]

This is to speak of death and destruction in the world of nature brought about by humans for their own benefit. Nature itself also depends on death for its self-regulation and survival. Witness the key role that programmed cell death plays in the healthy development of the chromosomes and molecular structures that make up the basic building-blocks of life and the constant surrender and self-limitation of species which underlies the whole process of evolution.

Then there is the extent to which Jesus' words apply to the human condition. We know that in our lives it is constantly necessary to die to the old, the stale and the selfish if we are to grow and progress. In St John's Gospel Jesus' saying about the corn of wheat is immediately followed and amplified by his statement that 'He that loveth his life shall lose it; and he that hateth his life in this world shall keep it unto life eternal' (John 12:25). This is a hard and difficult doctrine to accept.

We now know that the author of the Fourth Gospel may have come from a narrow and persecuted Christian community which saw itself as being set against the world and that this fact may well have coloured his theology. Yet it is not just in this gospel that we find the notion that it is only by dying to self and attachment to the world that people can find their true identity: the same point is made in every one of the gospels. Indeed, we find it twice in Matthew (10:39 and 16:25) and Luke (9:24 and 17:33) as well as once in Mark: 'For whosoever will save his life shall lose it; but whosoever shall lose his life for my sake and the gospel's, the same shall save it. For what shall it profit a man, if he shall gain the whole world and lose his own soul?' (Mark 8:35).

The image of the corn of wheat buried in the ground reminds us of the difficult, unpalatable kernel of Christian discipleship – that it is about denying ourselves, taking up our own crosses and following the *via dolorosa* which Jesus trod. This is not its only message, however. It also speaks of the transfiguring glory of resurrection. This is the fruit of sacrifice, the triumphant and certain outcome of its costliness and pain.

It is extremely important that we hold on to this aspect of sacrifice. If we understand it only in terms of crucifixion and without the element of resurrection, we reduce it to a negative doctrine of self-destruction and humiliation. It is the image of the abundant fruit which is produced when the grain is buried and dies with which Jesus concludes his statement. Significantly, when St Paul uses similar language it is to explain the Christian idea of transfiguring resurrection:

What you sow does not come to life unless it dies. And what you sow is not the body which is to be, but a bare kernel, perhaps of wheat or of some other grain. But God gives it a body he has chosen, and to each kind of seed its own body. . . . So it is with the resurrection of the dead. What is sown is perishable, what is raised is imperishable. It is sown in dishonour, it is raised in glory. It is sown in weakness, it is raised in power (1 Corinthians 15:36–8; 42–3).

Jesus is also surely thinking of himself when he tells his disciples about the corn of wheat. Certainly, the graphic picture that he paints seems to describe perfectly his own impending death, burial and rising again. Several Christian poets and mystics through the centuries have seen the Easter story in these terms. The seventeenth-century radical Puritan, Gerard Winstanley, imagined the dead Christ as 'lying in the grave, like a corn of wheat buried under the clods for a time'.[23] Early this century John MacLeod Campbell Crum penned his beautiful and justly popular Easter hymn which brings together so many of the strands of meaning in Jesus' apparently simple statement.

Now the green blade riseth from the buried grain,
Wheat that in dark earth many days has lain;
Love lives again, that with the dead has been:
    Love is come again
    Like wheat that springeth green.

In the grave they laid him, Love whom men had slain,
Thinking that never would he wake again,
Laid in the earth like grain that sleeps unseen:
    Love is come again
    Like wheat that springeth green.

Forth he came at Easter, like the risen grain,
He that three days in the grave had lain,
Quick from the dead, my risen Lord is seen:
    Love is come again
    Like wheat that springeth green.

When our hearts are wintry, grieving, or in pain,
Thy touch can call us back to life again,
Fields of our hearts, that dead and bare have been:
    Love is come again
    Like wheat that springeth green.

There is one further symbol of sacrifice which is particularly dear to the hearts of all members of the Church of Scotland. The burning bush from which God speaks to Moses is the emblem of our church and the phrase which describes it in Exodus 3:2 *'nec tamen consumebatur'* (yet it was not consumed) is our motto. Fire has, of course, been an essential element of sacrifice in most of the great religions of the world. The smoke rising from the altars on which victims were slain and burnt was seen as the medium which carried human offerings to the gods and through which the divinities descended. It was in this sacred scent that the worlds of earth and heaven met and intermingled. Central to Israelite temple worship were the *'olâs* or burnt offerings whose sweet savour was 'pleasing in the sight of Yahweh'. In Hinduism the fire god Agni has a crucial role as both the priest and victim of the sacrificial flame which mysteriously brings the gods to the gods.

Christianity may have dispensed with the actual element of fire in its worship, just as it has dispensed with the ritual slaughter of animals. However, the image of the eternal sacrificial flame which judges, purges and burns away sin and evil, while continuing to blaze in the hearts of the faithful, has remained especially potent to poets and hymnwriters. Perhaps no one has captured it better in words than Charles Wesley.

> O thou who camest from above
> The pure celestial fire to impart,
> Kindle a flame of sacred love
> On the mean altar of my heart.

> There let it for thy glory burn
> With inextinguishable blaze,
> And trembling to its source return
> In humble prayer and fervent praise.

> Jesus, confirm my heart's desire
> To work, and speak, and think for thee;
> Still let me guard the holy fire,
> And still stir up thy gift in me.

2

Osiris, Purusa and *zimsum*: creation as sacrifice

The subject of primal religion is rightly attracting more and more attention not just from anthropologists and historians of religion but also from Christian theologians. In the rites and beliefs of so-called primitive societies we can often discern the origins of practices and doctrines found in more complex and advanced cultures. The study of comparative religions has made us realize the extent to which the world's great faiths overlap and borrow from one another. It is now generally recognized how much Christianity owes not just to its Jewish roots but to other religious traditions found in the Middle East in the first century AD. More widely, scholars like John Hick and R. C. Zaehner have shown the extent to which the world's eight great faiths (Christianity, Judaism, Islam, Hinduism, Buddhism, Taoism, Shintoism and Sikhism) share common features deriving from their roots in the primal religions which were the first expression of the human quest for the eternal.

The practice of sacrifice is a central feature in all known primal religions. Indeed, as F. C. N. Hicks has observed, 'in practically every quarter of the globe religion as it emerges as such in a recognisable form is bound up with sacrificial practice'.[1] Some scholars have even argued that ritual came before belief and that the origins of religion itself lie in sacrifice. In their classic work on the subject Henri Hubert and Marcel Mauss see in sacrifice the genesis of the gods. Through the repetition of ceremonies involving an identical victim a particular personality is created and 'the accumulation of past sacrifices thus culminates in the creation of a god'.[2] Whether the practice of sacrifice did, indeed, engender religious beliefs

48

and myths or vice versa, is a matter of considerable debate. What is undisputed, however, is its ubiquity and potency in primal religions and its role as the critical point of intersection between this world and the next, the meeting place of humans and gods and the ultimate source of all energy and renewal, and, indeed, of life itself.

Much of the work that has been done on this subject has focused on the nature of the rites performed, the way in which the victims were viewed and the motives of those involved. This has tended to reinforce the distorted view of sacrifice as something done by humans to win the favour of or to placate the gods on the principle of *do ut des* – 'I give that you may give'. There is, however, a rather different and much deeper conception discernible in many primal religions: an understanding that as a continuing process of birth coming out of death, renewal and strength out of limitation and surrender, sacrifice is the principle of life itself in both the natural and the human world with origins that are divine rather than human.

One of the earliest and most widespread forms in which this understanding of the principle of life coming out of death and recreation through sacrifice came to be expressed and acted out was in the cult of the god who dies and rises again. Divinities of this kind were a marked feature of ancient nature religions and were associated particularly with the annual cycle of the seasons and the way in which crops experienced an apparent rebirth in spring having died in winter. James Frazer, the great Scottish anthropologist best known for his study, *The Golden Bough*, first published in 1890, was struck by the way in which primitive peoples 'pictured to themselves the growth and decay of vegetation, the birth and death of living creatures, as effects of the waxing or waning strength of divine beings, of gods and goddesses, who were born and died, who married and begot children, on the pattern of human life'.[3]

The ancient Egyptians who farmed the Nile valley were particularly conscious of this cyclical pattern of death and rebirth. Every autumn as the waters of the Nile receded, veg-

the swollen river irrigated the land and plants grew again. This experience may have contributed to the development of the cult of Osiris, the Nile god, who became second in importance among Egyptian deities only to Isis, the Sun god. From the period of the Middle Kingdom (*c.* 1900 BC) corn effigies of Osiris were buried in the ground during the autumn. The shoots that sprung out of them in the spring were taken to indicate the rising of the god from death. There is a striking parallel here with Jesus' words about the corn of wheat needing to fall into the ground and die if it is to bring forth fruit and with the hymn 'Now the green blade riseth'. A similar annual rite, long practised by the Arabs of Moab, was observed by Frazer:

> When the harvesters have nearly finished their task and only a small corner of the field remains to be reaped, the owner takes a handful of wheat tied up in a sheaf. A hole is dug in the form of a grave and two stones are set upright, one at the head and the other at the foot, just as in an ordinary burial. Then the sheaf of wheat is laid at the bottom of the grave, and the sheikh pronounces these words: 'The old man is dead'. Earth is afterwards thrown in to cover the sheaf, with a prayer, 'May Allah bring back the wheat of the dead'.[4]

Work by more recent historians of religion, notably J. Gwyn Griffiths, has suggested that the identification of Osiris with vegetation and fertility was a rather later development than pioneer anthropologists like Frazer thought.[5] It has, however, done nothing to diminish the essentially sacrificial nature of the cult which surrounded this particular Egyptian god and the extent to which it reinforced a primal understanding of life and rebirth coming out of death. Osiris was thought to have been murdered by his brother Seth, thrown into a sarcophogus and committed to the Nile. When he returned from the dead his brother slew him again, this time tearing his body into fourteen pieces and scattering them over the land. His dismembered body was later reassembled by

Isis, but not before its blood had irrigated the ground. In another later development of the cult Egyptian farmers annually slew a human victim, representative of the corn spirit, and scattered either his dismembered flesh or ashes over a field to fertilize it. Later on an animal victim was substituted. Those who had taken part in this ritual sometimes shared in consuming some of the victim's flesh or blood so that they might themselves secure the benefits of rising again after death. Osiris came to be seen as a saviour who could achieve for those who worshipped him the resurrection from death which he himself had achieved. He was, in the words of Frazer, 'the one who could raise the dead to life eternal just as he caused the seed to spring from the ground ... a god who fed his people with his own broken body in this life and who held out to them a promise of a blissful eternity in a better world hereafter'.[6]

These sacrificial developments in the cult of Osiris link with the widespread sense among ancient peoples that the continuation and renewal of life depended on the shedding and spilling of blood. This theme was picked up by several pioneer anthropologists and historians of religion. In his research into the religious beliefs and practices of the Semites William Robertson Smith found widespread evidence of the belief that fertility came out of sacrifice while Emile Durkheim's work on primitive societies in Australia highlighted the role of blood as a life-giving essence which was either poured out on the ground to promote fertility or drunk to promote immortality.[7]

The gradual emergence in Egyptian religion of a system of salvation centred on the figure of Osiris is paralleled by the development of similar cults in the ancient world based on worship of dying and rising gods and belief in the salvific and regenerative effects of blood and sacrifice. The ancient Greeks worshipped the slain and resurrected Dionysus with dark, bloody rites associated with the renewal of vegetation, the sun, the moon and the human soul. In later Hellenistic religion attention shifted to the figure of Adonis, who was personified by priestly kings or other members of the royal family periodically put to death to revive the god's ailing powers and improve fertility. In the eight-day festival of Adonia, which was celebrated in Assyria, Alexandria, Egypt, Judaea, Persia and Cyprus as well as in Greece and Rome, women first lamented Adonis' death and then rejoiced at his resurrection. It is the first stage of this festival which is referred to in Ezekiel 8:14 where the prophet is brought by God to the north gate of the temple in Jerusalem 'and behold, there sat women weeping for Tammuz' (Tammuz being the Phoenician name for Adonis). Phrygian mythology had its own dying and rising god of nature in the figure of Attis, who was personified each year by a human victim who was hanged on a pine tree. In a ceremony known as 'the Day of Blood' the high priest drew blood from the victim's arms which he presented as an offering while other priests gashed their bodies with knives to bespatter the sacrificial altar and tree with blood.[8]

A later cult in classical Greece, which was almost certainly derived from the Eleusinian mysteries, centred around the corn goddess Demeter (known as Ceres in Roman religion). She was hailed as the saviour who died and rose again to bring fertility to the earth and immortality to humans. The great spring festival of Dromenon marked both the renovation of the earth and the refertilization of human life. In the original rites of Demeter at Eleusis a reaped ear of corn was exhibited to worshippers as the central mystery of their religion. In other primal cults ears of newly ripened wheat were seen as possessing almost sacramental efficacy and were eaten by worshippers in the belief that they would convey the power of the corn god to rise after death.

Some Christian theologians have argued that Jesus' death and resurrection can be interpreted as a continuation and final consummation of this motif of the dying and rising God-Man found throughout the ancient world though conspicuously absent in Judaism. In his book, *Revelation and the Modern World*, for example, Lionel Thornton, an Anglican priest and member of the Community of the Resurrection at Mirfield until his death in 1960, put forward the view that when Jesus, the Son of God, took upon himself the role of divine-human priest king he was standing clearly in the tradition of the dying and rising gods of nature which had been departed from in Hebrew religion. Indeed, for Thornton, Jesus' death and resurrection fused nature with history and brought this tradition to completion.[9]

The sacrificial death of the gods, ritually represented and re-enacted by the slaughter of their human representatives, was not just associated by the ancients with the annual cycle of recreation in the world of nature and the gift of life after death for humans. Many primal religions are also characterized by a belief that the original creation of the world, and of human beings, was accomplished through a sacrificial act on the part of the gods. This idea is generally expressed in terms of a creation legend or myth in which the gods are portrayed as giving up some part of themselves in a way which is costly and generally involves the shedding of blood. In some cases, the whole world of matter is seen as growing out of the dismembered body of a god who has been killed. In other accounts the creating god is represented as making both humans and animals out of clay which has been mixed with his own blood.

Possibly the earliest expression of this idea is in the great Babylonic creation myth of *Enuma elish* which was probably composed in the early part of the second millenium BC. Following the pioneering work of Herman Gunkel at the end of the last century, Old Testament scholars are now almost universally agreed in seeing this myth as the main source lying behind the creation story in the opening chapters of the Book of Genesis. Essentially, the Babylonian myth portrays the creation of the world as the outcome of a fierce struggle between two deities, Marduk, god of the sun, and Tiamat, the monster-like god of water who represents the forces of chaos. In the conflict, Marduk subdues Tiamat and the world is formed out of the defeated deity's carcass which is split into two parts, the water above and the water below. The fertility of the land is achieved through his blood and decaying flesh.

Humans are created out of the blood of the demon Kingu to whom Tiamat had entrusted the Tablets of Destiny.

Similar myths which describe the entire created world as growing out of the dismembered body of a primordial being are found in other primal cultures. In Scandinavian mythology both human beings and the gods are seen as deriving from Ymir, a giant in human form and the first of all living creatures who was himself formed from melted drops of ice. Ymir fathered a race of giants some of whom killed him in his old age. His body was later raised from the deep by other offspring, the gods Odin, Vili and Ve, and was formed by them into the earth. Ymir's flesh became the land and his blood the sea. From his bones the gods made mountains and from his hair they made trees. His skull was placed on four raised pillars to be the vault of the heavens into which were put the sun, the moon and the stars. The most popular Chinese creation myth focuses upon a similar primordial being named P'an-ku whose eyes became the sun and moon and from whose body the mountains were formed.

Even more overtly sacrificial themes are to be found in the various creation myths contained in the sacred books of Hinduism. Like their contemporaries in other areas, the Aryan people who came into India in the middle part of the second millenium BC performed frequent sacrifices to gods associated with the world of nature. The purposes of these sacrifices seem to have been threefold: to establish communion with the gods; to remove or cover the taint of sin incurred through contact with 'taboo' objects; and only lastly and least importantly to win divine favour on the *do ut des* principle.

The whole business of sacrifice, or *Yajna*, came to assume enormous importance in Hindu religion. It was the central, if not the only, form of worship practised. Worshippers gathered round the sacrificial fire into which offerings such as butter, milk, meat, grains cooked in milk and goats were thrown in order to be consumed. Occasionally horses and even humans seem to have been sacrificed. The proper performance of these rituals became a matter of considerable importance and many of the great sacred texts of Hinduism were written as manuals describing the correct conduct of sacrifices. In common with the writings of other religious traditions, notably Judaism, they display a progressive shift of emphasis away from ritual slaughter and cultic offerings to a more 'interiorized' or 'spiritualized' understanding of sacrifice in terms of renunciation, asceticism and acts of compassion and charity. There is, however, no sense of the theme of sacrifice in any way diminishing in importance. Indeed, in many ways it becomes even more central as *Yajna* is seen less and less in terms of cultic ritual offered by humans and more and more as the pure creative force behind all life and being.

Several of the most important Hindu gods were associated with sacrifice. This is true both of the earlier Vedic period (from roughly 2000 to 1000 BC), where polytheism was dominant, and of the later age of the *Brahamanas* and *Upanishads* (around 1000 to 400 BC), which is characterized by a more monotheistic approach. Of prime importance among the Vedic deities were Agni, the god who as fire consumed the sacrifice and as priest offered it to the gods above and Soma, the intoxicating drink made from a fungus which in deified form became the central sacrificial libation. In the later Brahamanic period Prajapati, the supreme god who is Lord of the creatures, came to be identified with sacrifice as the force behind primeval creation and was conceived as having 'created the all out of himself'.

The notion that the creation of the world somehow came about out of sacrifice is found in the *Rig Veda*, that great body of hymns to the gods which were written down around 1200 BC. It is first expressed in somewhat obscure language in two creation hymns addressed to the immanent and mysterious god Visvakarman, 'the all-maker' who is described as 'thriving on sacrifice' and as 'sacrificing for himself' earth and heaven.[10] The contemporary Indian philosopher Rajenda Pandeya has suggested that these hymns reveal creation as having a spiritual rather than a material beginning in the form of a sacrifice with 'darkness covering the darkness, that is with the unique and opaque grossness of the primeval water as its first oblation. The sacrificer is the immanent God (Visvakarman) who activates by his radiant presence the opaque and gross primeval waters thereby setting the creative process in motion'.[11]

The fullest account of the creation of the world as an act of sacrifice in the *Rig Veda* is to be found in the *Purusa-Sukta*. This hymn, which was of considerable significance and influence in the development of Hindu religion, describes the entire universe, the world of matter and all physical forces as having come into being out of the primordial sacrifice of Purusa, a cosmic entity which mysteriously embodies the Supreme Being, humanity, all matter and senses, the male principle in the universe and the immortal substance of the human soul.

Purusa is portrayed at the start of the hymn as having a thousand heads, a thousand eyes and a thousand feet and as encompassing the world on all sides and standing out ten fingers' length beyond it. He alone is this Universe, what has been and what is to be. He rules over the gods and grows through sacrificial food. This sense of both immanence and transcendence, being wholly in and of the world and yet having an existence beyond it, is explained by the fact that when Purusa was sacrificed, the larger part of him rose to create the spiritual world of the heavens and the gods while just a quarter remained in the physical plane to form the universe and all that it contains. The actual creation of the world is represented as being brought about through a further sacrifice of this part of Purusa, regarded as Primal Man:

When the gods, with Purusa as the offering, performed the cosmic sacrifice, Spring became the butter of it, Summer the firewood, Autumn the oblation.

They consecrated on the sacred grass this sacrifice, Purusa, born in the beginning. With him the gods sacrificed, the Sadhyas and the Seers.

From this sacrifice, offered as a whole offering, the

ghee-mixture (the juice that flowed off) was collected; it made these animals – those of the air, of the jungle and of the village.

From this sacrifice, offered as a whole-offering, the stanzas of praise (the Rigveda) and the melodies (Samaveda) were produced; the metres were produced therefrom, the sacrificial formulas (Yajurveda) were produced therefrom.

Therefrom were produced horses, and whatever animals have cutting teeth on both jaws. Cattle were produced therefrom, therefrom were born goats and sheep.

When they divided the Purusa, into how many parts did they separate him? What did his mouth become? What his two arms? What are declared to be his two thighs, his two feet?

The Brahman (priestly caste) was his mouth, his two arms became the Rajanya (warrior caste); his two thighs are the Vaisya (artisan caste), from his two feet the Sudra (serf caste) was produced.

The moon sprang from his thought-organ, the sun was produced from his eye; from his mouth Indra (war-god and soma-drinker) and Agni (the Fire-god), from his breath Vayu (the wind) was produced.

From his navel arose the atmosphere, from his head the heaven evolved; from his two feet the earth, from his ear the directions. Thus they fashioned the worlds.[12]

Professor R. C. Zaehner elucidates the meaning of these verses as follows:

The World is nothing less than the disembodied body of Primal Man: it is the completed sacrifice, and all sacrifice is but a repetition and renewal of the creative act, and in the material remains of the sacrifice the whole cosmos, both spiritual and material, is contained – heaven and earth, gods and Vedas, the whole sacrificial system itself as well as *dharma* and truth, for 'the sacrificial altar is the uttermost ends of the earth and the oblation is the navel of the earth'.[13]

Although the *Rig Veda* portrays the gods as being responsible for the sacrifice which creates the world and which has Purusa as its victim, they themselves are at the same time somehow subordinate to it and under its power. Purusa is both subject and object – the ultimate author of the sacrifice which brings all things into being and yet also its victim. There is perhaps a foreshadowing here of the Christian understanding of Jesus Christ as both agent of creation, the Word by whom all things were made, and the crucified one who is sacrificed for the sins of the world. Just as Purusa is both the agent and the object of sacrifice, so Christ is both high priest and victim. This paradox is expressed in the cryptic but highly charged words of the penultimate verse of the *Purusa-Sukta* which are repeated in another of the great Vedic hymns, *Asya-Vamasya* (*The Riddle of the Sacrifice*): 'With the sacrifice the gods sacrificed to the sacrifice'.[14] The message being conveyed here is surely that in some mysterious way the principle of sacrifice lies at the very heart of creation with its own extraordinary power and energy to which even the gods are subject.

This theme is echoed in the *Brahamanas*, the prayer books containing detailed instructions for performing sacrifices which date from the period between 1000 and 800 BC. They too suggest creation coming out of an act of sacrifice by the gods and make even more of the idea that in it the gods have suffered and given up something of themselves. Prajapati, portrayed in the *Satapatha Brahamana* as having created the cosmos from his own substance, is described once he had produced it as 'fearing death' and being in need of the offerings which were brought by the other gods to restore and revive him. There is a somewhat similar story in the *Rig Veda* which portrays the fire god Agni as fleeing and hiding in the waters because of his fear of being destroyed through his constant sacrificial work. He is eventually coaxed out of his hiding place by the other gods on the promise that he will be given 'the pre-sacrifices and the post-sacrifices, the nourishing parts of the offering'.[15]

Cultic and ritual sacrifices thus remained important as a means of replenishing the diminishing strength of the gods and keeping them going so that they might continue the work of nourishing and sustaining creation. The general tendency of the *Brahamanas*, however, is to conceive of sacrifice much less in terms of a ritual to be performed by humans to secure favours from the gods and much more as the sacred energy that charges the whole cosmos, a mysterious force like electricity which sustains order and harmony throughout the universe. For Zaehner, the view expressed in the *Brahamanas* is that 'sacrifice and the world process are in some sense identical'.[16]

The linking of sacrifice with the principle of order is particularly important in the Hindu tradition. It is first clearly propounded in a short hymn in the *Rig Veda* which is concerned with the *Tapas*, or cosmic heat, produced in the sacrificial fire:

> Order and truth were born from heat as it blazed up.
> From that was born night; from that heat was born the
> billowy ocean.
> From the billowy ocean was born the year, that
> arranges days and nights, ruling over all that blinks its eyes.
> The Arranger has set in their proper place the sun and
> moon, the sky and the earth, the middle realm of space,
> and finally the sunlight.[17]

The images in this last verse are strikingly similar to those contained in passages in the Old Testament, notably in Genesis and the Psalms, which portray God as the great arranger of the cosmos. This idea is taken up in Joseph Addison's hymn 'The spacious firmament on high' and Beethoven's great creation hymn with its acknowledgement of the One 'who holds the numberless stars in their places'. In the Vedic tradition, however, the concept of order (or *Rta*) is not just confined to the physical sphere. It embraces the moral values of truth, creativity and justice which are seen as existing in the remains of the sacrifice.

This notion of sacrifice underlying the principles of order and harmony is further developed in the *Upanishads*, the third great corpus of Hindu sacred literature which is generally taken to have been composed between around 800 and 400 BC. In general the *Upanishads* continue the trend begun in the *Brahamanas* and stress the need for renunciation and self-denial rather than burnt offerings or blood-lettings. *Yajna* comes increasingly to be seen as a perpetual process which operates in human beings as well as in the universe. Self-sacrifice purges people and lifts them to immortality. The way to move from this world to the next and higher one is through absorbing the sacrificial fire within oneself.

The fullest development of this more 'spiritualized' notion of sacrifice is to be found in the *Bhagavad Gita* which is generally thought to have been written around 500 BC. It makes much of *karma*, a highly loaded term derived from the Sanskrit root *kri* which also finds its way into the English words 'create' and 'creation'. *Karma* also means 'sacred work' and is connected with the whole Vedic notion of sacrifice. The link made in earlier Vedic texts between creation and sacrifice is thus preserved in the *Bhagavad Gita*. While maintaining the cosmic aspects of this link, however, it is notable in advocating a more personal response to the dominant creative power of sacrifice in terms of individual acts of surrender and self-giving.

> Thus spoke the Lord of Creation when he made both man and sacrifice: 'By sacrifice thou shalt multiply and obtain all thy desires.
>
> By sacrifice shall thou honour the gods and the gods will then love thee. And thus in harmony with them shalt thou attain the supreme good.
>
> For pleased with thy sacrifice, the gods will grant to

thee the joy of all thy desires. Only a thief would enjoy their gifts and not offer them in sacrifice'.

Holy men who take as food the remains of sacrifice become free from all their sins; but the unholy who have feasts for themselves eat food that is in truth sin.

Food is the life of all beings, and all food comes from rain above. Sacrifice brings rain from heaven, and sacrifice is sacred action.

Sacred action is described in the Vedas and these come from the Eternal, and therefore is the Eternal everpresent in a sacrifice.

Thus was the Wheel of the Law set in motion, and that man lives in vain who in a sinful life of pleasure helps not in its revolutions.[18]

It is important to note here that while the stress is now on sacrifices made by individuals, the ground and origin of all sacred action, and therefore of all sacrifice, is still seen as being the Eternal. By offering themselves in acts of self-surrender, humans are in fact helping to keep the eternal wheel of sacrifice going round and living in harmony with the most basic principle of life.

Alongside this increasingly interiorized understanding of sacrifice, the later sacred texts of Hinduism also continue to present a picture of creation coming out of the dismembered body of a sacrificial victim similar to that found in the much earlier *Rig Veda*. The longest and probably the oldest hymn in the Upanishadic collection portrays the whole of created matter as having its origins in the sacrifice of a horse:

The dawn is the head of the sacrificial horse; the sun is its eye, the wind its breath, universal fire its mouth. The year is the self of the sacrificial horse, the sky its back, the atmosphere its belly, the earth the underside of its belly, the cardinal points of the compass its flanks, the intermediate points its ribs, the seasons its limbs, the months and half-months its joints, day and night its feet, the stars its bones, the clouds its flesh. Sand is the food in its stomach, rivers are its entrails, the mountains its liver and lungs, plants and trees its hair. The east is its fore part, the west its hind part. When it yawns, then there is lightning. When it shakes itself, then there is thunder. When it urinates, then there is rain.[19]

Like earlier texts, the *Upanishads* insist not just that the world came into existence through the power of sacrifice but also that it is held in being and continually renewed through the same agent. *Yajna* is the basis of both creation and recreation, an action in eternity which is the source of all energy and life. It is also an action of the gods in which the phenomenal world participates by providing the essential ingredients of *soma* and fire. Indeed, there is a wonderful reciprocity here which links the gods, humans and the physical world of matter in an interdependent chain. The gods subsist on what is offered to them from below just as humans subsist on gifts that come to them from the heavens above.

In this schema the sacrificial altar becomes the key point of contact between the human and divine worlds. The fire, as priest, consumes the oblation which sustains the gods and which simultaneously transmits their virtue to those taking part. The altar is also the place where creation is renewed. Each and every sacrifice represents a renewal, if not an actual repetition, of the original act of creation and a microcosmic representation of the continual and eternal process of destruction and renewal, death and resurrection which is going on throughout the cosmos. Nothing can endure if it is not continuously animated and reinvigorated through the power of sacrifice.

The importance of this continuous, sustaining, regenerative role of sacrifice in Hinduism and in other religious traditions was well brought out in the work of Mircea Eliade, the Rumanian-born philosopher and historian of religion who died in 1986. In his book, *The Myth of the Eternal Return*, he pointed to the way in which each and every Brahmanic sacrifice marked a new creation of the world. The construction of a sacrificial altar was conceived as a 'creation of the world' with the clay forming its base as the earth, the water with which it was mixed as the primordial water and the side walls as the atmosphere. Each stage of the construction of the altar was accompanied by the reading of verses describing the creation. Eliade also suggests that part of the purpose behind these sacrifices was an attempt to restore the primordial unity and harmony which had been lost at the moment of creation because of the suffering and surrender involved on the part of the gods and the violence and bloodshed which accompanied it.[20]

This sense that through sacrifice creation could be both repeated and renewed was not peculiar to the Hindus. Eliade finds it also among the Fijians, the Polynesians and other primal peoples. It is at the basis of what he calls the myth of eternal return:

> The death of the individual and the periodic death of humanity are necessary, even as the three days of darkness preceding the 'rebirth' of the moon are necessary. The death of the individual and the death of humanity are alike necessary for their regeneration. Any form whatever, by the mere fact that it exists as such and endures, necessarily loses vigour and becomes worn; to recover vigour, it must be reabsorbed into the formless if only for an instant; it must be restored to the primordial unity from which it issued; in other words, it must return to 'chaos' (on the cosmic plane), to 'orgy' (on the social plane), to 'darkness' (for seed), to 'water' (baptism on the human plane, Atlantis on the plane of history), and so on.[21]

We are brought back here to the central tragic mystery of all existence: that life proceeds from death, progress from suffering and surrender. We are back, too, to Christ's words about the need for the corn of wheat to fall into the ground and die before it can bring forth fruit and to the significance of his own descent into the depths for three days before his resurrection. We are also close to the symbolism at the heart of the Christian sacrament of baptism as expounded by Paul where we die with Christ in order that we may be reborn.[22]

In other respects, however, we seem to be very far from traditional Judaeo-Christian teaching on creation. There is no place in the Genesis story for corn gods, sacrificial horses or primordial beings being dismembered to create the world. At first sight, at least, and certainly as it has traditionally been interpreted, there is no suggestion of sacrifice or suffering on the part of the creator God. Rather the picture is of an omnipotent God fashioning the entire world out of nothing seemingly without effort or any loss of power. This certainly is how many contemporary Old Testament scholars see it. In the words of William Dyrness, 'The job of creating the world contained no struggle for God as it so often does in Near Eastern mythology'.[23] Even the much more radical Claus Westermann agrees that 'There is no sign at all of any struggle between God and *tehom* (the deep) corresponding to the struggle between Marduk and Tiamat'.[24] Neither Jewish nor Christian worship has traditionally been conceived of as in any way renewing or sustaining the flagging creative powers of the Almighty. Nor has mainstream Christian theology had any time for a myth of eternal return. Its worldview is historical and linear rather than cyclical, with a definite beginning and a definite end. Creation, like redemption, has generally been conceived of as a once-for-all sufficient and complete event in history and not as some continuous process which depends on the constantly renewing and energizing power of sacrifice.

This traditional view of creation transmitted through Judaism to Christianity has not been without its dissenters, however. There have always been those Christians whose understanding of creation and the role of God within it has been more akin to that found in other religions. In the latter part of the twentieth century they have been joined by a growing number of distinguished theologians influenced by such strong contemporary movements as patripassianism and process thought and by images of God as the Crucified One or the Divine risk-taker. There has been much more readiness to think and talk in terms of God's brokenness and vulnerability and to see creation as a continuous, open-ended process involving risk and exposure to the world rather than a far-off and long-completed historical event accomplished by a remote and distant deity. It is, indeed, much more possible now for Christians to conceive of creation as a continuous sacrificial act on the part of God which involves costly love, self-limitation and surrender.

Even within the Old Testament there are hints which suggest that creation may not be quite the simple, straightforward divine 'zap' of traditional Judaeo-Christian cosmology. There are a number of passages which echo the *Enuma elish*'s portrayal of a battle and which specifically portray God as having taken on and defeated Rahab, the primeval dragon and chaos monster:

By his power he stilled the sea;
by his understanding he smote Rahab (Job 26:12).

Thou didst crush Rahab like a carcass,
thou didst scatter thy enemies with thy mighty arm
(Psalm 89:10).

Was it not thou that didst cut Rahab in pieces,
that didst pierce the dragon? (Isaiah 51:9).

Although the impression created by these passages is of a decisive victory gained by God over Rahab, the sea monster, they also leave a lingering sense of the continuing presence of the forces of chaos, represented particularly by the restless power of the sea which was so much feared by the Israelites. The theme of chaos has received considerable attention among Old Testament theologians in the twentieth century, thanks largely to the pioneering work of the great German scholar, Herman Gunkel. In his seminal work, *Creation and Chaos*, published in 1895 he used the term *chaoskampf* to describe the dominant theme of the opening chapters of Genesis. Classical Jewish and Christian theology have traditionally portrayed God as creating the world out of nothing – *ex nihilo*. Many modern scholars of the Hebrew Bible, however, follow Gunkel in interpreting the Genesis stories rather as describing a process whereby order and form are fashioned out of chaos. In this, they stand in a tradition which reaches back at least as far as the second-century Greek apologist, Justin Martyr, who held that 'God created all things out of formless matter'[25] and which finds expression in Isaac Watts' magisterial paraphrase of Psalm 90:

> Before the hills in order stood,
> or earth received her frame,
> from everlasting thou art God,
> to endless years the same.

At the beginning of the creation account in the first chapter of Genesis the Holy Spirit is pictured as moving over the face of the primeval waters. God goes on to divide the waters from the waters, an action explicable in terms of Hebrew cosmology where the earth was envisaged as floating on water and the heavens as being stretched out like a giant umbrella to hold back the water surrounding the cosmos. In this, there are close parallels both with the Babylonian creation myth and with the creation hymns in the *Rig Veda* where Indra, the king of the gods, is depicted on the bed of the primordial ocean while Brahma, the prototype of creativity, hovers overhead. While Genesis goes on to describe the watery forces of chaos being reined in and tamed by God, they never lose their unpredictable power to upset the order and harmony of creation. Indeed, they continue to be portrayed as an ever-present threat throughout the New Testament until the Book of Revelation triumphantly declares that at the new creation there will be no more sea. Even in the apparently confident strains of that marvellous nineteenth-century hymn on creation, 'Eternal father, strong to save' there is a recognition that the restless wave and the mighty ocean will not always keep to their appointed limits.

It is notable that many scientists should recently have

become interested in chaology, the study of the apparently random disorder which seems to characterize the behaviour of all matter. Increasingly physicists, mathematicians and astronomers are stressing the instability and unpredictability at the heart of the physical world. Chaos seems to be ever present as a background and counter-force to order and harmony just as it is ever present in the Genesis story of creation. Can we go so far as to say that the Creator God of the Judaeo-Christian tradition is, in fact, constrained and limited in some way by the forces of chaos, that there is a dark region of disorder which he cannot ever totally eliminate? If so, then we are acknowledging the motif that runs through so many of the primal creation myths and through so much modern science: the interplay of chaos and order, chance and necessity, unpredictability and purpose. We are also affirming, as the Bible surely affirms and as several modern theologians want to stress, the very close link between creation and redemption. Indeed, we may well want to see them as inseparable and to view God's creative activity as a continuing process of redemption and salvation from the forces of chaos and disorder. This is surely being true to the witness of the Hebrew psalmists and prophets who portray God not as a divine conjuror magicing into existence something out of nothing but rather as the one who works unceasingly to sustain order and purpose and to fashion form and meaning out of chaos.

Is it also possible for the Judaeo-Christian tradition to go further and acknowledge as the primal religions do that the agency which, under and through God, achieves this work of creation is sacrifice, understood not in terms of the cultic offering of victims but rather of self-limitation and costly self-giving? This surely follows from the understanding of creation outlined above.

What can it mean to speak of creation as a victory over hostile forces, a defeat of the forces of chaos? If God creates 'from nothing', there can be no eternally existent opposite principle to God, as there is in dualistic systems of thought where forces of good and evil are for ever balanced against each other. The Old Testament itself does not ask such abstract, philosophical questions, but we may surely say that the picture of redemption from chaos (Gen. 1:1–3) means that creation involves God in cost and pain from the very beginning. God is always sustaining his creation and keeping it from falling into nothing. In creation God gives freedom to something over against himself; he limits himself by the freedom of others, his creatures, and becomes vulnerable to their decisions.[26]

The whole question of the cost to God of creation is a very important one which has rightly come to concern many theologians in the present generation. If we are coming to a view that creation does in a very real sense represent a sacrifice on the part of God then the biblical image of the One who fashions order out of chaos is of central importance. Chaos and disorder are states of wild and unrestrained excess, self-indulgence and lack of restraint. To create order and harmony requires setting boundaries and imposing limits and this is just as much true for the creator as for the material which is being shaped and given form. The potter working with clay (an image which is, of course, used to describe God's continuing creative work in the Old Testament), the artist contemplating a black canvas, the composer embarking on a new piece are all in some senses constrained and limited both by the nature of the medium in which they are working and also by principles and conventions of their art. Nothing valuable, and certainly nothing orderly and structured, is created without considerable effort and cost, nor without some surrender of the wilder excesses and temptations to which we are all subject, creative artists perhaps more than most. The twentieth century has, of course, seen a widespread abandonment of the principle of sacrifice in creativity, as in so many other areas, and a positive cult of the chaotic, the unstructured and the formless. The utterly trivial and brutalizing nature of so many of the products created in this flight from any kind of limitation and restraint surely serves only to highlight the connection between order and sacrifice in the creative process.

Interestingly, this connection has been made in Christian theology, though not in the context of creation. In his treatise on *The Christian Sacrifice* Eugene Masure makes the observation that 'before sacrifice there was nothing achieved. After sacrifice order has appeared'.[27] This remark is made about the sacrifice of Christ on the Cross but could it not equally apply to the activity of God in creation? In somewhat similar vein Colin Gunton has commented in his recent study of the atonement that sacrifice 'has to do at least in part with the ordering and reordering of life both in the cosmos and in relation to God'.[28] Again, this remark is made specifically about Christ's sacrifice on the Cross. May we not justifiably extend it to the Trinitarian God's work of creation? We can, indeed, do this while keeping the focus firmly Christocentric and by resting on a fundamental tenet of orthodox Christian doctrine, namely that creation was and is carried out by God *per verbum*, through the agency of the Word. It is the doctrine that is stated so splendidly and sonorously in the opening verses of St John's Gospel: 'In the beginning was the Word, and the Word was with God, and the Word was God. He was in the beginning with God; all things were made through him and without him was not anything made that was made'. The Word has, of course, been identified throughout Christian theology with Jesus Christ, the pre-existent Logos, who dwells with his Father from before time and is the special agent of both creation and redemption. There has also been a clear connection made between Christ the Word and the bringing of order out of chaos, as in the New Testament miracle stories of Jesus stilling the storm and walking on water and in John Marriott's great hymn inspired by the Genesis creation story. 'Thou, whose almighty Word chaos and darkness heard, and took their flight'.

Now one of the most distinctive and characteristic marks of the Word as it is incarnated in the person of Jesus Christ is that of sacrifice. If this principle lay at the basis of his life and work on earth, then is it not also likely to have characterized

his role as agent of creation? We are now much more conscious than in former times that we cannot radically separate
the first and second Adams, the Garden of Eden and the
Garden of Gethsemane, creation and the Cross. Rather we
understand them as part of a continuum in the great Christian
drama of creation and redemption. If that is indeed the case, is
it not reasonable and right to see something of the element of
sacrifice which is represented on the Cross as being present
also in the activity of creation?

But what kind of sacrifice? We are presumably not talking
about the slaughter and dismemberment of a primordial being
like Osiris, Ymir or Purusa. Yet perhaps the underlying
message of these primal creation myths may not be so different from the notion that Christians are in the process of redis-
covering at the heart of their own understanding of God and
his relationship with his world. What these stories speak of is
a brokenness at the basis and origin of all life, a sense that
creation is a matter of self-giving and surrender. Is there not a
very real sense in which the Trinitarian God of Christianity
has a dismembered body just as much as Prajapati, the Hindu
Lord of the Creatures? The words of Jesus at the Last Supper
are surely supremely relevant here. Did he not tell his disciples, 'This is my body which is broken for you' and are we
not enjoined at every communion service to break bread in
remembrance of him? In this context the word 'remember' is
surely not so much the opposite of forget as of 'dismember'.
What Christ offers the world is his broken body. We as his
body on earth are also broken and divided. What we are
called to do through our participation in the Lord's Supper
and through costly works of reconciliation, justice and mercy
is to re-member his broken body, to help in the immensely
painful task of putting together all that has been destroyed
and severed by the forces of evil and chaos. There is another
interesting parallel here with Hinduism. The ground-plan of a
Hindu temple, or *Vastu-Purusha-Mandala*, is conceived of as
a sacred space in which that which has been scattered and
dismembered in the primal sacrifice from which everything
came is brought back together again.

I shall be returning to the sacrifice and sufferings of Jesus and to the specific connection between the Cross, creation and recreation. I have introduced the theme at this point where the focus is on God and the cost and pain to him of creation because I find it impossible to view the Christian God except by reference to the One in whom he has uniquely revealed himself. It is most obviously through the brokenness of Christ that we can come to an appreciation of the brokenness of God and to an understanding of creation, like redemption, as a sacrifice which involves costly self-giving and surrender. This is by no means the only way, however, in which modern theologians have come to understand and embrace the notion of creation as a sacrifice on the part of God. Many have found equally if not more suggestive the concept of risk and the related notion that in giving freedom to his creatures God has significantly limited his own freedom and made himself to some extent dependent on factors outside his own control.

Viewing creation primarily as a risk taken by God is not a new idea in the Judaeo-Christian tradition. It is expressed in radical and somewhat irreverent terms in the Jewish *Talmud*, the collection of stories, laws and sayings drawn up by the rabbinical sages of Babylon and Palestine in the first seven centuries AD:

> Twenty six attempts preceded the present genesis, all of which were destined to fail. The world of man has arisen out of the chaotic heart of the preceding debris; he, too, is exposed to the risk of failure, and the return to nothing. 'Let's hope it works' exclaimed God as he created the world, and this hope, which has accompanied all the subsequent history of the world and mankind, has emphasized right from the outset that this history is branded with the mark of radical uncertainty.[29]

In many ways recent developments in science, particularly in the fields of quantum physics and biology, have served to increase our sense of the radical uncertainty at the heart of the

71

universe and the importance of the element of unpredictability in the behaviour of both animate and inanimate beings. For one eminent scientist-theologican, such considerations have been important in reinforcing a sense of the risk taken by God in creation.

If God willed the existence of self-conscious, intelligent, freely-willed creatures as an end, he must, to be self-consistent, logically be presumed to have willed the means to achieving that end. This divine purpose must be taken to have been an overriding one for it involves as a corollary an element of risk to his purposes whereby he renders himself vulnerable in a way that is only now becoming perceivable to us. This idea that God took a risk in creation is not new but is now, I am suggesting, reinforced and given a wider context by these biological considerations.[30]

Other recent explorations of this theme, which include the important collection of essays edited by Richard Holloway under the title *The Divine Risk*, tend to put the emphasis on the risk that God takes in creating something outside himself with whom he must have a relationship and which has its own freedom and integrity. In his book, *The Christlike God*, John V. Taylor speaks of 'this huge adventure, this precious world' created by 'God the self-giver who for love lets it be, with all its risk'.[31] Bernard Brasnett in *The Suffering of the Impassible God* sees God laying aside his impassibility and allowing suffering to come upon him at the hands of his creation: 'God suffers because by the act of creation He so placed Himself that if man sinned it meant suffering for God'.[32] Paul Fiddes is another contemporary theologian to make much of the notion that God's suffering extends to his creative activity and is not confined to his work of redemption.

Common to these and other recent treatments of creation theology is a sense that in creating the world God somehow limited his own omnipotence and freedom. The process is often described as a giving up or passing over to his creation of the radical freedom to be itself. This is well expressed by Peter Baelz:

> In creating a world with a character and independence of its own, one that is no mere extension of God's own thought; and, more particularly, in creating human beings whose responses are freely their own rather than programmed reactions to inbuilt instructions; God has to limit himself and his power over the world. When Love wills to create human beings who can freely love in return in a fully personal relationship, Love can create only by letting go – even when the letting go results in a journey into a far-off country. The lyric-writer may 'rather have a paper doll to call his own than have a fickle-minded real live girl'; but the true lover desires the beloved's true love, which he can never command or commandeer. So too with God. The cross in the heart of God from the beginning of time is a cross of creation as well as a cross of redemption. Or, rather, since the risk-laden process of loving into being is all of a piece, it is a cross of everlastingly creative, redemptive and consummative self-giving.[33]

There is, of course, a traditional Christian doctrine which speaks of the self-limitation and letting go of God. It is the notion of *kenosis*, the process of divine self-emptying and self-humiliation, which is derived from Philippians 2:5–8. *Kenosis* has traditionally been taken to apply only to the second person of the Trinity, and specifically to the incarnate Christ on earth, but John Moses is surely right to argue for its wider application:

> It is customary to speak of God's self-emptying in relation to the incarnation, but the incarnation cannot be separated from the continuing and unbroken activity of creation and redemption. The self-limitation, the self-emptying, the self-giving of God are seen in His sovereign act of creation; namely, that it is His will that there shall be created beings who stand alongside Him or even, perhaps, over against

Him. The whole thrust of the Biblical story is of God going out of Himself, calling to Himself a people with whom He establishes a covenant relationship, enabling His purposes to be discerned in the events of history but guaranteeing the freedom of man to respond or withdraw. The great Biblical themes of grace, of creation, of election, of covenant, of revelation, of redemption speak of the God who gives Himself to His creation. God exercises His sovereignty in such a way that He puts Himself at risk. Creation, incarnation and redemption belong together. The self-limitation and self-emptying speak of humility and the patience, the suffering and the sacrifice of God.[34]

There is, in fact, a kenotic text in the Hebrew scriptures as well as in the New Testament. The thirty-fifth verse of Psalm 18, 'Thy right hand supported me and thy gentleness made me great', has been interpreted in the rabbinic tradition, and especially in the Jewish mystical movement known as the *Kabbalah* which flourished in the Middle Ages, as meaning 'Thou showest me thy greatness through the humiliation of thyself'. The Kabbalists, who first appeared in the thirteenth century, developed a whole theory of God's *kenosis* in which they discerned a progressive self-emptying and humiliation of the divine being through history. This kenotic tendency was particularly associated with God's activity in creation and in some parts of the *Kabbalah* it was interpreted in a way that echoes the idea of the broken or dismembered body which needs to be re-membered: 'Before God created the Universe, He abandoned a part of Himself to leave an emptiness in which we and the world could exist in freedom. In the emptiness are scattered sparks of His shattered divinity. It is our duty to redirect them back to God – to reassemble and reunite him, so to speak'.[35]

One particular Kabbalistic mystic, Isaac Luria, who lived in the middle of the sixteenth century, developed this idea of God's self-abandonment in creation. The word which he used for it was *zimsum* which means concentration or contraction. Luria argued that the existence of the universe has only been made possible by a 'shrinkage process in God' in which he withdraws into himself. In order to bring about the existence of something out of nothing, God has released a certain sector of his being, a primal empty space from which he has withdrawn. Creation is, therefore, an act of sacrifice, a self-imposed exile within the Godhead, a *passio Dei* rather than an *actio Dei*, a 'self-withdrawal of God from himself into himself'.[36]

Luria himself developed the concept of *zimsum* as a way of coming to terms with the idea of creation being out of nothing, or *ex nihilo*. I have to say that I am not entirely happy with his notion of God withdrawing into himself in order to create: that seems to be altogether too much of an inwardly directed action on the part of the One whose overwhelming characteristic is his outwardly directed grace and overflowing love. Interpreted more in terms of God's giving away something of himself, however, the notion of *zimsum* can provide a helpful perspective for understanding what happens in creation and one that is just as appropriate if the process involved is conceived of as the fashioning of form and order out of chaos rather than the more traditional *creatio ex nihilo*.

The great contemporary German Reformed theologian Jürgen Moltmann, has found the concept of *zimsum* extremely suggestive and has used it to develop what might be described as a kenotic theology of creation.

God 'withdraws himself from himself to himself' in order to make creation possible. His creative activity outwards is preceded by this humble divine self-restriction. In this sense God's self-humiliation does not begin merely with creation, inasmuch as God commits himself to this world: it begins beforehand, and is the presupposition that makes creation possible. God's creative love is grounded in his humble, self-humiliating love. This self-restricting love is the beginning of that self-emptying of God which Philippians 2 sees as the divine mystery of the Messiah. Even in order to create heaven and earth, God emptied himself of his all-plenishing omnipotence, and as Creator took upon himself the form of a servant.

This points to a necessary correction in the interpretation of creation: God does not create merely by calling something into existence, or by setting something afoot. In a more profound sense he 'creates' by letting-be, by making room, and by withdrawing himself.[37]

It is interesting to note in passing that much the same kind of language was being used at the turn of the century by P. T. Forsyth. His starting point was not the notion of *zimsum* but rather the biblical concept of *kenosis* which he interpreted in terms of the self-reduction or self-retraction of God, a process which he saw as fundamental to creation and even more to evolution.

It is only thus that growth is made possible and evolution started on its career. No evolution is possible on other terms, none unless the goal is the start. . . . Evolution is a mode of the self-limiting power innate in a personal infinite. And only so is it possible. The conditions of time must lie within the possibilities of Eternity, the growth of man within the infinite mobility of the changeless God.[38]

Something of this same sense of creation as an act of limitation as well as an act of power on the part of God, a letting be and a letting go which puts the Creator in a two-way relationship with his creatures is to be found among the expounders of process theology. The founders of this influential modern movement, the American philosophers Alfred North Whitehead and Charles Hartshorne, reacted against what they saw as the false and alien models of God which have for so long dominated the thinking of the Christian Church. They felt that the traditional attributes of omnipotence, impassibility and immutability owed much more to Greek philosophical ideas and Roman imperialism than to the Christian revelation of God in human form as a humble and vulnerable Galilean peasant. In place of the traditional amalgam of Roman emperor, 'unmoved mover' of Greek philosophy and harsh law-maker of Hebrew tradition, process theology puts forward a less static and self-sufficient God who suffers and feels and is in some senses dependent on his creation.

In this respect, as in others, process theology brings Christianity closer to ideas found in other faiths. One of the striking features of the creation stories in many primal religions is their sense that the gods are not wholly self-sufficient and need renewal and regeneration. This, of course, is why sacrificial offerings by humans come to be so important. Now there is only so far that Christians can go along with this idea: there is no suggestion in either the Bible or in Christian tradition that God is in need of renewal or regeneration. We are specifically told that 'he does not faint nor grow weary' (Isaiah 40:28) and that it is those who wait on the Lord who will renew their strength. Nor is there any explicit suggestion that God is dependent on the sacrifices of his creatures, however construed. There are, however, numerous references in both the Old and New Testaments to the acceptability and pleasingness to God of sacrifices which come from the heart and express a real sense of contrition and cost. The Bible is also clear in its portrayal of a close ongoing relationship between God and his creation, inanimate as well as animate. It is a mutual relationship to which both sides contribute, the Lord through his sustaining providential care and love, creation through its offering of a sacrifice of praise, whether it be the mountains skipping like rams or the trees of the field clapping their hands.

The continuing aspect of this interaction between God and his creatures is very important. Thanks partly to the influence of process thought and also to the impact of contemporary science, there is now a much greater tendency among Christian theologians to see creation as an ongoing, open-ended process rather than a once-and-for-all event which happened millions of years ago and is now over and done with. Fewer and fewer people now treat the opening chapters of Genesis as a literal historical or scientific description of how creation took place. It is regarded rather as myth, that word being understood not as the opposite to truth but rather as a category of story which contains much wisdom and important timeless truths. The principle of evolution has come to be accepted by most Christians as totally compatible with their faith. Indeed, it is completely consistent with the doctrine of providence and with the biblical witness to a God who is not simply standing back and watching the world that he has set in motion tick away like a giant clockwork toy, but is rather 'working still' (John 5:17), continually sustaining, recreating and transforming it.

Those Christians who still cling to a literal interpretation of the Genesis story often protest that the theory of evolution and the notion of continuous creation diminish the power and self-sufficiency of God. Their point is well put by Geoff Chapman of the Creation Resources Trust: 'One may ask why an all-powerful, omnipotent God would waste millions of years in cruel evolutionary experimentation, when all he needed to do was speak. There is no hint in Scripture that God did or would use a process of evolution'.[39] The actual state of the natural world as we know and observe it, however, surely forces us to put the question the other way round and to ask how such manifest waste, violence and suffering throughout creation can be squared with the existence of a deity who is both benevolent and omnipotent. There is, in fact, one very significant passage in the New Testament which does acknowledge the waste and futility of the whole evolutionary process and in so doing presents creation as both a continuing and a painful activity for God. It is Paul's description of the creation groaning in travail, being subjected to futility and in bondage to decay and 'waiting with eager longing for the revealing of the sons of God' (Romans 8:19–22).

This is a difficult passage to exegete. It clearly portrays the created world as existing in a state of frustration and imperfection. This state is not simply the consequence of sin, however, as Paul specifically says that the world's condition is not one that has been brought about by its own choice. His words, of course, point forwards in an eschatalogical direction to the final summing up and perfection of all things in Christ, and for Paul this means particularly in and through the sacrifice of Christ. What they also convey very clearly about the here and now is a strong sense of unfinished business and of creation as a process which is still ongoing.

One of the most striking aspects of this much-quoted passage is surely Paul's comparison of the sufferings of creation to the groans of a woman in labour. 'Up to the present, as we know, the whole created universe in all parts groans as if in the pangs of childbirth' (Romans 8:19–22, REB). It has always surprised me that with its love of metaphor and analogy the Christian tradition has never made more of this parallel and applied it to God's creative activity. I suppose it is because of the masculine and patriarchal character of the Church and so much theology. But if we are made in the image of God, then surely on the principle of the *analogia entis* between the human and the divine, this is an image worth exploring further. Childbirth is the supreme human experience of creation: it is in many ways a sacrificial experience, a bringing into being of life in a way which is profoundly holy yet also bloody, painful and costly. May not God's activity in creation have something of the same character? At the end of the passage quoted above on creation as a process of self-restriction on the part of God, Jürgen Moltmann is surely right to observe that 'The creative making is expressed in masculine metaphors. But the creative letting-be is better brought out through motherly categories'.[40]

There are some biblical passages which do seem to draw an analogy between the human process of childbirth and God's creative activity. One is to be found in the Book of Ecclesiastes 11:5 'As thou knowest not what is the way of the spirit, nor how the bones do grow in the womb of her that is with child, even so thou knowest not the works of God who maketh all'. The main point being made here is to stress the unfathomability of God's works and particularly to point to the impenetrable mystery of suffering. Yet it is significant that the miracle of the child forming in the womb is put alongside the wonders of creation. Then there is that wonderful passage in Isaiah 49:15 when the Lord's continuing love for his people Israel despite all their wanderings is compared to that of a mother for her child: 'Can a woman forget her sucking child, that she should not have compassion on the son of her womb?'

The process of childbirth is curiously close to that of death. This is not just because in many parts of the world it is accompanied by high rates of mortality and even with our advanced medical techniques it remains a time of potential danger to the life of any mother. Nor is it just because of the pain and the blood and the mother's sense of pouring out her strength and her life and being left spent and exhausted. There are deeper and more mysterious primeval forces which link the coming of life and its going. In no human life have birth and death been more closely and ambiguously intertwined than that of Jesus of Nazareth. This ambiguity is well brought out in the concluding lines of T. S. Eliot's *Journey of the Magi* when the wise men reflect on exactly what it is that they have witnessed at Bethlehem:

Were we led all that way for
Birth or Death? There was a Birth, certainly,
We had the evidence and no doubt. I had seen birth and
    death,
But had thought they were different; this Birth was
Hard and bitter agony for us, like Death, our death.

It is apt that we should have been brought from creation via birth and death to the Cross of Christ, for Christians at once the supreme symbol of sacrifice and the place where God and his creatures meet. In primal religions, as we have seen, sacrifice, or more particularly the sacrificial ritual, is the point at which earth and heaven intersect, where humans commune with the gods and where the cosmic energy is generated to keep the world turning. This is how the sacrificial cultus in early Chinese religion is described in the *Li Chi*:

The aura of earth ascends, the aura of heaven descends.

Negative and positive meet in friction. Heaven and earth are in commotion, drummed by thunder-claps, fanned by wind and rain stirred by the four seasons, warmed by sun and moon. Thus all transforming processes arise.[41]

There is something of the same sense of elemental upheaval in St Matthew's description of the moment of Jesus' death on the Cross when not only was the veil of the temple rent from top to bottom but 'the earth did quake, and the rocks rent; and the graves were opened' (Matthew 27:51). Here, too, there is a sense of the transforming power of sacrifice. It is on and by the Cross that the frustration, the futility and the suffering of the world is taken up to heaven, to be transfigured and absorbed by God. It is the supremely transforming and integrative event in the cosmic as well as the human dimension – the meeting point of chaos and order, death and birth, suffering and salvation.

This sense of the transforming, creative, energizing power of sacrifice has perhaps been most fully articulated in the Christian tradition by certain theologians of the Eastern Orthodox churches. In seeking to explain the thinking of one of the most notable of them, the early twentieth-century Russian theologian, Nikolai Berdiaev, F. W. Dillistone produced a remarkably potent image of the power of sacrifice. It is at once thoroughly Christian, with clear echoes of the emblem of the burning bush discussed in the last chapter, and yet also strongly suggestive of ideas found in other faiths, notably the Hindu concept of *agni*, the eternal fire which is both sacrificial priest and victim:

I find myself imagining a series of concentric spheres. At the heart of the system is a burning centre. This burning centre may be described in terms of sacrifice and particularly of the sacrificial *Lamb*: or in terms of suffering and particularly of the suffering *Servant* of humanity: or in terms of the sequence of birth – passion – death – resurrection. This fire burns perpetually and is not consumed. This fire is the energy which activates the whole of the cosmos.

In a kind of pulsating movement all things are transfigured as they are drawn towards the burning centre from which they originally withdrew. . . . He that is near me is near the fire. Through suffering, fulfilment. Through sacrifice, renewal. Through death, newness of life.[42]

This is, surely, precisely the meaning that the passion, crucifixion and resurrection of Jesus Christ carries, or should carry, in Christian teaching. Yet in the West at least we have been rather reluctant to see the sacrifice of Christ as having creative and recreative power and to follow Berdiaev's insistence that 'when the blood of Christ shed upon Calvary touched the earth, earth became a new thing'.[43] We are accustomed to taking the Cross as a symbol of sorrow and shame or as the instrument of atonement and redemption. We are much less ready to see it as a sign or an agent of creation and new birth. Maybe this reluctance derives from unease about linking the Cross too closely with the recurrent theme in many primal religions of the slaughter of a god-man on a tree to bring life and regeneration. This is a striking feature of cults associated with dying and rising gods of nature. We have already noted in Phrygian mythology the figure of Attis, who in human form was hanged each year on a pine tree. The institution of Easter as the festival to commemorate the death and resurrection of Christ almost certainly represented an attempt by the Roman Church to Christianize and assimilate the celebrations of the death and resurrection of Attis which were held throughout the Empire in spring. According to Norse mythology Odin, father of the gods and of men, sacrificed himself on a great ash tree: he remained hanging on the tree for nine nights and through his sacrifice gained the power to overcome evil forces and also his own rejuvenation.

The tree on which Odin hung, Yggdrasil, was thought to stand at the centre of the world and was conceived of as the tree of life and knowledge as well as of death. Many primal religions had a similar sense of a cosmic tree of sacrifice standing at the meeting place of the three zones of earth, heaven and hell. This tree was often associated with the genesis of the world and the emergence of human life. It was also seen as a source of regeneration to all living creatures and as a means of ascent from earth to heaven. In the Siberian Tungus, for example, the soul of the shaman was seen as climbing up to God by means of a tree. Anthropologists and historians of religion have pointed to the popularity in many cultures of rites designed to renew creation which involve the felling of a tree standing near the centre of the world and the setting up of a sacrificial stake fashioned out of its wood. This stake then became a pillar or ladder, connecting earth and heaven. The sacrificer, mounting the stake, believed that he was ascending to the heavenly region and offered his sacrifice in order that creation might be renewed.[44]

The Bible does not make an explicit association between the tree of life planted by God in the Garden of Eden and the tree of Calvary on which Christ died. Many Christian artists and poets down the centuries, however, have seen them as standing on the same spot. In early Germanic art the Cross is often represented as a living tree and is sometimes depicted as being intertwined with an ash tree which stands like a pillar supporting the cosmos. John Donne wrote a poem to express his opinion that 'Paradise and Calvarie, Christ's Crosse and Adam's tree, stood in one place'. Once again, this theme has been taken up particularly in Eastern Orthodox theology. John of Damascus wrote: 'The tree of life which was planted by God in Paradise prefigured this precious Cross. For since death was by a tree, it was fitting that life and resurrection should be bestowed by a tree'.[45] A homily of the pseudo-Chrysostom speaks of the Cross as a tree which 'rises from the earth to the heavens. A plant immortal, it stands at the centre of heaven and earth; strong pillar of the universe, bond of all things, support of all the inhabited earth; cosmic inter-lacement, comprising in itself the whole medley of human nature'. The Byzantine liturgy for the day of the exaltation of the Holy Cross sings of 'the tree of life planted on Calvary, the tree on which the King of kings wrought our salvation . . . which springing from the depths of the earth has risen to the centre of the earth ... and sanctifies the Universe unto its limits'.[46]

The power and significance of the Cross of Christ is surely not diminished or weakened in any way by a realization that it was prefigured in earlier religions and that it belongs to a universal mythology of sacrifice focused upon the tree of life and death. Indeed, the reverse is true: it is only by putting Calvary into this wider context that we can comprehend its full cosmic dimension and begin to come to terms with the mysterious power of sacrifice to create and recreate and the tragic truth that life proceeds from death.

There can be little doubt that the essential pattern of universal regeneration through a central cosmic sacrifice, of the attainment of eternal life through the efficacy of a sacrificial stake, were motifs which had established themselves firmly in the human imagination long before the Christian era. The transfiguration of Calvary was therefore assured. This was the new tree of life: this was the noble tree of sacrifice: this was the central ladder linking earth to heaven.[47]

Most, if not all, of the world's primal religions conceive of the creation and recreation of the world as a work of sacrifice. Such a view encapsulates several important truths. It recognizes the extent to which creation, like sacrifice, is a continuing process of making holy, bringing a sacramental order and harmony out of chaos, producing wholeness out of separation and fashioning fullness, form and variety out of emptiness and undifferentiated mass. It also underlines the imperfection and incompleteness of creation, its ambiguities and frailties and its constant need for renewal, redemption and transfiguration. Above all, it recognizes and acknowledges the deep pain and cost of all this to the creator. At the root of this view of creation as sacrifice is an understanding of the process that leads from birth through life to death and on through resurrection to new birth and new life. This is the fundamental message of the cults of Osiris and Attis, the dying and rising gods of nature, Purusa, the dismembered primordial man, and Odin, hung on the tree that stands at the centre of the world.

For Christians these same truths are expressed through belief in a God who constantly sacrifices himself in and through creation by costly self-giving and self-emptying. The power and the depth of that sacrifice is shown most vividly at Calvary where his own and only son, the God-Man who is the Logos and special agent of creation, is broken and dismembered through crucifixion. Set in this perspective, the Cross is not just an emblem of suffering and shame, although it is that assuredly: it is the instrument of creation as much as redemption, the tree of life which renews all and the sacrificial pillar which supports the entire cosmos.

3

The sacrifice of God is a broken spirit: sacrifice in the Old Testament

You cannot read far in the books that make up the Hebrew Bible and the Christian Old Testament without coming across references to the cultic slaughter of pigeons, sheep and goats and their presentation as burnt offerings to God. While the theme of sacrifice is certainly ubiquitous in the Hebrew scriptures, however, it is not treated in a uniform or a static way. The word itself is used with several different meanings and there is a discernible shift in emphasis away from cultic ritual involving the slaughter of victims and towards the moral qualities of repentance, obedience and selflessness. The great prophets of the eighth and seventh centuries BC were particularly concerned with promoting this movement from outward to inner sacrifice.

Following the lead of William James, many scholars have seen the Old Testament as developing a steadily more 'spiritualized' view of sacrifice and progressing from crude notions of propitiating a capricious deity towards an understanding of God as the One who reveals himself in a series of compassionate acts and draws a response in the form of worship and dedication.[1] There is undoubtedly much truth in this analysis but it can also be misleading. It tends to downplay the very demanding and physical concept of sacrifice as a life of utter dedication and service that replaced the notion of cultic offering. It can also encourage the erroneous view that when sacrifice is mentioned in the early books of the Bible it is always in terms of the propitiation and appeasement of an angry deity. In fact, a brief excursus through Genesis reveals that from the very beginning the Israelites saw God as the author of sacrifice as well as its recipient and had a sense of its importance as a fundamental principle of life.

It is true that the first sacrifice recorded in the Bible, made by Noah just after the flood subsided, looks at first sight like a straightforward, and successful, attempt to win the favour of God:

> Then Noah built an altar to the Lord, and took of every clean animal and of every clean bird, and offered burnt offerings on the altar. And when the Lord smelled the pleasing odour, the Lord said in his heart 'I will never again curse the ground because of man, for the imagination of man's heart is evil from his youth; neither will I ever again destroy every living creature as I have done' (Genesis, 8:20–1).

Yet this is more than a matter of bribing God with a pleasant smell. Noah's burnt offering was in part a thank offering for deliverance from the flood. It also needs to be seen in the context of the covenant that is about to be made between God and Noah and through him with all humanity. At the heart of the Hebrew scriptures is the portrayal of God's relationship with his people Israel as a covenant sealed and renewed by sacrifice.

This theme is clearly evident in the next detailed account of a sacrifice which is found in Genesis 15. Here Abraham makes an offering of a heifer, a goat, a ram and a pigeon following God's promise to him in a vision that he will have descendants. At night a smoking furnace appears and a burning lamp passes between the pieces of the sacrificial animals that he has cut up and laid out. With this dramatic sign the Lord makes his covenant with Abraham, promising that his descendants will have the whole land from the Nile to the Euphrates. Here, as in the rituals of so many primal religions, sacrifice is presented as the meeting place of the human and divine and also as the starting point for a great historic happening – in this case the foundation of a new tribe.

The third detailed treatment of the theme of sacrifice in

Genesis is the powerful and disturbing story of Abraham's readiness to offer up his son, Isaac, at the call of God and the last-minute substitution of a ram caught in the thicket as the sacrificial victim. The key message of the Akedah, as it is known, is usually interpreted as being the importance of utmost faith and trust in God. This is certainly a crucial dimension of the story of Abraham and Isaac. Indeed, Mircea Eliade has pointed out that it is the element which distinguishes this particular sacrifice from others recorded in the literature of Paleo-Semitic religion. Sacrifice of the first-born was, in fact, a common practice in the ancient Middle East. First children were often regarded as the offspring of gods and their sacrifice restored to the particular divinity involved the substance and effort expended and exhausted in maintaining the world. We are back to the role of sacrifice in regenerating the gods discussed in the last chapter. Whereas for most people in the Paleo-Semitic world the sacrifice of their first-born child was a custom, the purpose of which was perfectly intelligible, however, for Abraham it is an act of pure faith. He does not understand why it is necessary yet he is prepared out of faith to do it. The Akedah indicates the extent to which the notion of true sacrifice as an obedient and trusting heart was present at a very early stage of the development of Hebrew religion.[2]

The story of Abraham and Isaac has another and even more significant message. It is contained in the statement 'God will provide himself the lamb for a burnt offering' (Genesis 22:8), a verse on which the whole Christian doctrine of providence is substantially founded. This promise, which is fulfilled in the dramatic incident of a ram caught in the thicket, underlines the extent to which God himself is the author of the sacrifice with complete responsibility for it. His action in substituting an animal for a human victim is unique to the Genesis account of the Akedah and is not found in versions of the story found in other traditions. The Jewish scholar, Hyam Maccoby, has pointed out that in the Midrashic version, Isaac is indeed sacrificed. Normally an event with such cosmic significance, leading as it does to the foundation of an entire people, would always have been associated with human sacrifice. Yet the Genesis account provides a unique double twist – not only is God prepared to accept an animal sacrifice but he himself provides the victim.[3]

In his book, *The Sacred Executioner*, Maccoby goes on to show that the Akedah is by no means unique in having been altered by the authors of Genesis to eliminate the idea of human sacrifice. Exactly the same happened with the stories of Cain, Lamech and Ham which all involve human sacrifice in other sources such as the *Midrash* and the Kenite tradition. He suggests that the editorial changes introduced by the Israelites mark a crucial stage in human moral development whereby notions of personal repentance and responsibility begin to replace the idea that blame and guilt can be transferred and expiated through ritualized sacrifice.[4]

Significant as this process of 'spiritualization' undoubtedly is, we should not lose sight of the clearest message coming out of the Abraham and Isaac story as told in Genesis, which is that God is the author of sacrifice. The German biblical scholar Markus Barth is surely right to suggest that the Akedah shows sacrifice to be willed by God: 'by sacrifice God wants to reveal and to prove his faithfulness to his past promise and gift, and by the same sacrifice He wants to promise even more abundant blessing in the future'.[5] Alongside the close connection between sacrifice and covenant, we now have the crucial role of sacrifice as revelation. In the provision by God of the ram for Abraham to slaughter and offer up in place of his son Isaac we also have the clearest indication possible that sacrifice is a gift of God to humankind, rather than a gift of humankind to God: 'By this gift God reveals, and tests, installs and unites. The beneficiary of the sacrifice is always man. . . . Through sacrifice God gives to man what man has not deserved and what he cannot give to or secure for himself, namely blessing and power'.[6]

This message that sacrifice has its origin and source in God is reiterated in the early books of the Old Testament. It is expressed both in a general portrayal of Yahweh as the one who gives himself in a careless and costly way to his people (as denoted by the use of the verb *ahab* in such passages as Deuteronomy 7:7 and 7:8) and much more technically in relation to the mechanics of the Israelite temple cult in a verse such as Leviticus 17:11: 'The life of the flesh is in the blood; and I have given it for you ... to make atonement for your souls; for it is the blood that makes atonement, by reason of the life'. It is important to keep this overriding sense of sacrifice as a provision and gift of God in mind as we come to look at the worship of ancient Israel and specifically at the bewildering variety of offerings which are described in such detail in the books of Exodus and Leviticus.

Throughout the period covered by the Old Testament, both before and after the building of the Jerusalem temple, during the exilic period and after the return and rebuilding of the temple, three different kinds of sacrificial ritual were performed by the priests of Israel. These involved respectively burning either animal flesh, a flour-based mixture or incense to produce a sweet smell; slitting the throats of birds and animals so that blood was shed; and offering up fruit and grain as the first-fruits of the harvest. Of the three, the burnt offerings or *'olâs* are most frequently mentioned. As in Vedic and Chinese traditions, particular significance was attached to the aromatic smoke which ascended from the sacrificial altar towards the heavens and which was seen as the element in which human and divine interaction and communion took place. While the Canaanites had linked the coming of God (or *kebôd Yahweh*) to the autumnal equinox when the rays of the dawning sun miraculously kindled the sacred fire on the altar, the Israelite priests stressed the perpetual nature of the altar flame and the permanent dwelling of the *kebôd Yahweh* in the tabernacle. The idea of fire was laden with religious significance: 'Burning something was seen as a way of "giving" it back to God. Fire was a means of theophany and a symbol of God's presence. It had a purifying or sanctifying power, but it also could serve, on occasion, as a means of divine chastisement'.[7]

The second form of sacrifice, slitting the throats of birds and animals, was often a preliminary to burning them as an 'olâ. It was, however, of extreme significance in its own right as the means of releasing blood. Once again, we are back to the dark symbolism of primal religion and its sense of blood as the vital life-force that needed to be shed and poured out to renew the potency of the community. As we have already seen, it was such blood sacrifices made by Noah and Abraham that were particularly associated with the making and sealing of covenants between God and his people Israel. They continued to have this association in later temple worship, though they were also associated with the atonement and expiation of sin and guilt. The third category of sacrificial offering, which involved neither burning nor blood-letting but the setting aside of fruit and grain to be laid on the altar, derived from the widespread ancient custom of offering the first-fruits of each crop to the deity, in thanksgiving for a successful harvest and in hopeful anticipation of more to come. Such offerings were clearly required by Mosaic law, as laid down in Exodus 23:19: 'The first of the first fruits of your ground you shall bring into the house of the Lord your God'.

Although each of these three kinds of sacrificial offering had its own distinct identity and purpose, they were often combined in a single ritual. Indeed, the typical sacrifice in Israelite worship involved a blending of the blood-letting and the burnt offering in six stages. First the worshipper drew near to God with his offering. Then he laid his hands on the victim's head. Next he slew the victim. Only at the fourth stage, which involved presenting the blood of the victim to God either by pouring it or dashing it against the altar, did the priest take over performance of the sacrifice. The victim's flesh was then burnt so that its odour might ascend to heaven and finally, if it had not all been consumed, the roasted meat was eaten by priests and male worshippers.

These cultic sacrifices seem to have had three main purposes. First they were seen as providing the means whereby humans could be drawn nearer to God and he nearer to them. This communion aspect was particularly apparent in the feasts in which priests and male worshippers shared in consuming the burnt offerings in whose savour God himself was also taking delight and participating. These offerings were not restricted to the roasted flesh of slaughtered birds and animals. Cereal offerings were mixed with oil and water and baked to produce unleavened bread and cakes which were also sometimes eaten. Passages such as Leviticus 6:8–30, 7:1–21 and Numbers 18:10–11 show the strict rules which surrounded what could and could not be eaten, and who could partake in sacrificial feasts. They also underline the holiness of the food. Restricted and awesome as they were, these common meals, eaten in the presence of God, were also festive and celebratory occasions. At times they could have a much wider focus and provide an element of social welfare. In Deuteronomy 16:1–12 those offering sacrificial animals are commanded to share the meat with the poor, the homeless, foreigners and slaves.

The second broad purpose of the sacrifices was to offer praise and thanks to God. Many of the *'olâs* and offerings of first-fruits fell into this category. So did other kinds of offerings, such as those prescribed in Exodus 25, which include gold, silver, brass, fine linen, goats' hair, rams' wool, badgers' skins, shittim wood, oil, spices and onyx stones. Significantly, these offerings are mentioned in the context of the confirmation of God's covenant with his people. Animals and cereals sacrificed for this purpose as gift offerings were wholly consumed by fire on the altars and not saved to be eaten by worshippers.

The third category of sacrifices were those designed to atone for or expiate sin and guilt. There is a clear overlap in purpose between these sin and guilt offerings, which seem to become more and more numerous from the seventh century onwards, and the communion offerings. Both are designed to bring humans closer to God but with the former this process is conceived in terms of putting right a relationship which has been disturbed by sin. Most blood sacrifices fell into this category, reflecting the idea expressed in Leviticus 17:11 that 'the life of the flesh is in the blood . . . and it is the blood that makes atonement by reason of the life'. Central to this notion of sacrifice as the God-given remedy for sin was the idea that blood shed according to the carefully prescribed ritual of the cult somehow had the power to cover and blot out wrongdoing both at an individual and at a communal level (see Leviticus 1:4 and 16:33, Numbers 15:25 and Ezekiel 43:26).

Significant new ideas as to the purpose of sacrifice were introduced with the institution of two annual rituals which came to assume enormous importance in Israelite religion, as they still do in contemporary Judaism. The feast of the Passover commemorated the event which had happened on the eve of the exodus from Egypt when the blood of a slaughtered lamb had been daubed on the lintel of every household as a sign to the Angel of the Lord to pass over and not seize the first-born child. During the post-exilic period, from around 500 BC, commemoration of this event moved from the home to the temple and became a cultic act rather than a domestic ritual. The passover lamb was henceforth slaughtered on the altar and a new purpose for sacrifice was introduced – the power to avert evil.

The origins of the other great institutionalized sacrifice of Judaism, the Day of Atonement, lie in a passage in Leviticus where the Lord lays down complex instructions for Aaron as to the performance of a sin offering which involves two goats. One is to be slaughtered in the traditional way but the other is to be kept alive:

Aaron shall lay both his hands upon the head of the live goat and confess over him all the iniquities of the children of Israel, and all their transgressions in all their sins, putting them upon the head of the goat and shall send him away by the hand of a man into the wilderness: and the goat shall bear upon him all their iniquities unto a land not inhabited (Leviticus, 16:21–2).

In Israelite temple worship this injunction came to be observed by the high priest entering the Holy of Holies on one day of the year to offer atonement for the sins of the whole people. More generally, of course, it has given rise to

93

the idea of the scapegoat who carries the sins of others and in Christian theology to the notion of substitutionary atonement.

So far, I have avoided suggesting that propitiation was a significant element in the Israelites' understanding of the purposes of sacrifice. There are Old Testament scholars who argue that it was. William Dyrness, for example, writes about sacrifice in the Old Testament that 'the central idea is the process of ransoming or restoring to favour by means of suitable payment ... in addition to this is also the idea of propitiation ... further, Old Testament sacrifices were substitutionary'.[8] The general consensus among scholars, however, is that the sin offerings made by the Israelites were conceived of in expiatory rather than propitiatory terms with the sacrificial victims being regarded as representatives of, rather than substitutes for, the lives of the offerers.

There do certainly appear to be examples of propitiatory sacrifices in the Hebrew Bible. One such is recorded in 2 Samuel 24:25 where David offers up his oxen so that the Lord may not bring down plague on the land. There is also at least one case where God himself seems to initiate a sacrifice in order to propitiate himself. In Job 42:7–10, he tells Eliphaz the Temanite and his friends that his wrath is kindled against them and that they had better take seven bullocks and seven rams and offer them as a burnt offering. In both these episodes, however, the dominant note is not that of propitiation. In the case of David's sacrifice, the stress is on the costliness of his offering: the king refuses the offer of free oxen for his sacrifice from a friend, telling him, 'No, but I will buy it off you for a price; I will not offer burnt offerings to the Lord my God which cost me nothing' (2 Samuel 24:24). This note is common to many of the accounts of sacrifice in the Old Testament: what is offered up is always something of value. In the story from Job, the emphasis is on God as the initiator of the sacrifice. If he himself is both its author and its recipient, can the sacrifice really be described as propitiatory?

What is undoubtedly found in the Old Testament is a theology of the divine acceptance of sacrifice. Indeed, the phrase 'the pleasing odour of sacrifice' occurs more than forty times. Yet the overall image conveyed is not that of a greedy and sadistic deity who revels in the smell of freshly shed blood and burning flesh. The God of the Hebrew scriptures is in no sense to be compared to the voracious man-eating plant in the musical 'The Little Shop of Horrors' which grows by gorging itself on the blood of its hapless human victims. The dominant message is rather of the appropriateness and acceptability of sacrifice as the God-given means for divine-human communication and particularly for the repairing and restoring of relationships broken by sin and selfishness.

Not every kind of sacrifice was seen as pleasing to God. The Hebrew prophets railed against the mere mechanical performance of ritual slaughters and burnt offerings, which was unaccompanied by any sense of real repentance or self-giving on the part of worshippers:

'What to me is the multitude of your sacrifices?' says the Lord; 'I have had enough of burnt offerings of rams and the fat of fed beasts; I do not delight in the blood of bulls, or of lambs, or of he-goats (Isaiah. 1:11).

To what purpose does frankincense come to me from Sheba, or sweet cane from a distant land? Your burnt offerings are not acceptable nor your sacrifices pleasing to me (Jeremiah 6:20).

For I desire steadfast love and not sacrifice, the knowledge of God, rather than burnt offerings (Hosea 6:6).

They love sacrifice, they sacrifice flesh and eat it; but the Lord has no delight in them (Hosea 8:13).

They shall not pour libations of wine to the Lord; and they shall not please him with their sacrifices (Hosea 9:4).

Even though you offer me your burnt offerings and cereal offerings, I will not accept them and the peace offerings of your fatted beasts I will not look upon (Amos 5:22).

Will the Lord be pleased with thousands of rams, with ten

thousands of rivers of oil? Shall I give my first-born for the sin of my soul? (Micah 6:7).

These statements were made at a time when Israel was facing serious external threats from the Assyrians and Babylonians. It was also internally weakened by oppressive rule, inequality and injustice. The prophets pointed out that what the Lord required of his people in such a situation was not ritual offerings but lives sacrificially devoted to righting these social and political evils. Micah continued the rhetorical question begun above my asking 'What does the Lord require of you but to do justice, and to love kindness and to walk humbly with your God?'.

Similar denunciations of propitiatory cultic offerings can be found in other religious traditions at very much the same time. In Hinduism the almost mechanical sacerdotalism of the *Rig Veda* gives way to the Upanishadic stress on costly acts of renunciation which will bring about the identification of the individual self (*atman*) with the cosmic divine reality (*Brahman*). The attitude taken to sacrifice in the *Mundaka Upanishad* is almost identical with that of the Hebrew prophets:

> These deluded men, regarding sacrifices and works of merits as most important, do not know any other good. . . . But those who practise austerity and faith in the forest, the tranquil knowers who live the life of a mendicant, depart freed from sin, through the door of the sun to where dwells the immortal, imperishable person.[9]

The same stress on inner rather than outward sacrifice is to be found in the Buddhist religion which began to emerge in north-east India in the sixth century BC. It is clearly brought out in a story which tells of a ruler who consults the Brahmans when his kingdom is afflicted by plague and drought. They tell him that he must offer up a sacrifice and thus build a bridge to the world of the gods. The king is uneasy about following this advice, asking himself 'what connection may there be between righteousness and killing animals?'. He agrees to make a great sacrifice of a thousand human victims but promises that no one who behaves honestly will be immolated. The result is a moral revolution among his subjects who devote themselves to selfless good neighbourliness. The pestilence disappears, rain returns and the nation becomes prosperous again. The moral of the story is clear: 'Injuring animals never tends to bliss but charity, self-restraint, continence and the like have this power'.[10]

Much the same message was to be preached a thousand years or so later in the Koran. Unlike Buddhism, Islam did not repudiate animal sacrifice but the followers of Muhammad were enjoined to regard it not as a ritual offering which had propitiatory power in itself but as a symbol of self-surrender.

> The flesh of the animals sacrificed is not to be wasted but it should serve as food for the poor and needy. Thus, while inwardly laying down one's life in the cause of truth, it is to be borne in mind that outwardly a Muslim should devote himself to the service of humanity. . . . It is not the outward act of sacrifice which is acceptable, but the deep meaning of sacrifice which underlies it.[11]

It is important that this common thread which runs through Judaism, Hinduism, Buddhism and Islam is not interpreted as a repudiation of the whole notion of sacrifice. It does certainly mark a shift away from emphasizing the efficacy of the cultic offering *per se*, but there is no lessening of belief in the power of sacrifice, nor any diminution of the symbolism associated with it. The stress comes to be put on the inner disposition of the worshipper and the sacrificial fire being kindled within each heart. This change of emphasis undoubtedly represents a process of 'interiorization' but I am less certain that it also involves the spiritualization claimed by many scholars. The kind of sacrifice which the Hebrew prophets, the *Upanishads* and the Buddha are calling for is not just a matter of disposition and outlook – it is a whole way of life and as such is profoundly practical and physical.

This dimension comes over clearly in the Psalms. At first sight the message of these great hymns of the Hebrew people might seem to be that sacrifice is redundant: 'Sacrifice and offering you do not desire but my ears you have marked for obedience' (Psalm 40:6). However, the point being made here is similar to that made by the prophets: what God wants is not the performance of cultic acts but the much more demanding offering of lives based on the principle of self-giving together with the sacrifices of praise and thanksgiving which are mentioned so often (Psalm 27:6; 50:23; 69:30; 107:22 and 116:17). In the words of Colin Gunton, 'Sacrifice became for some of the Psalmists a way of speaking of the true worship and form of life required by God of his people'.[12]

There is one particular verse in the Psalms which has come to haunt me almost as much as Jesus' words about the need for the corn of wheat to fall into the ground and die. It is the statement that 'the sacrifices of God are a broken spirit; a broken and contrite heart, O God, thou wilt not despise' (Psalm 51:17). I have quoted it in the form in which it appears in the Authorized Version because this is most faithful to the original. Hebrew scholars whom I have consulted are emphatic that the word *zibhē*, which is the most commonly used word for sacrifice in the Old Testament, is in a construct relationship with the word *'elohīm* (God) which corresponds to our genitive. Indeed, they suggest that a literal translation of the first part of this verse would be 'The sacrifice of God is a broken spirit'.

If this really is the case, then we may have here a remarkable biblical testimony to the sacrificing nature of the God who reveals his innermost self through his brokenness. We also have a clear articulation of the theme of the pathos of God which has gripped many Jewish and Christian scholars in the twentieth century following the lead of Rabbi Abraham Heschel who in 1936 first seriously challenged the apathetic theology of medieval Judaism and classical Christianity, with their close dependence on classical Greek ideas that change and passion are evidence of corruption. Heschel argued that the Hebrew prophets in fact developed a 'pathetic theology'. Unlike Aristotle, they did not portray God as being in a state of *apatheia*, free from passion and suffering. Rather they saw him as being affected by the actions and passions of his people and moved by them not just to anger and condemnation but to pity and to suffering himself. Heschel contrasted this Israelite perspective, which is of course the foundation for the Christian view of God, with the outlook of virtually all other religions which regard their divinities as jealous and self-centred. 'Pathos, on the other hand, is not a self-centred and self-contained state; it is always, in prophetic thinking, directed outward; it always expresses a relation to man'.[13]

Most modern translations convey a rather different sense of the meaning of this verse. The Revised Standard Version renders it as 'The sacrifice acceptable to God is a broken spirit', the New Jerusalem Bible as 'sacrifice to God is a broken spirit' and the Revised English Bible as 'God, my sacrifice is a broken spirit'. Hebrew scholars assure me that these translations involve distorting the meaning of the original, but even if we are to accept them, the verse still has an important message, although one considerably less radical and distinctive than that proposed above. In this more common version the psalmist is reiterating the teaching of the prophets that it is the offering of broken and contrite hearts rather than the performance of cultic rituals which God desires from his people. Whichever interpretation is preferred, we are pointed towards the mysterious connection between brokenness and holiness which lies at the heart of both the paradox and the power of sacrifice.

There are two other important passages in the Old Testament which express both the power and centrality of sacrifice. The first is that much-loved prophecy about the time when the wolf shall dwell with the lamb and the leopard shall lie down with the kid; when a little child shall put his hand on the adder's den and 'they shall not hurt or destroy in all my holy mountain' (Isaiah 11:1–9). This moving vision of the harmony that will prevail in the animal kingdom when the rule of righteousness is established has obvious affinities with the description of the Garden of Eden in Genesis. Otto Kaiser has rightly pointed out, however, that it is not a mere search for security projected back into the primal period. 'We should rather assume that here we have the expression of a sensibility which is aware of the primal guilt in all life, which can only survive through the death of other life.'[14] In his commentary on this passage he goes on to say that far from being a piece of mere wishful thinking, it is both a direct promise of what will come about in the last days and also a clear call to action here and now:

> The important thing is to regain a feeling for the primal vitiation of our lives, to recognize that our own life is always made possible by the sacrifice of other life and is fulfilled only by surrender to other people. The result of this would be a new reverence for life, primarily for the life of other people, and then, by virtue of the unity of all life, reverence also for the life of animals. That alone could set clear limits to what we do with the life of others. So it could succeed in making sure that the life of animals and of human beings continued to be worth living.[15]

The other great Old Testament statement about the power of sacrifice also occurs in Isaiah, although it is almost certainly the work of a different author. It is the 'suffering servant' passage (Isaiah 52:13–53:12) which speaks of the redemption and healing brought about by the wounds of the one who is led like a lamb to the slaughter. The sacrificial imagery here is inescapable. The Hebrew word used to describe the suffering servant, *asham*, belonged to the temple cult and was applied to blood offerings which were seen as making restitution for wrongdoing. It is variously translated as an offering for sin (Revised Standard Version), a sin offering (New Jerusalem Bible) and a guilt offering (New International Version). Two modern translations use the word 'sacrifice'. The Good News Bible has: 'The Lord says, "It was my will that he should suffer; his death was a sacrifice to bring forgiveness" ' while the Revised English Bible prefers: 'Yet the Lord took thought for his oppressed servant and healed him who had given himself as a sacrifice for sin'. Unfortunately, the original Hebrew text is ambiguous, making it impossible to determine which of these translations, with their very different emphases, is more accurate.

There is also a wide divergence of view as to the identity of the suffering servant. Many scholars share Geoffrey Ashby's belief that it is the kingdom of Israel as a whole:

> In this new vision, Israel is the servant, prepared to undergo humiliation and suffering and to be herself the sacrifice or at least the opening movement of the sacrificial symphony, through which the alienation of the world of nations from its true Lord and Creator is to be removed. This is the kingship of the future, the leadership that will open the way through sacrifice for the world of nations to approach its Lord. . . . Isaiah was saying, 'I show you a new way to fulfil your election by your Lord – the way of sacrifice, involving suffering and death'. This is the kingly path, not one of national triumph or self-sufficiency.[16]

If the suffering servant passage is about the destiny of the people of Israel, then it has proved remarkably prophetic. The Jews have been despised, persecuted and humiliated more than any other race. Ashby even suggests that the holocaust of the Second World War 'is a fulfilment of Isaiah's plan for Israel and should be a message to the Christian Church that, if they really consider themselves to be the new Israel, this is what they must accept for themselves – sacrifice, suffering and holocaust. After all the very word "holocaust" means a burnt-offering, totally consumed by fire. This is the telos of the royal trajectory and this is true kingship'.[17] Many readers will be disturbed and made profoundly uneasy by these words. Yet Ashby is not alone among twentieth-century theologians in seeing the holocaust in sacrificial terms (see p. 214).

Most Christians, of course, have identified Isaiah's description of the man of sorrows who is acquainted with grief and who has healed us by his stripes not with the kingdom of Israel but with the figure of Jesus. Traditionally read in churches on Good Friday, it seems to point forward in an uncanny way to Christ's passion and crucifixion and to give these events a clearly sacrificial purpose. The suffering servant passage provides one of the most important links between the theology of the Old and New Testaments. It does this by focusing on the redemptive healing power of sacrifice, conceived not in terms of ritual cultic offerings but as costly self-giving on the part of God.

4

The cult and the Cross: sacrifice in the New Testament

The theme of sacrifice bulks as large in the books that make up the Christian New Testament as it does in the Hebrew Bible. It is most obviously apparent in the use of explicitly sacrificial language, drawn largely from the Israelite cult, in connection with Jesus and particularly his passion and death. There is also a good deal of exhortation directed at those who would follow him to lead selfless lives and offer themselves as living sacrifices. At a deeper level the crucifixion-resurrection continuum which runs as a key motif through the gospels and epistles expresses the central sacrificial principle of 'through death to life'.[1]

I should say at the outset that there is far from a consensus among scholars as to whether the New Testament does, in fact, portray the life, death and resurrection of Jesus in sacrificial terms. On one side, Robert Daly is emphatic that 'the Christ event is clearly presented to us in the New Testament as a sacrificial event', Colin Gunton finds the description of the life and death of Jesus in terms of sacrifice to be 'the dominant New Testament metaphor' and John Moses argues that 'the notion of the death of Jesus as a sacrifice is so significant within the New Testament that no theory of atonement can stand within the Christian tradition if it does not incorporate the element of sacrifice'.[2] On the other side, Ernst Käsemann and Gerhard Friedrich lead a group of German scholars who are profoundly uneasy about interpreting the New Testament in these terms. Somewhere in the middle is Stephen Sykes, who while wanting to retain sacrifice as a central category in Christian theology, feels compelled to admit that 'the New Testament evidence ... does not immediately suggest that the idea of sacrifice is the prime category for the interpretation of the death of Christ'.[3]

Even among those who are certain that the New Testament does speak of Jesus in sacrificial terms, there is considerable disagreement about exactly what is at issue. Is it his death, his passion or the whole 'Christ event' of his life, death and resurrection? Several theologians, following the lead of F. C. N. Hicks, have argued that limiting the notion of sacrifice to Jesus' death on the Cross has produced an unhealthy and distorted concentration among both Catholics and Protestants on the bleeding heart and being washed in the blood of the lamb.[4] Yet it is undeniable that New Testament writers take up Jewish ideas about the efficacy of blood sacrifices and apply them to the death of Jesus.

This raises another important question. Is the sacrificial language found in the New Testament there primarily in order to explain the significance and saving power of Jesus Christ to a predominantly Jewish readership brought up in a culture where sacrificial offerings involving the shedding of blood were the recognized way of atoning for sin and establishing a right relationship with God? This is the view of E. O. James: 'In an age saturated with sacrificial ideas, and against the background of the highly developed Levitical conception of the priesthood, the death, resurrection and ascension of Christ were interpreted as a priestly oblation to reconcile God and man'.[5] There is certainly no doubt that several of the most striking images applied to Christ by New Testament writers are taken from the world of Israelite sacrificial ritual. At times they portray him as the Passover lamb, ritually slaughtered to avert danger and to confirm the deliverance and salvation of the Israelites; while on other occasions they interpret his death in terms of the ceremonies associated with the Day of Atonement. Their purpose, most explicitly pursued in the Epistle to the Hebrews, seems to be to locate Jesus' death and resurrection within the context of the Jewish cult and to establish that his single self-offering has achieved what tens of thousands of 'olâs have failed to do and effectively atoned for the sins of the world.

Other scholars, however, have seen a radical discontinuity between Jewish and New Testament ideas of sacrifice. For William James the Christian doctrine of atonement represented a reversal of the general process of 'spiritualization' found in Judaism and other religious traditions.[6] This is also the view of Hyam Maccoby:

> It is quite mistaken to see the Christian concept of sacrifice as arising naturally out of the Jewish sacrificial system, or as providing the climax to which it tended. On the contrary, the natural tendency of Judaism was in Christianity catastrophically reversed. The whole tendency of the Jewish system was to *reduce* the importance of sacrifice; the very term 'sacrifice' is a misnomer in relation to the majority of the offerings of the Jerusalem Temple, where in general the tone set was that of a communal meal with God, with the aim of thanksgiving rather than of redemption. In Christianity the age-long Jewish process of sublimation disappears as if in a sudden bout of psychosis. We are back at the primitive level at which the abyss opens and panic requires a victim.[7]

If the New Testament does approach sacrifice in a radically different way from the Old, then this may be because there were other traditions influencing its writers. Martin Hengel has pointed to the prevalence of sacrificial ideas in Hellenistic culture. They included the notion of heroic apotheosis achieved through death, the nobility of laying down one's life for the sake of country, friends or some other higher cause and a sense of the benefits achieved through the suffering of the innocent.[8] It may well be that the authors of the New Testament, most of whom were steeped in Greek culture, drew on these ideas as well as on the ubiquitous motif of the dying and rising hero-god in their portrayal of the death of Jesus.

This raises another series of questions. Assuming that the Cross of Christ is represented sacrificially in the New Testament, is it seen in Jewish terms as the offering of a passive victim or in Greek terms as a voluntary self-sacrifice? Who exactly is doing the sacrificing? It can hardly be those who put Jesus to death: they have no sense of making a cultic offering but rather see themselves as carrying out the judicial execution of a criminal. Jesus is killed by soldiers, not priests, and he dies on a cross rather than an altar. Does this not make him the victim of betrayal or murder rather than a sacrificial lamb? Is he, indeed, a victim at all? Does he make a voluntary sacrifice of himself or is he driven by a combination of utter obedience to God and a dark messianic conviction that the Son of Man has to suffer and die? What sense does it make to speak of him, as the prayers and hymns of the Church throughout the ages have done, as both priest and victim? Who is the author of his sacrifice and to whom is it directed? If it is difficult enough to think of Jesus as both priest and victim, it is even more confusing to work out the role of God in the death of his Son. Is God both offering Jesus and accepting him as a sacrifice? Is he in fact sacrificing himself to himself?

Attempts have been made to reconcile these apparent contradictions within the framework of the Trinitarian relationship, most notably by Jürgen Moltmann in *The Crucified God*. Yet we seem to be left with a schizophrenic God who is not wholly his own master.

> In the Christian myth, God the Father plays two roles at once: He is the sad, sacrificing father, and He is also the father-god who demands the sacrifice in appeasement of His anger at the original sin of mankind. God denies His fatherly feelings in order to bring about a sacrifice to Himself. As self-denying parent, God bows to some dark necessity beyond His control; but as father-god, He is himself that necessity.[9]

Beyond all these questions lies the contentious issue of what exactly Jesus died for and how his sacrifice, if that is what it was, is to be interpreted. Is it primarily expiatory, propitiatory or exemplary? Does the offering of his blood somehow cover and blot out sin in a manner which is akin to, if infinitely more efficacious than, the action of the Jewish holocausts? Does his death propitiate and satisfy the righteous wrath and indignation of God and reconcile him with his wayward creation? Or is it rather primarily an example to us, pointing out the way of suffering and self-sacrifice that we must take if we are to be followers of Christ? Should Jesus' sacrifice be seen as vicarious, substitutionary or representative? What is the most appropriate way to understand it today: through biblical images like suffering servant, lamb of God or great high priest; through metaphors drawn from the courtroom and the counting house, which speak of ransom, debt, advocacy, mediation and paying the price for sin and which have appealed so much to the Church through the ages; or through contemporary anthropological concepts such as the sacred executioner or the neutralizer of violence and aggression?

Finally there is a clutch of even more vexed questions as to the efficacy and particularity of the event that took place on Calvary in the mid-30s AD. Was Jesus' crucifixion a unique sacrifice which had the effect of destroying utterly the power of death and cancelling out all sin for all time, or does it point to an eternal process of sacrifice which is at the heart of the being of God, in which Christ is constantly engaged and in which we all participate? If it really is true that, in the words of the Book of Common Prayer, by suffering death on the Cross Jesus Christ 'made by his one oblation of himself once offered a full, perfect, and sufficient sacrifice, oblation and satisfaction for the sins of the whole world', then why is it that nearly 2,000 years later the world seems more steeped than ever in sin and evil? Quite apart from the evidence, or lack of it, as to its efficacy, what is the presumed causal relationship between the historical event of the Cross and the enormous atoning achievement which it is supposed to have brought about? How did one man's crucifixion change the whole destiny of creation and break the power of sin and death? If the crucial factor was Jesus' utter obedience to God, then could not Abraham equally well have done it? If it was his laying down of his life for the sake of others, then what about all the other martyrs and heroic figures who have died in order to save others? If it was because he offered his sacrifice as the Son of God then we are back to the whole question of the sense and the necessity of God demanding a sacrifice from himself.

It would be the height of folly and presumption to suggest that I can even begin in this chapter to offer an answer to this host of questions which have preoccupied theologians for centuries and on which thousands of volumes have been written. Rather, I propose the more modest task of reviewing the use of sacrificial language in the New Testament in the hope that this may at least shed some light on the issues raised above, as well as on the general theme of the power of sacrifice. I will look first at Jesus' own teachings and his statements about himself as they are presented in the gospels. I will then examine the treatment of his death and passion in the three synoptic gospels, in the Johannine literature and in the Epistle to the Hebrews. Finally, I will look at those books in which what might be called a sacrificial Christology is most fully worked out, the Pauline epistles. This is not, of course, to proceed in a chronological direction: Paul's letters are almost certainly the earliest documents in the New Testament. Their advanced sacrificial Christology cannot, therefore, be seen as the culmination of a developing tradition of which we see the beginnings in the gospels. I wonder if they do not rather reflect a view held by many in the immediate aftermath of Jesus' death, from which subsequent writers backed away, as many have continued to back away ever since, because of their uneasiness with its disturbing and even tragic portrayal of the Saviour of the world and the God who sent him.

Jesus' own references to sacrifice as reported in the gospels echo the line taken by the Hebrew prophets. He twice quotes approvingly Hosea's words about mercy being more desirable than sacrifice (Matthew 9:13 and Matthew 12:7) and is delighted to be told by a scribe that to love God and your neighbour as yourself is 'more than all whole burnt offerings and sacrifices' (Mark 12:33). Like the prophets, he does not condemn cultic offerings but stresses that they only have value when they are accompanied by a spirit of forgiveness and charity: 'If you are offering your gift at the altar, and there remember that your brother has something against you, leave your gift before the altar and go; first be reconciled to your brother, and then come and offer your gift' (Matthew 5:23). This is a rare example of Jesus speaking about the cultic sacrifices of Jewish temple worship in direct terms. More often he refers to them metaphorically as in the cryptic words recorded in Mark 9:49: 'For everyone shall be salted with fire and every sacrifice shall be salted with salt'. Salt was sprinkled on the animals killed and burned in cultic sacrifice to add to their savour. Jesus applies this imagery to his followers as he does again in his famous utterance, 'You are the salt of the earth' (Matthew 5:13). In the words of F. C. N. Hicks, 'The salt is the dedicated life of Christians. So they are to have salt, the secret of the life which issues from self-dedication, in themselves and that is a common life in them all'.[10]

Jesus' repeated emphasis on the importance of self-sacrifice as the foundation of discipleship is one of the most distinctive elements in his teaching. The theme of costly self-giving underlies the important trio of parables found in Chapter 15 of Luke's Gospel, which tell of the lost sheep, the lost coin and the prodigal son. It is expressed more bluntly in the remark which he makes to his disciples in Caesarea Philippi: 'If any man would come after me, let him deny himself, and take up his cross, and follow me. For whoever would save his life will lose it; and whoever loses his life for my sake and the gospel's will save it' (Mark 8:34–5). Similar words recur in Luke 9:23 and Matthew 10:39 and 16:25. This call for the utter surrender of self is reinforced by his grim reminders to his disciples that the reward for those who follow him will be suffering and servitude (Mark 10:30, 44). When James and John, the sons of Zebedee, ask that they might sit respectively on his right and left hand in glory he responds, 'The cup that I drink you will drink; and with the baptism with which I am baptized you will be baptized' (Mark 10:40). This statement seems to promise an active and continuing participation in

Jesus' sacrifice on the part of his followers as they drink the cup of sorrow and are baptized into suffering.

This kind of teaching was unprecedented in the circles in which Jesus moved. While both Jews and Greeks accepted the inevitability of suffering and recognized the nobility of selfless service, they did not make these principles prerequisites for salvation. Jesus' message was nothing less than that the only way to light was through darkness, the only way to glory and fulfilment was through sacrifice and surrender and the only way to the kingdom of eternal life was through death, understood spiritually in terms of dying to self, as well as physically. In many ways this had more in common with the mythology of primal religions with their dying and rising gods and their appreciation of the cycle of life, death and rebirth than with either Hebrew religion or Greek philosophy.

Jesus' teaching was encapsulated in his words about the need for the corn of wheat to fall into the ground and die (John 12:24–5). I have already suggested that he seems to have intended this statement to apply also to himself. Certainly, he is portrayed in the gospels not just as urging self-sacrifice on others but as accepting it for himself. From the time of his ready submission to baptism at the hands of John there is a strong sense that he is, in the words of F. W. Dillistone, 'under constraint to go down into the darkness of the waters, to pass through the river of affliction, to follow the pathway of self-humbling and self-identification with the poor in spirit, in the fulfilment of His vocation'.[11] Jesus' call on his disciples to take up their crosses comes hard on the heels of his prophecy of his own impending suffering and death which itself follows Peter's identification of him as the Christ. His prophecy 'that the Son of Man must suffer many things and be rejected . . . and be killed' (Mark 8:31), which runs as a recurring motif through Mark's Gospel, comes to take on clearly sacrificial overtones: 'The Son of Man came not to be served but to serve, and to give his life as a ransom for many' (Mark 10:45).

These verses seem closely to echo the language of Isaiah 52:13–53. Martin Hengel has argued that alongside the psalms the suffering servant passage constituted the most important portion of the Hebrew scriptures for Jesus and he has identified it as the source of ten direct quotations and thirty-two allusions in the New Testament.[12] The extent to which Jesus consciously applied Isaiah's words to himself is a matter of considerable debate among New Testament experts. There is also disagreement as to whether he took them to have sacrificial connotations. Yet it is surely hard to read the remarks quoted above from St Mark's Gospel without agreeing with Vincent Taylor that Jesus did, indeed, see himself as the fulfilment of Isaiah's prophecy and 'must have thought of His suffering as a sacrificial offering in which men might participate'.[13]

There is also a strongly sacrificial theme in the synpotic gospels' treatment of the last supper. All three identify it as a Passover feast and Mark begins his account of its preparation with a reminder that it coincides with the time when the Passover lamb is slaughtered (Mark 14:12). Jesus' words at the supper, 'This is my blood of the new testament, which is shed for many for the remission of sins' (Matthew 26:28), clearly suggest an atoning sacrifice. Yet in their descriptions of the actual event of the crucifixion the authors of the synoptic gospels eschew sacrificial language: Jesus is portrayed as a victim of cruelty and mockery and not as the object of a cultic offering.

If Christ's crucifixion is portrayed in the gospels as being a judicial execution or a foul murder, can it really be seen as a sacrifice? Those theologians who feel that it can have traditionally made a distinction between the event itself and Jesus' approach to it. Their position is classically stated by Thomas Aquinas in that part of the *Summa Theologiae* where he deals with the question 'Did Christ's passion achieve its effect by being a sacrifice?' His considered view is that 'On the part of those who put Christ to death, the passion was a crime: on the part of Christ, who suffered out of love, it was a sacrifice. And that is why Christ is said to have offered this sacrifice and not those who slew him'.[14] Many modern theologians, particularly, though not exclusively, Roman

Catholics, have echoed this argument and stressed Christ's self-offering as the key element which makes the crucifixion a sacrifice. For Eugene Masure, 'the death of Christ on Calvary is a sacrifice not in so far as it is a juridical murder carried out by executioners, or a sin on the part of the Pharisees, but in so far as it is the self-immolation of God's son'.[15] In similar vein, J. F. McHugh writes that 'the essence of Christ's sacrifice lies not in the fact that he was put to death, but in the fact that he willingly accepted death', while I. U. Dalferth notes that

> in speaking of Christ's death for us in terms of sacrifice, the New Testament does not refer to a ritual act of killing but uses sacrifice as an interpretative symbol to communicate the soteriological meaning of his death to its audience. It is not the act of killing at the crucifixion (which was a judicial execution, not a ritual slaying) but Christ's self-offering culminating in his acceptance of death which it is at pains to emphasize.[16]

Protestant theologians are, if anything, even keener to stress the voluntary nature of Jesus' sacrifice. Thus Colin Gunton writes that 'as a sacrifice of himself, the death of Jesus was a free and voluntary human act'.[17] This does not seem to me, however, to take full account of the strong sense conveyed in the gospels of his death as a dark necessity to which he bows in a spirit of obedience and acceptance. The words which he utters in the garden of Gethsemane, 'Father, if thou be willing, remove this cup from me: nevertheless not my will, but thine, be done' (Luke 22:42), speak of resignation and obedience at least as much as, if not more than, of willing self-sacrifice. The theme of the inevitability of Jesus' death runs through all the gospels and is particularly marked in Luke's account of the passion. He certainly does not flinch from it – 'When the days drew near for him to be received up, he set his face to go to Jerusalem' (Luke 9:51). Indeed, he accepts the 'rightness' of the passion, at least retrospectively, as indicated by his post-resurrection appearance on the road to Emmaus where he expounds all the prophecies concerning himself and asks the disciples 'was it not necessary that the Christ should suffer these things, and enter into his glory?' (Luke 24:26). Yet this overwhelming stress on inevitability and necessity surely invalidates a portrayal of Jesus' suffering and death simply in terms of a free and voluntary self-sacrifice. Is there not rather a sense here of his submission to the dark and mysterious power of sacrifice, that simultaneously tragic yet life-giving principle at the heart of the cosmos, which as the Son of God he is destined to reveal and release?

One has to go on and ask, indeed, whether in their treatment of his passion and crucifixion the synoptic gospels in fact portray Jesus as a free agent in any real sense. Traditional Christian theology, liturgy and hymnody have always spoken of him as both high priest and victim, the one who offers and the one who is himself the perfect sacrifice for sin. Yet the gospels stress his passive status as victim to the virtual exclusion of any priestly role and portray him very much as the object rather than the author or subject of the events which make up the passion narrative. I follow here the very convincing and deeply moving argument of W. H. Vanstone in his book *The Stature of Waiting* which points to the change that comes over Jesus with his arrest in Gethsemane – from active public ministry to a state of almost total passivity. In being handed over, Jesus passes from action to passion, from subject to object, from doing things himself to having things done to him and it is in this condition that he achieves his great work of salvation. This new state that he enters is a profoundly sacrificial one of surrender and abandonment. Yet it is wrong to conceive of it simply in terms of voluntary and willing self-sacrifice. Vanstone is extremely careful to distance himself from any notion that Jesus courted or purposed his own death. On the contrary, what he sees, and this surely is also what the gospels record, is a man who allows himself to be put into a situation the outcome of which does not lie in his own hands, a situation of utter dependence and total receptivity. Vanstone himself compares it to the situation of those who are ill or incapacitated and whose most characteristic experience is of having things done to them. This can hardly be described in terms of voluntary or willing self-sacrifice. It is rather the experience of suffering, or in Vanstone's own phrase, the stature of waiting.[18]

I suspect that one of the main factors leading theologians to over-stress the voluntary nature of Jesus' sacrifice has been their desire to avoid any suggestion of propitiation. Yet we can surely hold to an interpretation which makes more of the inevitability and unavoidability of Christ's passion and see it as something that happens to him rather than something that he wills on himself without invoking the heretical demons of propitiatory atonement or penal substitution. Indeed, such an interpretation is surely more in keeping with a view of God as the one who himself suffers than as the angry and affronted deity who needs to be propitiated. The accounts of the passion and crucifixion in the synoptic gospels raise very important issues about the dividing-line between involuntary suffering and voluntary self-sacrifice. In particular, they raise the question of whether suffering has to be self-willed and voluntary in order for it to have sacrificial efficacy. The desolate words which both Mark and Matthew record Jesus uttering on the Cross, 'My God, my God, why hast thou forsaken me?' hardly convey the notion of willing self-sacrifice. They sound from the very depths of human experience, the authentic and anguished cry of all who experience unwanted pain and suffering. They take us, too, far beyond the realms of cultic sin offerings to a deeper and more inclusive understanding of the Cross as a sacrifice for suffering as much as for sin (see pp. 256–7).

When we turn from the synoptics to the Fourth Gospel, we seem to find a clearer and bolder use of sacrificial imagery in connection with Jesus' death. There is a more explicit identification of Jesus with the Passover lamb, provided by God and slain to expiate sin. The author of St John's Gospel has Jesus on the Cross on the eve of the Passover when the lambs are being slaughtered. He also records the 'Lamb of God' sayings which are not found in the synoptic gospels, most notably, the great statement 'Behold the Lamb of God, who takes away the sin of the world' (John 1:29). Several scholars see the Akedah theme as central to the Fourth Gospel and point to the sacrificial significance of the 'blood and water' described as coming out of Jesus' side after his death (John 19:34). The first epistle of John, which is often taken to be by the same author as the Gospel, views Jesus' death in sacrificial terms, with its efficacy lying in the blood which washes away sin (1 John 1:7).

However, in other respects the Fourth Gospel offers a less sacrificial interpretation of Jesus' death than the synoptics: the recurring motif is not his offering of himself but his lifting up (John 3:14, 8:28, 12:32–4). His death is portrayed not as an expiatory sin offering but in terms of the glorification and revelation of the Son of Man. Several scholars, following the lead of Rudolf Bultmann and Ernst Käsemann, see the concepts of expiatory or vicarious sacrifice as being wholly absent from the theology of the Fourth Gospel.[19] Bultmann even suggests that the 'Lamb of God' sayings were interpolated by a later ecclesiastical redactor to introduce the idea of atonement which was otherwise missing. In a similar way, 1 John with its explicitly propitiatory and expiatory language is seen as having been written to counter the absence of these ideas in the Fourth Gospel.

Certainly the author of John's Gospel seems to be at pains to distance Jesus from the cultic sin offerings of Jewish temple worship. He makes a good deal of Jesus cleansing the temple and removing those selling oxen, sheep and doves for sacrifice. More dramatically, he has Jesus calling for the temple to be destroyed and speaking of his own body as the true temple (John 2:19–21). This last remark is amplified by his words to the Samaritan woman that true worship is 'in spirit and in truth' (John 4:23). The clear implication here is that with Jesus' coming worship is liberated from the temple with its ritual offerings and sacrificial cults. God is to be worshipped through Christ, the new temple, and in terms of inner disposition and not outward performance of cultic rites.

Like the synoptics, the Fourth Gospel puts great stress on the theme of self-sacrifice: while they show Jesus commending it to his disciples as a way they should follow, John has him more often applying it to himself or to God – 'For God so loved the world that he gave his only begotten Son (John 3:16); 'I am the good shepherd: the good shepherd lays down his life for his sheep' (John 10:11); 'Greater love has no man than this, that a man lay down his life for his friends' (John 15:13). When this principle of self-giving is extended in the Johannine literature to be a maxim of Christian discipleship it is on the basis of an exemplary theory of atonement understood in terms of the begetting of self-sacrificial love: 'By this we know love, that he laid down his life for us; and we ought to lay down our lives for the brethren' (1 John 3:16). It is significant that all of these statements seem to follow the Greek idea of the nobility of laying down one's life for others rather than the Hebrew concept of atonement for sin or the notion of propitiating an angry God. As we have already noted, there is a strong propitiatory emphasis in 1 John (see especially 1 John 4:10), but this is in marked contrast to the overall tone of the Fourth Gospel.

There is also much less stress in John's Gospel than in the synoptics on the inevitability of Jesus' death and on his passive role as an object and victim. If his filial obedience in laying down his life is stressed, then so also is his complete freedom to do with it as he likes: 'For this reason the Father loves me, because I lay down my life, that I may take it again. No one takes it from me, but I lay it down of my own accord. I have power to lay it down and I have power to take it again' (John 10:17–18). This verse epitomizes the Fourth Gospel's positive portrayal of the crucifixion as the means of Jesus' exaltation and rising to glory. There is little sense of tragedy or suffering: instead of the expressions of Godforsakenness recorded by Matthew and Mark, Jesus' utterance from the Cross is the triumphant cry 'It is finished' (John 19:30).

With its key motif of the descending and ascending God-Man, John's Gospel comes closer than any other book in the New Testament to echoing the idea of the dying and rising gods of primal religion. Its portrayal of the Cross as a means of exaltation and glorification perhaps also parallels primal myths about the sacrificial tree which supports the cosmos like a pillar and provides a ladder on which to climb from earth to heaven. The Fourth Gospel as a whole makes much of the central sacrificial principle that life comes out of death. Significantly, it makes the raising of Lazarus from the dead the climax of Jesus' public ministry. The theme of resurrection is also at the heart of its triumphant theology of the Cross where death is presented not as a final destination, but as a departure, 'a loss which is turned into gain, a giving up of life which is made the means whereby that life is received back again renewed, transfigured, and fulfilled'.[20]

Nowhere in the New Testament is sacrificial language more boldly and dramatically applied to the Cross of Christ than in the Epistle to the Hebrews. Its overriding aim is to locate the death of Jesus in the context of Hebrew cultic offerings and to present him as the ultimate high priest who, through shedding his own blood, has made a perfect atonement for sin:

> For if the sprinkling of defiled persons with the blood of goats and bulls and with the ashes of a heifer sanctifies for the purification of the flesh, how much more shall the blood of Christ, who through the eternal Spirit offered himself without blemish to God, purify your conscience from dead works to serve the living God? (Hebrews 9:11–14).

Again and again the author of Hebrews stresses that Jesus Christ's one offering has done what all the ministrations of priests throughout the centuries have failed to do: it has provided a complete and final sacrifice for sin.

> He has no need, like those high priests, to offer sacrifices daily, first for his own sins and then for those of the people; he did this once for all when he offered up himself (Hebrews 7:27).

> Nor was it to offer himself repeatedly, as the high priest enters the Holy Place yearly with blood not his own; for

then he would have had to suffer repeatedly since the foundation of the world. But as it is, he has appeared once for all at the end of the age to put away sin by the sacrifice of himself (Hebrews 9:25–6).

This note of finality and sufficiency has been widely picked up by liturgists and hymnwriters. It has found its way into many eucharistic services which stress the efficacy of the single oblation once offered by Christ as 'a full, perfect, and sufficient sacrifice and satisfaction for the sins of the whole world'. It has also inspired many great evangelical hymns:

Jesus, my great High Priest,
Offer'd his Blood and died:
My guilty conscience seeks
No sacrifice beside:
His powerful Blood did once atone,
And now it pleads before the Throne.

. . .

Not all the blood of beasts,
On Jewish altars slain,
Could give the guilty conscience peace,
Or wash away the stain.

But Christ, the heavenly Lamb,
Takes all our sins away;
A sacrifice of nobler name
And richer blood than they.[21]

It is unfortunate that the message from the Epistle to the Hebrews which has been taken up in the worship and song of the Church should be so blood-soaked and sin-centred and dwell so much on the finality of Christ's sacrifice. There is another theme running through this book which is less often heard in prayers and hymns. It is the notion of the continuing sacrifice of Christ, 'the great high priest who has passed through the heavens' (Hebrews 4:14) and 'who is able for all time to save those who draw near to God through him, since he always lives to make intercession for them' (Hebrews 7:25). This ongoing sacrificial activity of the risen and ascended Christ is just as important as his once-for-all sacrifice made on earth. In the words of E. O. James, 'the central theme of the Epistle to the Hebrews is . . . the perpetuation in the eternal world of the perfect sacrifice once offered on the Cross in time and space'.[22]

Two Scottish theologians have particularly stressed this vital eternal dimension to Christ's sacrifice. For William Milligan, Professor of Biblical Criticism in Aberdeen University during the 1860s and 1870s, 'the lesson constantly enforced in the Epistle to the Hebrews is that the high priesthood of Christ is "fulfilled" by His work in heaven; that only after His Resurrection is He in a position to exhaust the functions of that office; and that His offering is not completed until, within the heavenly sanctuary, He presents Himself to the Father in all that perfection of service which the Father claims'. Milligan sees Christ making two distinct sacrifices, dying on the Cross to bear the penalty of human sin and to enable all to pass with him through death to life, and eternally offering himself to his father in heaven in joyful gratitude and praise to enable us to return to God. 'Without the former, that death would be wanting out of which alone the corn of wheat can spring up in life. Without the latter, there would be no springing up of the corn of wheat at all.'[23] Donald Baillie, Professor of Systematic Theology at St Andrews University for 20 years from 1934, also set much store by the doctrine which he saw worked out in the Epistle to the Hebrews:

The atoning work of Christ, as Priest and Victim in one, is not confined to His Passion on earth and did not end with his death on the Cross. That work on Calvary was indeed a finished work, a perfect sacrifice made once for all on earth. Yet it was the beginning of a priesthood which goes on for ever in the unseen realm, in heaven, in the Holy Place beyond the Veil, into which our High Priest entered through death, and where he 'ever liveth to make intercession for us', being continually 'touched with the feeling of our infirmities'.[24]

Alongside this stress on the continuing sacrifice of Christ beyond the Cross, the Epistle to the Hebrews also points to the importance of his followers continuing to lead sacrificial lives. His death may have made cultic offerings utterly redundant but it has in no way obviated the continuing need for this kind of living sacrifice. Readers of the epistle are exhorted to 'offer up to God a sacrifice of praise continually . . . to show kindness and to share what you have with others . . . for such are the sacrifices which God approves' (Hebrews 13:15–16, REB). They are also urged to tread the *Via Dolorosa* and embrace a life of suffering and sorrow, remembering that 'the Lord disciplines him whom he loves, and chastises every son whom he receives' (Hebrews 12:6). There are echoes here of Jesus' words to his disciples in Mark 10:39–44 and of other passages in the New Testament which suggest that Christians should accept and even welcome suffering as a test of their faith and as a response to and a sharing in Christ's suffering (like, for example, 1 Peter 2:19–21 quoted on p. 248). The author of the Epistle to the Hebrews goes beyond other New Testament authors, however, both in the vehemence of his conviction that suffering is beneficial and a mark of God's love and, more radically, in applying this principle to Jesus himself when he states that 'it was fitting that he, for whom and by whom all things exist, in bringing many sons to glory, should make the pioneer of their salvation perfect through suffering' (Hebrews 2:10). The point is reiterated in Hebrews 5:8–9 where Jesus' perfection through the things he suffered is put forward as the essential prerequisite for assuming his role as source of eternal salvation.

The principle of perfection through suffering, which is extended in Hebrews to the whole of humanity, is at first sight morally repellent. It suggests a callous and cruel God who achieves his work by inflicting misery and sorrow on his creatures to test and strengthen them. The notion that Jesus was especially singled out for this treatment by his Father and visited with afflictions in order to be perfected seems particularly distasteful. Yet are we perhaps not being pointed back here to a God who suffers himself and who with his Son creates, sustains and redeems through the power of sacrifice – that same power through which all things live and move and have their being? As the Alpha and Omega, the author and the finisher of the race that is set before us, the redeemer and the perfector of creation, Christ has, indeed, been made perfect through suffering and through abandoning himself utterly to his Father. Through him, and specifically through sharing his suffering and abandonment, the whole groaning and travailing creation moves painfully towards its completion and fulfilment. That suffering has in some sense come from God but not in the form of a calculated reign of terror and tribulation. Rather it is the inevitable and unavoidable overflowing of the pain and passion of one who himself acts and communicates through the power of sacrifice. Perhaps in our age of patripassianism it is not too much to suggest that God makes himself perfect through suffering as he expresses and fulfils his creative and redeeming nature by means of deeply costly self-giving.

The writings of St Paul provide the most complex and varied treatment of the subject of sacrifice in the New Testament. As with the Fourth Gospel there has been considerable debate as to whether they do in fact express a sacrificial theology. German scholars are once again much more reluctant to acknowledge this element than their British and American counterparts.[25] Yet it is surely impossible to read Paul's letters without gaining a strong sense of the central importance of the theme of sacrifice to their author. There are numerous allusions to Israelite cultic offerings and the death of Jesus is described in terms which are clearly sacrificial. Even more explicitly than the author of the Fourth Gospel, Paul identifies Jesus with the Passover lamb: 'Christ our passover lamb is sacrificed for us' (1 Corinthians 5:7). In Ephesians 5:2 he is described as 'a fragrant offering and sacrifice to God' and on three other occasions as a sin offering (2 Corinthians 5:21, Romans 8:3, 3:24). Paul also refers to the cleansing, atoning powers of the blood of Christ (Ephesians 2:13) and makes frequent use of the Greek word ὑπερ (hyper) with its strong sacrificial connotations (2 Corinthians 5:14, Romans 5:6, Galatians 2:20, Ephesians 5:25). In writing about the last supper he stresses Jesus' sacrificial action in shedding his blood and breaking his body for his followers (1 Corinthians 11:23–7). He also gives a significantly sacrificial slant to the Eucharist by making a direct connection between Christian participation in the body and blood of Christ through breaking bread and sharing the cup and the 'partnership in the altar' forged by Israelite worshippers eating their burnt offerings (1 Corinthians 10:16–19).

In speaking of Jesus as a sacrifice for sin, Paul is very careful to insist that the initiative lies with God and to portray him as the author of the sacrifice. 'For our sake he made him [Christ] to be sin' (i.e. a sin offering) (2 Corinthians 5:21); 'Christ Jesus whom God put forward as an expiation by his blood' (Romans 3:25, see also Romans 8:3). He speaks of God giving up his son – 'He that spared not his own Son, but delivered him up for us all' (Romans 8:32; see also Romans 4:25). Significantly, the word used here, παραδιδόναι or *paradidonai*, also occurs three times in the suffering servant passage from Isaiah in the Septuagint, the Greek translation of the Hebrew Bible. It is also the term used to describe the handing over of Jesus in the Gospel passion narratives. Several scholars suggest that Paul's use of it is designed to convey not just the costliness of the sacrifice which God makes of his Son in the process of dealing with sin but also the sense that he is giving up part of himself. Hyam Maccoby sees Paul as taking over and Christianizing the notion of the sacrificial death of a god found in pagan mystery religions and associated with such figures as Attis and Odin. Martin Hengel, on the other hand, finds Paul's concept of the God who gives up his Son and thereby surrenders part of himself more original.[26]

There is certainly no suggestion in Paul's writings of either God or Christ being sacrificed by humans so that they may be regenerated or brought back to life. The emphasis is rather on God's costly self-giving and perhaps, too, his self-emptying in parallel with and as a corollary of the *kenosis* of his Son 'who, though he was in the form of God, did not count equality with God a thing to be grasped, but emptied himself, taking the form of a servant, being born in the likeness of men. And being found in human form, he humbled himself and became obedient unto death, even death on a cross' (Philippians 2:5–8). This passage, which clearly echoes Isaiah's description of the suffering servant, has often been taken to suggest a sacrificial Christology. For Edward Irving, the early nineteenth-century Scottish Pentecostalist, Christ's sacrifice lay precisely in his humiliation, his becoming man and being made flesh.[27] Michael Ramsey, the mid-twentieth-century Archbishop of Canterbury, felt that these two verses in Philippians showed that the Son of God made his deity 'the occasion of an act of self-sacrifice towards mankind'.[28] More generally, the verses have been the starting point for the development of 'kenotic' Christologies which have generally been associated with an exemplary theory of atonement, a call to Christians to live humbly and sacrificially and a portrayal of Jesus as one who throughout his life reversed the usual human aspiration to be upwardly mobile and consciously descended not just through the social scale but into the very depths of human experience and misery.

All three of these elements are clearly present in Paul's writings, particularly, perhaps, the theme of Christ's descent into the deep (see Romans 10:7, Ephesians 4:9). Like the author of the Fourth Gospel, he develops a descent-ascent motif but in his case it follows the death of Jesus and involves a descent into hell before the double ascent of the resurrection and ascension. The suggestion that Jesus descended briefly into hell following his death is not, of course, peculiar to Paul. It is to be found in the synoptic gospels, notably in Matthew 12:40: 'For as Jonah was three days and three nights in the belly of a whale, so will the Son of man be three days and nights in the heart of the earth'. The reference in 1 Peter 3:19 to Jesus going and preaching to the spirits in prison is also generally taken to describe a descent into hell to preach to the damned and offer them a way of release and salvation. It was reflection on these texts which led to the incorporation of the phrase 'He descended into hell' into the historic creeds of the Church formulated in the fourth century. The notion of Jesus' descent into hell is extremely important for establishing the universality of his mission and showing that no one is beyond the reach of his saving love. It also presents him as one who has himself sunk sacrificially to the very depths of human despair and Godforsakenness.

For Paul the descent of Jesus into the deep is the essential condition for his resurrection to eternal life. In seeking to explain the central Christian paradox that life comes out of death he finds himself echoing Jesus' own words about the corn of wheat: 'What you sow does not come to life unless it dies. And what you sow is not the body which is to be, but a bare kernel, perhaps of wheat or of some other grain' (1 Corinthians 15:36-7). It is significant that Paul uses this analogy in an attempt to get across the idea of resurrection to a readership which found it very difficult to grasp and was much happier with notions of immortality and some kind of continuing existence for the soul without the radical discontinuity of death and rebirth. He wants to stress both the reality and the necessity of physical death as the seed-bed for new life and the radical transformation which the individual Christian undergoes in the process of resurrection: 'What is sown is perishable, what is raised is imperishable. It is sown in dishonour, it is raised in glory. It is sown in weakness, it is raised in power. It is sown in a physical body, it is raised a spiritual body' (1 Corinthians 15: 42-4).

These statements point us to what is perhaps Paul's most original contribution to Christian theology, his unique understanding of our mystical participation in Jesus' death and resurrection. It derives from his distinctive Christology which identifies Jesus as the second Adam, the representative man, the new and true humanity. Central to Paul's thought is the notion that the sacrifice of Jesus Christ is not substitutionary but representative. It is not an event external to us or which happens on our behalf; it is an activity in which we are intimately caught up and involved in the most direct way possible. We die with Christ and this means that we no longer live for ourselves but for, in and through him. 'I have been crucified with Christ: the life which I now live is not my life but the life which Christ lives in me; and my present mortal life is lived by faith in the Son of God, who loved me and gave himself up for me' (Galatians 2:19–20, REB). In this context Christ's sacrifice shows what is the true nature and end of human life. The crucified Christ is the image of God in which humans are created (Romans 2:12–21, 8:29; Colossians 1:15; Ephesians 2:10). The principles of limitation and surrender are revealed not to be inimical and alien to life but fundamental to its fulfilment.

> If Christ's death is a sacrifice, then the death of the true man, Jesus Christ, and the limitation of every man's life in time, are not tragic features which disturb or interrupt an otherwise wonderful process of continuous 'incarnational' influx of the divine into the material. Rather, it is revealed by the true man that all humanity must and can stand before God only in accepting the limits which God has set up by creating time.... True humanity does not last only till death comes. It includes the acceptance of death from God's hand. True life is not life despite death, but resurrection and life of the dead.[29]

This motif of life through death and resurrection has a continuous application throughout our earthly existence and is not just confined to the process of physical death. Only those who continually identify themselves with the dying and rising of Christ experience authentic life and participate in the full humanity revealed in his representative sacrifice. For Paul this identification comes in an important measure through the sacraments of the Church. In baptism we drown with Christ and rise from the incompleteness and imperfection of our previous existence to a new life in him. Through the Eucharist we are fed with the holy mysteries of his body and blood and join ourselves to him by re-membering his passion and crucifixion and showing forth his resurrection. Our participation in the dying and rising of Christ also involves leading lives which are grounded on the principle of sacrificial love and self-giving. This is what lies behind Paul's insistence that the seat of sacrifice has shifted with Christ from the temple to the body. The proper performance of cultic rites has been replaced by the proper disposition of the human heart and proper behaviour towards others. Christians are the new temple, a holy priesthood continually offering sacrifices to God, not, as in the old dispensation, in the form of burnt offerings and the blood of animals but of themselves. 'I appeal to you therefore, brethren, by the mercies of God, to present your bodies as a living sacrifice, holy and acceptable to God' (Romans 12:1).

The fact that Paul uses the word 'bodies' in connection with this new kind of offering should make us think twice before talking in terms of a 'spiritualization' of sacrifice. What he urges on us is a highly physical form of sacrifice which, to paraphrase Watts' great hymn, demands our souls, our lives, our all. This is reinforced by Paul's conception of Christians as having the role of sacrificial victims as well as that of priests. On at least two occasions he refers to himself and his friends in these terms: 'we are the aroma of Christ in God' (2 Corinthians 2:15); 'I am now ready to be offered' (2 Timothy 4:6). This kind of language almost seems to call into question the idea that Christ's sacrifice on Calvary was all-sufficient and ended the need for any further offerings to God. Paul does, in fact, make one very interesting statement on this subject. It is so important that I will give it in three different translations:

I Paul . . . now rejoice in my sufferings for you, and fill up that which is behind of the afflictions of Christ in my flesh for his body's sake (Colossians 1:24, RSV).

It makes me happy to be suffering for you now, and in my own body to make up all the hardships that still have to be undergone by Christ for the sake of his body, the Church (Colossians 1:24, Jerusalem Bible).

It is now my joy to suffer for you; for the sake of Christ's body, the church, I am completing what still remains for Christ to suffer in my own purpose (Colossians 1:24, REB).

Most commentaries on this passage insist that it does not imply any incompleteness or deficiency in the redemptive value of the Cross. On the contrary, they see it as indicating that 'anyone who continues his [Christ's] work must share his suffering'.[30] Yet one might reasonably ask why, if Christ's death and resurrection represented a final and decisive victory over sin and death, there should be any need of further suffering. The determination of theologians to cling to the notion of the total sufficiency of the sacrifice on Calvary has produced some rather unattractive and unconvincing theories. Charles Moule's suggestion that this passage points to 'a quota of sufferings which the whole Church, the corporate Christ, has to exhaust before God's plan of salvation is complete' seems to introduce the idea that God's purposes for the world are somehow predicated on continuing suffering.[31] Frances Young seems to me to produce an equally unsatisfactory and untidy exegesis with her statement that 'while the death of Christ was really sufficient, there was at least a small part left over which his followers could play in the redemption of the world, namely to suffer in the drive to spread the Gospel of salvation to all mankind'.[32]

I cannot see how we can take Paul to be saying anything other than that the crucifixion of Jesus is not the end of the story of the awesome and mysterious power of sacrifice as the great engine of creation and redemption in the world. However decisive and unique it was, the particular manifestation and instantiation of that power which took place at Calvary is not the last word. There is still unfinished business and ongoing work to be done. Is this not also the unmistakable message conveyed to us by the sorry state of our groaning and travailing world 2,000 years after Jesus died on the Cross? At the tail-end of the twentieth century do we not pray to God, if anything, with more fervour and urgency than John Wesley did 250 years ago to 'make the sacrifice complete'?

It would be all too easy to take Paul's words as suggesting that somehow our task is to make up the deficiency in Christ's sacrifice by our own sufferings and trials, so letting him off the hook and diminishing the further sufferings which strictly speaking he should undergo for us. That, however, would be to ignore his overwhelming sense of our total participation in the sufferings of Christ and Christ's in ours. Paul would not have used the language that Charles Wesley did about making our own sacrifices complete (see p. 305): His firm conviction was that there is just one sacrifice, the eternal sacrifice of Christ to which all that we give up and suffer in our lives here on earth is mysteriously linked. We can only make sense of his words in Colossians 1:24 by relating them to his sense of our total participation in the dying and rising of Christ and our coming to live in and through him.

> Paul does not mean merely that the Christian experiences the sufferings of Christ after Him in thought, imagination, or sympathy, nor merely that his own actual sufferings are endured with Christ or for the sake of Christ (though all these ideas are present), but that his own actual sufferings are a real participation in Christ's sufferings, suffered by virtue of his communion with Christ.[33]

The unmistakable message of Paul is surely that Christ goes on suffering. He comes back to this theme again in 2 Corinthians 1:5: 'The sufferings of Christ abound in us'. This does not simply mean that we continue to carry round with us the marks of Jesus' passion. It points us to the truth that he is caught up and present in all suffering and sacrifice. It also identifies an eternal cosmic dimension to the sacrifice of Christ which transcends its particular historical instantiation at Calvary. In the words of William Temple, 'the self-giving of Christ is an eternal action; to give himself is his very nature'.[34] Seen in this perspective, the Cross has an existence far beyond the temporal and geographical confines of first-century Palestine. We can affirm with Origen that 'Christ remains on the Cross as long as one sinner is left in Hell' and share Pascal's disturbing conviction that 'Jesus will be in agony until the end of the world'.[35]

This is not to diminish the significance of Calvary or the uniqueness of the sacrifice made there by Jesus: it is to put it in a wider and more positive context. Understood as the supreme instantiation in time of the eternal principle of sacrifice which is at the heart of the being of God, the Cross ceases to be a crude emergency operation mounted to rescue fallen humanity. In the oft-quoted words of Charles Dinsmore: 'There was a cross in the heart of God before there was one planted on the green hill outside Jerusalem. And now that the cross of wood has been taken down, the one in the heart of God abides'.[36] The Cross at Calvary remains supremely important as the historical actualization of that sacrificial heart which continually beats in the Godhead. The unique character of the sacrifice made by Jesus is not taken away by a realization that sacrificial self-giving is also the eternal work of his father. Paul Fiddes is surely right to insist that we can and must hold on to the idea of 'a God who suffers universally and yet is still present uniquely and decisively in the sufferings of Christ'.[37]

This eternal dimension of Christ's sacrifice has not been made nearly prominent enough by most churches. Too often, they have followed a distorted and partial version of the teaching in the Epistle to the Hebrews and preached that sacrifice was brought to an end at Calvary. The doctrine of the once-for-all oblation and all-sufficient satisfaction for the sins of the world achieved on the Cross is deeply flawed, and seriously at odds with the theology of the New Testament, in two ways. It links Jesus' sacrifice narrowly and exclusively to sin and it suggests finality and completeness. Only one of the four gospels reports Jesus' words on the Cross as being 'It is finished'; the others quote expressions of Godforsakenness and uncertainty which hardly suggest the successful conclusion of a mission. Yet this is the way that Jesus' death is so often portrayed by the Church and, indeed, by academic theologians. Let me take as an example these words which appear in an article on sacrifice in a recently published *Theological Dictionary of the New Testament*: 'The purpose of sacrifice is finally fulfilled in the personal act of Christ, in the voluntary and unique offering up of his life. Sacrifice is thus brought to an end in him'.[38]

Now this remark is true enough if 'end' is used in a strictly teleological sense of the kind Eugene Masure had in mind when he wrote that to sacrifice a thing is to lead it to its end.[39] As the Alpha and Omega, and as part of the Trinitarian Godhead, Christ is, indeed, both the source and the destination of all sacrifice. I suspect, however, that this is not the point which the author of this article is trying to make: he wants to assert that the death of Jesus on the Cross brought an end to all sacrifice. This is manifestly not the case. It did confirm the redundancy of cultic offerings to atone for sin, the unacceptability of which to God had long been pointed out by the Hebrew prophets. In all other respects, however, it represented more of a beginning than an end of sacrifice. This is most directly true in respect of the high priestly role of the risen and ascended Christ who goes on offering himself to his Father in heaven. More widely, the sacrifice of Christ lays out the path of surrender and self-giving as the one for Christians to follow and by which they come through him to God. We are not just dealing here with an exemplary theory of atonement; we are being shown the way to God which is also the way of God – the way of sacrifice.

Paul Fiddes makes a helpful distinction between the act of atonement accomplished on the Cross which is historical and once-for-all and the activity of salvation which is ongoing. He also rightly stresses that the power of the Cross lies in its capacity to evoke a response.[40] It is only in so far as that response is made and goes on being made in sacrificial living that Jesus' own offering becomes fully efficacious. This point is also well made by Vincent Taylor when he distinguishes the offering of Jesus and the sacrifice that it made possible. The sacrifice is more than the offering and is not complete without the response on which its entire value depends. Jesus' offering 'while it is perfect, is not a counter in some process of celestial arithmetic. It is rather the vehicle of man's aspiration, the centre of his hope, the wings of his prayer. It is the "one true, pure, immortal sacrifice" only as it is appropriated by personal faith, in corporate worship and in sacrificial living . . . . Man himself approaches God by a way the stones of which he has not cut; he finds access to the Father through the self-offering of Jesus'.[41]

This is where the burnt offerings and blood-lettings of the Israelite cult which are so often alluded to in the New Testament and which so repel us today become relevant. The whole basis of the cult, as of so much religious ritual, was the notion that sacrifice is the way through which humans can approach God and God approaches his creatures. So, indeed, it is, if not quite in the manner that the Israelites thought. They conceived of animal sacrifices and burnt offerings as the means by which the veil of the temple could be penetrated and the Holy of Holies entered. The rending of the temple veil at the moment of Jesus' crucifixion signalled that the performance of these cultic rites is not the way for humans to enter God's presence. It lies rather in pursuing the paths of mercy and peace and sharing in the passion and crucifixion of Christ. The broken and contrite heart, the humble spirit, the life of surrender and self-giving and not the slaughtered ram or the roasted pigeon are the means of entering the Kingdom and making the sacrifices acceptable to God. Above all, entrance into the Holy of Holies comes by participating in Christ, through the sacraments, through faith and through sacrificial living. This is 'the new and living way which he has opened for us through the veil, that is, through his flesh' (Hebrews 10:19).

The body of Christ thus comes to be conceived of as the new sacrificial temple. It has both a public and a private dimension in the corporate institution of the Church and in the body of the individual believer which is 'a temple of the Holy Spirit' (1 Corinthians 6:19). The physicality of this imagery is important in guarding against the over-spiritualization of the New Testament doctrine of sacrifice. Yet there is undoubtedly a strong spiritual emphasis in the portrayal of Christ as the cornerstone of the new temple: 'Come to him, to that living stone, rejected by men but in God's sight chosen and precious; and like living stones be yourselves built into a spiritual house, to be a holy priesthood, to offer spiritual sacrifices acceptable to God through Jesus Christ' (1 Peter 2:4–5). Robert Daly had described these as 'easily the richest two verses on the meaning of sacrifice in the entire Bible'.[42] They bring together the Old Testament's stress on the divine acceptability of sacrifice and the New Testament's transformation of the cult by making Jesus Christ the cornerstone of the new temple. They also clearly indicate the priestly calling of Christians to be the living stones of God's house through their self-offerings. It is, indeed, in this distinctive New Testament concept of the body of Christ as the new temple that the two meanings of sacrifice come together and where to give up is also to make holy.

Understanding the figure of Christ in terms of categories drawn from the Israelite cult is thus not without its enduring importance and value. For a start it preserves the idea of sacrifice as the key point of intersection between earth and heaven, the medium through which God comes to us and we approach him. Marcus Barth is surely right to suggest that it also provides important safeguards against over-subjective and individualistic views of our relationship with God and Christ:

> If Christ's death were not preached and interpreted in terms of Hebrew sacrificial stories, laws, institutions, festivals, Christians might feel condemned or freed for all kinds of enterprises. They might be tempted to dream of an immediate 'personal' relationship to Christ which would exclude or overlook the relationship God has already established between Himself, His Messiah and the members of His indestructible people. The fiction they contrived would be a Christ shaped for the individual; the glory of Israel (Luke 2:32) and the 'saviour of the world' (John 4:42; 1 John 4:14) would be forgotten or neglected.

Theirs would be a community of despisers of the Old Testament, of possible antisemites, and certainly of rugged individualists.[43]

As well as preserving objectivity, the cultic language which is so often used about the person and work of Jesus Christ in the New Testament also keeps the sacrificial initiative firmly with God. It preserves the Hebrew understanding of sacrifice as the means by which the Lord sealed his covenant relationship with his people. To quote Barth again,

> the gift of redemption is not a work of Jesus alone, or a fiction of human belief in that Jesus. It is willed and inspired by the Triune God. . . . The Bible calls Christ's death a sacrifice because it wants to attest that the humanity of Jesus and His death were willed by God, inspired by the 'eternal Spirit', manifested as the eternal will, accepted in glory before human faith discovered in them, or before human belief ascribed to them, redeeming power.[44]

This brings us to the New Testament's all-important presentation of sacrifice as revelation. Christ's sacrifice reveals the costly character of the relationship between God and his creatures. It also takes us to the very heart of the being of God, revealing him as the one who gives up that which is most precious and surrenders himself totally and unconditionally to the world. In the words of John Moses, 'What Jesus does in the extremity of risk to which He hands Himself over is to display in the most dramatic form the character of God whose purposeful activity is marked by self-limitation and self-emptying'.[45] Again and again, as we have seen, the New Testament, following the Hebrew Bible, portrays God as the author and initiator of sacrifice through his own costly self-giving and not as an angry deity who needs to be propitiated. As Charles Moule has observed, 'It is a grave misfortune that the misleading word "propitiation" has gone into English scriptures at Romans 3:25 and 1 John 2:2 and so into the Prayer Book. The very initiative is God's: how then can God be said to be propitiated? He is the subject of the verb, no longer its object'.[46]

Sacrifice thus comes to be the key to the incarnation as well as the atonement. God reveals himself and becomes flesh in the form of a sacrificial victim. To that extent the traditional distinctions between incarnation and atonement fall away and they become merged in the continual process of creation and redemption. John Donne was surely right to preach on Christmas Day that 'the whole life of Christ was a continual Passion. . . . His birth and death were but one continual act, and His Christmas Day and His Good Friday are but the evening and morning of one and the same day'.[47] In similar vein Simone Weil remarked that 'the birth of Christ is already a sacrifice. Christmas ought to be as sad a day as Good Friday'.[48] Such statements may seem excessively morbid and depressing. They do indeed, acknowledge the deep vein of tragedy that runs through all human existence and through the central Christian mystery of the broken and crucified Son of God. Yet there is triumph in the tragedy – through the power of resurrection and the sacrificial truth that life comes from death. There is also purpose – the consistent steadfastness of God who is eternally working to bring his creation to perfection. Through taking the theme of sacrifice as the key to understanding both revelation and incarnation, we are led also to a deeper and fuller view of atonement than the rather crude mixture of emergency rescue operation and financial/legal transaction which is still preached in many churches. We are taken beyond the specific event of the Fall to what is in technical theological terms a prelapsarian view of God's costly crusade against the forces of evil and alienation, chaos and disorder (i.e. it starts before the Fall and not afterwards as a reaction to it). This is not to lose the intimate connection between sacrifice and the expiation of sin which is pointed to again and again in the New Testament and to which I shall return in Chapter 9. Nor is it to detract in any way from the view that there are deep flaws and imperfections both in creation and in our relations with God which need to be put right. It is, however, to assert that the work of reconciliation and redemption is fundamental to God's eternal character and is not the result of something that has gone wrong. The very last book of the Bible presents us with the supreme image of eternal sacrifice, the Lamb slain from the foundation of the world (Revelation 13:8). Yes, there is tragedy here, and suffering and death and mystery a plenty; but it is tragedy that is not futile, suffering that can redeem as well as destroy, death that issues into eternal life.

What does this mean for us? If Jesus Christ is not just the one who supremely reveals the nature of God but also our beginning and our end, the inclusive and representative man in whom we participate and will be united as he gathers all things together at the last, then the principles of self-giving and limitation and the motif of life through death which he embodies must be at the heart of our human existence. Sacrifice is indeed the way, the truth and the life. It is not some unfortunate burden that we have to shoulder because of our sin but rather the basis of our lives as creatures made by God, redeemed by Christ and living under his Cross. There is a clearly exemplary element in Christ's sacrifice: his manner of living and dying presents a perfect model for us. Yet there is much more to it than this. The sacrifice of Christ is not just a morally edifying tale but nor is it simply the final and completely efficacious sin offering. It is the decisive expression of the underlying principle which animates the whole of God's work of creation, redemption and perfection through which he draws all to himself and makes all holy. It involves us by evoking the response and inviting the participation without which its power is not realized and fulfilled. When Jesus says, 'I, if I be lifted up, will draw all men unto me' (John 12:32), he is pointing to the mysterious unifying power of the Cross. It is a power which is essentially creative and enabling, luring us to live in the sacrificial way that he has taught us and shown us through his life and death.

This theme has been taken up by many twentieth-century theologians as they have struggled to express the kernel of New Testament teaching in contemporary terms. For Paul

Tillich, free participation rather than substitution marks the character of the divine suffering revealed on the Cross.[49] Rudolph Bultmann argued that believing in the Cross does not mean looking at some mythical process that has taken place outside our world or at an event that is objectively visible and that God has somehow reckoned to our credit. Rather, it means accepting the Cross as our own and allowing ourselves to be crucified with Christ.[50] For Robert Daly the concept of the Christian life, both in its individual and its corporate aspects, as the new temple produces a specifically New Testament concept of sacrifice which is neither cultic nor liturgical but practical and ethical. It establishes that 'Christian life is not primarily a ritual celebration, nor merely an intellectual adherence to a body of truths; it is primarily a participation in Christ by means of personal commitment to an active life of service and self-giving love'.[51]

So the New Testament preserves all the power, the reciprocity and the mystery which is implicit in the primitive notion of sacrifice as the meeting place of earth and heaven and the means through which humans commune with and participate in the divine life. What it does, however, is to alter the focus of sacrifice from the cult to the Cross. Like the smoke from burnt offerings, but with infinitely greater efficacy, 'the pure celestial fire' of Jesus' sacrifice reaches down to earth and up to heaven. In it is both the concentrated self-giving of God through the birth, life, death and resurrection of his incarnate Son and the concentrated offering of human life to the Father.

5

Martyrs and mystics: images of sacrifice from Irenaeus to St John of the Cross

Given its prominence in scripture, it is not surprising that sacrifice should have been a major theme in Christian theology and spirituality down the centuries. The next three chapters will explore some of the ways in which it has been treated from the early days of the Church up to the present day.

At first sight, the early Church might seem the last place to find sacrificial imagery and language. In a world steeped in the practice of blood offerings, what distinguished the early Christians most clearly from their contemporaries was their lack of sacrificial rituals. Unlike the Jews and adherents to Hellenistic pagan cults and mystery religions of the East, those who followed Jesus did not offer sacrifices to the gods. This was a major factor in their unpopularity: Christians were looked on as atheists because of their refusal to acknowledge or make offerings to the pagan deities. There was a widespread view that this snub to those on whose favour human prosperity and good fortune were seen as depending would result in natural disasters, crop failures and defeat in battle. The refusal of those in the new 'Jesus movement' to offer animal sacrifices also threatened the livelihood of many farmers who made their money by providing beasts for ritual slaughter. As Christianity spread through the Mediterranean world those supplying livestock and fodder complained that they were being put out of business because of the downturn in sacrificial activity.

As far as the Roman authorities were concerned, Christians were suspect and regarded as potentially subversive because of their refusal to perform sacrifices to the emperor. When

Pliny was sent as governor to the Black Sea province of Bithynia around AD 112 he decided to test the loyalty of the Christians he encountered there by insisting that they make an offering of incense and wine to a portable statue of the emperor which he carried round for the purpose. Those who refused were punished. In the savage persecutions initiated by the Emperor Decius in the middle of the third century, those suspected of being Christians were required to make sacrifices to the pagan gods and partake of the flesh of the victim. A signed confession of participation in such sacrifices, confirmed by two witnesses, was required. Those who refused were first tortured and then put to death.

In this atmosphere it is hardly surprising that early Christians were often hostile to the whole concept of sacrifice and saw it as essentially pagan. Early apologists such as Justin Martyr denounced Jewish as well as pagan cultic offerings. Cyprian, Bishop of Carthage during the savage Decian persecutions, preached a series of chilling sermons about what happened to those Christians who let sacrificial food pass their lips. One who came to Communion found that the Eucharist turned to ashes in his hands. A baby who had been fed on bread soaked in wine from a pagan libation howled in church during Communion and refused to touch a drop of wine from the chalice. The bishop taught his flock that demons sat on the pieces of meat which were offered on pagan altars and swarmed in the accompanying smoke and incense.[1]

There is a noticeable absence of sacrificial language in early eucharistic liturgies. The word 'altar' was very rarely used to describe the table on which Lord's supper was celebrated. The general feeling was rather, to quote Irenaeus, Bishop of Lyons at the end of the second century, that 'the altar is in heaven (for towards that place are our prayers and oblations directed); the temple likewise is there'.[2] Similarly, there seems to have been little or no sense in the early church of a sacerdotal priesthood and it is not until well on in the third century that such terms as *sacerdos* and *heirus* are used of Christian ministers. Although, as might be expected, it is a matter of some debate among scholars, there is general agreement that the Eucharist was not initially associated with the offering of a sacrifice but rather with a commemorative and communal breaking of bread.

Yet for all their hostility to pagan sacrifice and their unease about importing its principles and symbols into Christian worship, the early fathers of the Church wrote extensively and approvingly on the theme of sacrifice both as a category for understanding the life and death of Christ and as a principle for Christian discipleship. Frances Young, who along with Robert Daly has been instrumental in uncovering and analysing the vast literature on this subject in the early Christian centuries, is in no doubt about 'the central importance of sacrificial imagery in the early Church's thinking'.[3]

The range of sacrificial imagery found in the writings of the early fathers, and the theology which it suggests, is much more limited than in the New Testament. They were constrained both by their desire to distance themselves from Jewish ideas and practices and by the limitations imposed by the principles of Greek philosophy in which they had been schooled. In particular, they were strongly influenced by the notion of divine impassibility and the Aristotelian concept of God as the unmoved mover. This made it quite impossible to entertain any idea of God suffering or sacrificing himself in the process of creation and redemption. Indeed, divine passibility came to be seen as a heretical doctrine and was specifically condemned in the Council of Chalcedon in AD 451.

This stress on the impassibility of God did at least have the virtue of allowing no room for the idea of propitiatory sacrifice. 'The Divine nature is not wanting in anything', wrote Clement of Alexandria at the beginning of the second century, 'being itself full and affording all things to every creature which is in need. So the Divine nature cannot be propitiated by sacrifices or offerings, nor is it allured by them.'[4] Yet although they were adamant that God was not to be moved by bloody or burnt offerings, the early fathers followed the Hebrew prophets in arguing that he was pleased to accept the sacrifice of a pure heart and dedicated life. Their thinking on this subject was much influenced by the writings of the Hellenistic Jew, Philo (20 BC to AD 50) who had argued that 'God does not delight in the fleshiness or fatness of animals, but in the blameless intention of the votary'.[5] Greek and Jewish influences combined to produce the notion of a 'reasonable' sacrifice, which was bloodless and involved the spiritual offerings of prayer and praise, a humble and contrite heart and virtuous behaviour – 'for sacrifice is not flesh but the pure and unstained life of a holy person'.[6] Philo was also instrumental in developing a particular allegorical under-standing of sacrifice which came to be taken up by the Alex-andrian school. He interpreted the progress of the human soul towards God in terms of a passing over from the material to the spiritual and from passions to virtues. In this journey the notion of Passover came to have special significance as expressing the sacrificial progression from intemperance and dissoluteness to patience and moderation, from fear and cow-ardice to courage and wisdom and from selfishness to charity. Once again, the twin influences of Judaism and Hellenism are very clear.

If God was, in fact, totally impassible and impervious to sacrifice, then some reason had to be advanced as to why it was important and worthwhile to make spiritual offerings to him. Building once again on the work of Philo, the early fathers developed the notion of a reciprocal gift relationship in which we return to God what he first gave to us. This understanding of sacrifice as a process initiated by God to enable humans to draw near to him and to instil the habit of giving is particularly developed in the writings of Irenaeus of Lyons:

> Now we make offering to Him, not as though He stood in need of it, but rendering thanks for His gift, and thus sanctifying what has been created. For even as God does not need our possessions, so do we need to offer something to God. . . . For God . . . takes our good works to Himself

for this purpose, that He may grant us a recompense of His own good things.[7]

Irenaeus' writings on the theme of sacrifice have a clearly Christocentric focus. He presents the sacrifice of Christ as the purpose of the incarnation: the Word became flesh in order to be able to offer Himself bodily for us. This is typical patristic Christology. Both Robert Daly and Frances Young see the early church fathers as understanding the life and death of Christ primarily in terms of sacrifice. Exactly what kind of sacrifice they had in mind, it is more difficult to say: no single image predominates and their writings display a mixture of Old and New Testament categories, including the suffering servant, the Passover lamb, the atoning sin offering and the blood which washes away sin.

The most detailed treatment of the theme of sacrifice in the patristic period comes from the pen of Origen (AD 185–254). Wanting very clearly to portray God as the author of sacrifice and not its object, he is unique in the early patristic period in his willingness to entertain the notion of divine suffering. Commenting on the text, 'He who did not spare his own Son but gave him up for us all' (Romans 8:32), he describes God as enduring 'a suffering of love' and develops a kenotic theology of the mutual humiliation and passion of Father and Son which in many ways anticipates twentieth-century attempts to express the doctrine of patripassianism within a Trinitarian framework.[8] The only other patristic suggestion of God's suffering love of which I am aware comes roughly 200 years later in Athanasius' *De Incarnatione*. It portrays God as making the sacrifice of Christ out of the depths of his love for creation and in order to reconcile tensions within himself between mercy and holiness, love and righteousness.

Origen's determination to avoid any hint of propitiation leads him to see Christ's sacrifice as an aversion offering by God to buy off the devil and liberate humanity from his clutches: 'The slain lamb of God is made, according to certain mysterious principles, a purification for the whole world ... according to the Father's love to man, he submitted to death purchasing us back by his own blood from the devil who had got us in his power'.[9] Locating Christ's death within the context of a cosmic battle between good and evil and seeing it as the ransom with which God paid off the devil was to become a popular way of viewing the atonement during the Middle Ages. In establishing this notion of an aversion offering, Origen is very careful to avoid any sense of substitutionary or vicarious atonement. Rather he sees Christ's sacrifice as representative and inclusive, involving the offering of all humanity in and through his perfect obedience. As for Paul, the participatory nature of that sacrifice is all-important: by a total identification with Christ, dying with him and rising with him, humans are restored to a perfect relationship with God. To that extent there is an atoning element to Christ's sacrifice but there is much more to it than that – it is a sacrifice of worship and obedience which both calls and binds all people into making their own self-offerings.

There is for Origen an intimate relationship between the sacrifice of Christ and the sacrificial worship and service of the Church, the new temple of which all Christians are living stones. There is also a great sense of the Christian life as a sharing in Christ's sacrifice and self-offering. The altar on which each of us is called to make our daily offering is the altar of the heart. Here we must sacrifice without ceasing through prayer, pure living and rigorous self-discipline. This is not an easy or comfortable business. Origen talks of the need to offer up our proud flesh as the sacrificial calf and quotes approvingly from Psalm 44: 'For thy sake we are slain all the day long, and accounted as sheep for the slaughter'. He suggests at one point that the Lamb of God takes away the sins only of those who suffer. In offering himself the Christian must be prepared to give up everything and be crucified with Christ. 'He keeps the sacrifice burning on the altar by renouncing his possessions, taking up his Cross and following Christ; by giving his body to be burned, and following the glory of the martyr.'[10]

We have moved a long way here from the Greek ideal of the good life as one of virtue, temperance and stoicism. For

Origen, as for many in the early church, the accent is on renunciation, suffering and self-denial. Sacrifice is seen as the distinguishing feature of the Christian life. Perfection lies in the total surrender and self-immolation of martyrdom, the life that blooms by shedding itself and which pours out its precious blood in imitation of Christ. It is not surprising in this climate, and in the context of persecution, that the cult of martyrdom developed so strongly in the early Christian centuries. The Greek word μαρτυρος (marturos) means a witness and originally had no sacrificial connotations. It came to acquire them when it was applied to those Christians whose witness to their faith took them to death in the jaws and claws of the wild beasts to whom they were thrown by the Romans. In so dying they were seen as imitating Christ and participating in his passion. Their deaths were also regarded by some as having a sacrificial efficacy. This concept had already been established within Judaism when the blood of those who had died during the period of Syrian oppression in the second century BC recorded in the Books of Maccabees was seen as having an expiatory effect and wiping out sin. To some extent the early church took over this view although it was very much subordinate to the notion that martyrdom involved an imitation of Christ.

The first Christian that we know of to court martyrdom as a way of coming close to Christ was Ignatius, Bishop of Antioch, who went to Rome to face death around AD 107–10. Seeing his approaching death as 'a sacrifice to God', he cited Colossians 1:24 in support of his view that Christians who died at the hands of persecutors were participating in and completing the atoning work of Jesus. He wrote to the Roman church authorities to beseech them not to do anything that would save him from being thrown to the beasts: 'Let there come on me fire and cross and conflicts with wild beasts, wrenching of bones, mangling of limbs, crushing of the whole body, grievous torments of the devil may I but attain to Jesus Christ'.[11] To our modern ears this kind of language sounds almost perversely masochistic but then we do not share the early Christians' overwhelming desire to participate in the sufferings of Christ and their sense that martyrdom was the supreme human self-offering. This comes out very clearly in the detailed and harrowing account of the martyrdom of Polycarp, Bishop of Smyrna, around AD 156. The events leading up to his death are portrayed as being very similar to those that preceded the crucifixion and, indeed, as having come to pass 'in order that to us the Lord might once again give an example of the martyrdom which resembles the Gospel story'.[12] Polycarp is clearly presented as offering himself as a sacrifice. Taken to the stake to be burned, 'he put his hands behind him and was bound, like a goodly ram out of a great flock for an offering, a whole burnt offering made ready and acceptable to God'.[13] The prayer that he makes just before the fire is lit includes a blessing to God 'that thou hast deemed me worthy of this day and hour; that I might take a portion among the martyrs in the cup of Christ . . . among these may I today be welcome before thy face as a rich and acceptable sacrifice'.[14]

As the cult of martyrdom developed, those who died for the faith were credited with possessing supernatural powers. Polycarp and his companions were credited with reaching 'such a pitch of noble endurance that not one of them let cry or groan escape him, showing to us all that in the hours of their torture Christ's martyrs were absent from the flesh, or rather that standing by their side their Lord conversed with them'.[15] The idea also grew that martyrdom provided a swift and sure route to heaven and that the prayers of martyrs could be especially efficacious for those left below on earth. The intercessions of St Perpetua, executed in Carthage in or around 203, were believed to reach the unbaptized dead. More specifically they apparently cured her brother from a cancerous growth. So was born the practice of praying through the martyrs and regarding them as a group of spiritual super-heroes with special powers and gifts of healing and intercession.

There is no doubt that martyrdom was a significant factor in the growth of the early church. Evidence tends to support the famous dictum of the early third-century African apologist Tertullian that 'the blood of the martyrs is the seed of the church'. Certainly, many people seem to have been converted to Christianity as a result of either witnessing or hearing about someone dying for the faith. This is by no means just an ancient phenomenon, of course. The meteoric rise of the Church in Uganda in the late nineteenth century seems to have followed directly from the martyrdom of thirty young courtiers who were burned in a single pyre by the Kabaka (king) after they had been found reading the scriptures. Within ten years there were 7, 000 baptized members and 50, 000 enquirers in a church established and inspired by martyrdom.

In the contemporary Western Church we are uneasy about martyrdom. Of course in a climate of tolerance and indifference towards religious beliefs and practices there is little if any opportunity for people to die for the faith. Does our distaste for what we perceive to be the fanaticism and masochism of martyrdom not also betray a certain lack of courage in our convictions and an unwillingness to make sacrifices for the sake of our faith? In churches in the so-called developing world, by contrast, martyrdom still has an enormous power and impact. The murder of Archbishop Janani Luwum in 1977 led to a significant revival of the Church in Uganda. The assassination of Archbishop Oscar Romero before his altar in El Salvador in 1980 had a similarly dramatic effect on Christians in Central and Latin America. Twentieth-century Europe has not been without its Christian martyrs but they have somehow had less effect in renewing the churches. Commissioners to the 1994 General Assembly of the Church of Scotland stood and observed a minute's silence in memory of Jane Haining, matron of a girls' home in Budapest who refused to leave her Jewish charges when Hungary was invaded by the Nazis and eventually died with them in June 1944 in the gas chamber at Auschwitz. We then sat down again and got on with the business of discussing the Church's falling roll and revenue.

Maybe, as in so many other areas, the churches in Europe and North America need to listen to Christians in the rest of the world and to take martyrdom more seriously as a pointer to the disturbing power of sacrifice and the uncomfortable truth that life comes out of death. John Witheridge, a former chaplain to the Archbishop of Canterbury, has commented on the renewal to which it so often seems to give birth: 'From the ashes of a saint's suffering has arisen again and again the fair phoenix of a faith rekindled and revived'.[16] We could perhaps do with pondering the words that T. S. Eliot put into the mouth of England's best-known martyr, St Thomas à Becket, pointing out that it is no accident that the Church celebrates its first martyr, Stephen, the day after celebrating the birth of Christ:

'A martyrdom is always the design of God, for His love of men, to warn them and to lead them, to bring them back to His ways. It is never the design of man; for the true martyr is he who has become the instrument of God, who has lost his will in the will of God, and who no longer desires anything for himself, not even the glory of being a martyr.[17]

Such thoughts do not accord with our modern anti-sacrificial mentality and our preference for an easier and more comfortable faith. Yet martyrdom is not simply about surrender and self-immolation. 'It is the most literal imitation of Christ. It is to accompany Christ to his journey's end. But to share in that death is to share too in the mystery of his resurrection. The extraordinary and miraculous fruits of martyrdom are vital signs of the power and wonder of Easter.'[18]

Few Christians have understood better this intimate connection between martyrdom and resurrection than the Irish monks who kept the Gospel light shining across Europe through the so-called Dark Ages from around AD 500 to 1000. Living in a broadly tolerant atmosphere where there was little call to die for the faith, they developed two other categories of martyrdom through which Christians would imitate Christ and sacrificially offer themselves to God. While red martyrdom involved physically laying down one's life for the faith, white martyrdom meant dying to self and to all attachments, leaving home and family and going into perpetual exile. Green martyrdom meant following a regime of fasting, hard labour and physically demanding prayer and vigils. Sometimes white martyrdom could be imposed as a kind of penance as may have been the case in St Columba's departure from his beloved Ireland for Iona. Others became perpetual pilgrims voluntarily, seeking their own desert or place of resurrection where they could die to themselves and rise again in Christ.

This is why the holy men of Celtic Christianity sought out the most barren and inhospitable islands and rocks for their hermit caves and monasteries. They were deliberately imitating God's *kenosis* in Christ, emptying themselves of comforts and security and making themselves exposed and vulnerable. Exactly the same sacrificial principle lay behind the flight of many Egyptian and Syrian monks from the cities to the desert in the fourth and fifth centuries. They also were white martyrs seeking resurrection through dying to self. Their withdrawal from the pleasures and distractions of the world to lead lives of severe austerity and asceticism laid the foundations for the monastic movement which swept across both Eastern and Western Christendom. Thomas Merton, that great twentieth-century exemplar of monasticism, has written eloquently about the principle of sacrifice which directed the life of the desert father:

> He could not retain the slightest identification with his superficial, transient, self-constructed self. He had to lose himself in the inner, hidden reality of self that was transcendent, mysterious, half-known and lost in Christ. He had to die to the values of transient existence as Christ had died to them on the Cross, and rise from the dead with Him in the light of an entirely new wisdom. Hence the life of sacrifice, which started out from a clean break, separating the monk from the world. A life continued in 'compunction' which taught him to lament the madness of attachment to unreal values. A life of solitude and labour,

poverty and fasting, charity and prayer, which enabled the old superficial self to be purged away and permitted the gradual emergence of the true, secret self in which the believer and Christ were 'one Spirit'.[19]

This intimate if paradoxical connection between self-sacrifice and self-fulfilment, death and resurrection, is the key to understanding the spirituality of the Irish monks who were so close in outlook to and so influenced by the desert fathers. Those who see Celtic Christianity as an easy, self-oriented faith akin to the contemporary New Age movement could hardly be more wide of the mark. The Celts had a profound sense of the tragic element in creation and in the life of God. They were acutely conscious of the mystery of suffering and the grounding of life in death. They could hardly be otherwise when they lived so close to nature. Not that they were morbid, for they saw both death and resurrection as natural processes. The great ninth-century Irish philosopher theologian John Scotus Eurigena likened them to the setting and rising of the sun and the burial of a seed in the ground before it can bring forth a plant. Their theology is symbolized in the distinctive image of the Celtic Cross where the circle of creation is transfigured and bisected by the Cross of sacrifice and redemption. They saw God as the supreme sacrificer whose most overwhelming characteristic is his continuous costly offering of himself to his creatures. In the considered words of Saunders Davies, a Welsh-speaking priest who has deeply studied the subject, 'this self-giving of God to mankind, evoking our self-giving to God is the essence of Celtic spirituality. It affirms that new life can only come out of sacrifice and suffering'.[20]

The fasting and mortification, endless genuflections and self-flagellation, gloomy penitentials and stern disciplines that such an outlook inspired in the monasteries of Ireland and their offshoots on mainland Britain may seem unattractively and even dangerously masochistic to us today. We have lost that sense which our ancestors had, derived originally from Paul and more directly from Origen and the early Greek fathers of the Church, of life as a sacrifice to be offered to God. If that meant self-denial and limitation, then it also involved the joyful sacrifice of praise. We have lost, too, that sense of sacrifice as the way to blessedness which was the central concern of the greatest of the later Latin fathers, St Augustine of Hippo, and which underlies the famous definition which appears in his book, *De Civitate Dei* (c. 410):

A true sacrifice is every work which is done that we may be united to God in holy fellowship, and which has a reference to that supreme good and end in which alone we can be truly blessed. And therefore even the mercy we show to men, if it is not shown for God's sake, is not a sacrifice. For though made or offered by man, sacrifice is a divine thing, as those who called it sacrifice (literally sacred action) meant to indicate. Thus man himself, consecrated in the name of God, and vowed to God, is a sacrifice in so far as he dies to the world that he may live in God.[21]

Augustine's definition clearly establishes sacrifice as having its origin in God rather than with human beings. It also offers a suggestion as to its purpose. Sacrifice provides the way by which we lose ourselves in union with God and so fulfil our ultimate destiny. There are echoes here of Irenaeus' argument that while God does not need sacrifices, he gives them to us because we need them for our fulfilment and contentment. It is through acts of self-giving, mercy and compassion that we can be freed from the tyranny of self and the curse of being curled in on ourselves. Sacrifice thus becomes the basis for human happiness and fulfilment. We are also presented with a clear link between the two meanings of the word 'sacrifice' – it is by giving ourselves up for God's sake that we are made holy.

The key phrase here is 'for God's sake'. Augustine is very clear that what constitutes sacrifice, as opposed to mere benevolence, is the dedication of what we do to God. Given this dedication, any action, however mundane, can be sacrificial. It is not the doing of it but the doing of it for God. This is the principle expounded so beautifully in George Herbert's poem 'The Elixir', quoted on page 24 and in John Keble's hymn, 'New every morning is the love':

> If on our daily course our mind
> Be set to hallow all we find,
> New treasures still, of countless price,
> God will provide for sacrifice.

> The trivial round, the common task,
> Would furnish all we ought to ask,
> Room to deny ourselves, a road
> To bring us daily nearer God.

For Augustine, as for Paul and the earlier fathers, all sacrifice is related to the supreme sacrifice of the Cross and is in some sense a participation in it. 'The sacrifice of Christ is the basis or fundament of the Church, which is his body'.[22] This corporeal aspect is very important to Augustine. Commenting on Romans 12:3–6, he reflects: 'This is the sacrifice of Christians: we, being many, are one body in Christ'. As the great high priest, Jesus offers not just himself but all of us to God 'so that we might be the body of so great a head'.[23] This is not a matter of substitution but of mystical participation, both visibly through the Eucharist and invisibly through the sacrifice of the broken heart and the charitable act. Stephen Sykes has identified the key themes in Augustine's theology of sacrifice as communication and gift. There is no room here for the idea of propitiation. Rather sacrifice is seen as a reciprocal process in which God comes to us and we come to him in response with Christ as the mediator and bearer of the two-way gift.

Sadly, the post-Augustinian Western Church lost the biblical and patristic view of sacrifice as something that originates from God and saw it as something done by humans to God. The elements of reciprocity and participation were lost and the idea of propitiation became dominant. The Eucharist became increasingly detached from the invisible sacrifice of a broken heart to stand on its own as a cultic ritual with its own inherent and self-sufficient efficacy, resting on the mechanical actions performed by the priest rather than the inner disposition or outward behaviour of the worshippers.

This institutionalization of sacrifice represented the triumph of pagan influences within the early medieval Church. As persecution gave way to imperial favour and patronage in the aftermath of Constantine's conversion, the Western Church began to ape secular power structures. Ministry gave way to sacerdotalism as clergy assumed the garb of pagan priests, communion tables were replaced by high altars and bishops took to wearing the imperial purple. The hard path of sacrifice practised and preached by Christ and the early fathers and involving a self-offering of mind, body and spirit, was abandoned in favour of a broader and easier way which marked a return to the heresies of vicarious substitution and propitiation and culminated in priests being paid to celebrate private masses. As it became more and more institutionalized, sacrifice was diminished in power and scope and confined to the place from which Christ had liberated it, the temple, understood in its narrow cultic sense and not in the broader terms of the individual or corporate body of Christ.

With this shift of emphasis from the internal to the external, sacrifice came increasingly to be seen as a remote legal or financial transaction in which there was little human involvement. Cold and calculating concepts from the lawcourt and the counting house such as debt and ransom came to predominate over biblical images of the suffering servant and the Lamb slain from the foundation of the world. Anselm (1033–1109) developed his influential theory of penal satisfaction which cast God in the role of a feudal overlord demanding honour from his vassals. Sacrifice was narrowly related to the removal of sin and its wider significance as the animating principle of creation was all but forgotten.

While these trends increasingly affected the Church in the Middle Ages, individual saints and mystics continued to preach and to practise a wider and more costly sacrificial gospel. St Bernard (1090–1153), abbot of the Cistercian monastery of Clairvaux, had a strong sense of the pain and travail involved in God's continual outpouring of his divine love on errant and suffering humanity. He saw the self-humiliation and self-giving of Jesus providing the pattern of life and behaviour into which Christians are drawn and called. In identifying with a life of sacrifice, they are redeemed from the limitations and defects of their humanity and become united with God in love and obedience.

St Bernard's near-contemporary, Peter Abelard (1079–1142), is generally credited with developing a subjective view of atonement in contrast to the rigidly objective theory of penal satisfaction associated with Anselm. 'Subjective' is, in fact, something of a misnomer for a position which in no sense denied the objective reality or efficacy of the Cross. What was distinctive was Abelard's insistence that its power lay in the ability to evoke a response. His view is often summed up in the dictum 'love begets love' but perhaps 'sacrifice begets sacrifice' better encapsulates it. The love which Abelard sees being displayed on the Cross, and transferred to us not so much through example as through a kind of transfiguring power, is not just general beneficence but rather costly surrender and self-limitation. This is the kind of love which enters our very hearts and souls when we follow Christ. The Cross exemplifies and expresses the creative enabling power of sacrifice.

> Alone thou goest forth, O Lord,
>   In sacrifice to die;
> Is this thy sorrow naught to us
>   Who pass unheeding by?
>
> Our sins, not thine, thou bearest, Lord;
>   Make us thy sorrow feel,
> Till through our pity and our shame
>   Love answers love's appeal.
>
> Grant us to suffer with thee, Lord,
>   That, as we share this hour,
> Thy cross may bring us to thy joy
>   And resurrection power.[24]

Another poem written three centuries later combines the primal theme of the sacrificial fire, Paul's image of the human body as the new temple and the kenotic language of Philippians 2:8. In *Discendi, Amor santo* ('Come down, O love divine') Bianco da Siena (*c.* 1350–1434), an Italian mystic, speaks of his earthly passions being turned to dust and ashes in the consuming heat of the divine love and of lowliness becoming his 'inner clothing'. Dating from the same period is a German monk's clarion call to Christians to take up the Cross of Christ and follow the way of suffering and sacrifice. *The Imitation of Christ* by St Thomas à Kempis (1380–1471) marks a significant break from the traditional teaching of mystics that the way towards union with God is through ever higher levels of ecstasy and contemplation. He sees it rather as involving the acceptance of suffering and 'conforming ourselves with the Crucified'. Thomas à Kempis was not preaching the glorification of suffering but he was adamant that it must be accepted not just as the inevitable condition of sinful humanity but as the way of the Cross and the only true path to friendship with Christ and union with God.

Perhaps the most original and comprehensive treatment of the theme of sacrifice in the Middle Ages comes from the pen of Dame Julian of Norwich, the anchoress whose *Revelations of Divine Love* have rightly become a key text in the revival of spirituality in the late twentieth century. Her approach is allusive rather than systematic but embraces a wide variety of sacrificial images, some of them highly original. In an interesting variation on the kenotic theme, she suggests that when Adam fell into sin and hell, God's Son fell into the deep of the Maiden's womb. She also makes much of Christ's descent into hell to rescue the spirits of the lost which she interprets as a sign of the universality of his mission which will not be over until the last soul has been rescued from damnation.

Dame Julian is one of very few spiritual writers to make use of the imagery of the pains of childbirth. She applies it not to God's act of creation but to the redemption secured through the death of Christ. Instead of comparing Jesus' sacrifice to that made by Abraham and locating it in a patriarchal context, she chooses the matriarchal image of the woman in travail:

> We know that all our mothers' bearing is [bearing of] us to pain and to dying: and what is this but that our Very Mother, Jesus, He – All-Love – beareth us to joy and to endless living? – blessed may He be! Thus he sustaineth us within Himself in love; and travailed, unto the full time that He would suffer the sharpest throes and the most grievous pains that ever were or ever shall be; and died at the last.
>
> The mother may give her child suck of her milk, but our precious Mother, Jesus, He may feed us with Himself, and doeth it, full courteously and full tenderly, with the Blessed Sacrament that is precious food of my life. . . . The mother may lay the child tenderly to her breast, but our tender Mother, Jesus, He may homely lead us into His blessed breast, by His sweet open side, and shew therein part of the Godhead and the joys of Heaven, with spiritual sureness of endless bliss.[25]

Another key theme for Julian is the oneness between our suffering and the suffering of Christ. She is clearly struck by St Matthew's picture of the darkness and earthquakes that accompany the crucifixion and interprets them as a response by the whole of creation to the event of the Cross rather in the manner described in the nursery rhyme 'All the birds of the air fell a sighing and a sobbing when they heard of the death of poor Cock Robin':

> I saw a great oneing betwixt Christ and us, to mine understanding; for when He was in pain, we were in pain. And all creatures that might suffer pain, suffered with Him: that is to say, all creatures that God hath made to our service. The firmament, the earth, failed for sorrow in their Nature in the time of Christ's dying. For it belongeth naturally to their property to know him for their God, in whom all their virtue standeth: when He failed, then behoved it needs to

them, because of kindness (between them) to fail with Him, as much as they might, for sorrow of His pains.[26]

Perhaps the most important and radical feature of the *Revelations of Divine Love* is its clear suggestion of an eternal dimension to the sacrifice of Christ:

> And when He had finished, and so borne us to bliss, yet might not all this make full content to His marvellous love; and that sheweth He in these high overpassing words of love: *If I might suffer more, I would suffer more*. He might no more die, but He would not stint of working. . . .
>
> And in these words: *If that I might suffer more, I would suffer more* I saw in truth that as often as He *might* die, so often He *would*, and love should never let Him have rest till He had done it. . . . For though the sweet manhood of Christ might suffer but once, the goodness in Him may never cease to proffer: every day he is ready to the same, if it might be.
>
> The same desire and thirst that He had upon the Cross (which desire, longing and thirst, as to my sight, was in Him without beginning) the same hath He yet, and shall [have] unto the time that the last soul that shall be saved is come up to His bliss.[27]

It is something of an anti-climax to turn from this marvellous mystical invocation of the eternal sacrifice of suffering love to the sterile debates between Catholics and reformers in the late fifteenth and early sixteenth centuries on the nature of the Eucharist and the doctrine of atonement. God's authorship of sacrifice and its essential participatory nature were lost sight of as the focus came to be on penal substitution on one side and mechanical performance of the Mass on the other. As the notion of propitiation reared its ugly head again on both sides, the protagonists in this period of acrimonious and debilitating dispute were much closer to one another, and much further away from the teachings of the Bible and the early fathers, than they would have cared to admit.

Yet from the unpromising soil of Puritan polemic and Roman reaction sprang another group of Christian preachers and writers with a wider and deeper grasp of the power and mystery of sacrifice. Those on the Protestant side stressed the importance of the spiritual sacrifices of prayer and worship in language similar to that used by the Hebrew prophets. William Gouge (1578–1653) a London Presbyterian minister, argued that 'prayer, singing of psalms, reading, preaching, hearing the Word and celebrating the Sacraments' are 'as the sacrifices of bullocks and calves, goats and kids, sheep and lambs, turtles, pigeons and sparrows; and all manner of meat and drink offerings'.[28] John Owen (1616–83), a Congregational divine, held 'every act and duty of faith' to have the nature of a sacrifice pleasing to God, while Thomas Hooker (1586–1647), a minister in New England, preached that Christians should follow Christ and 'offer ourselves . . . as a living sacrifice and acceptable'.[29] For Samuel Ward (1577–1640) of Ipswich:

> The whole duty of all men is to give themselves wholly to Christ, to sacrifice not a leg or an arm or any other piece but soul, spirit and body and all that is within us: the fat, the inwards, the head and the hoof, and all as a holocaust to him, dedicating, devoting ourselves to his service all the days and hours of our lives, that all our days may be Lord's Days.[30]

It is this Puritan stress on spiritual and ethical sacrifice that finds its way into the Book of Common Prayer, most obviously in the post-Communion prayer of thanksgiving: 'And here we offer and present unto thee, O Lord, ourselves, our souls and bodies, to be a reasonable, holy and lively sacrifice unto thee'. The alternative thanksgiving prayer expresses another favourite Puritan theme in its beautiful description of our participation in the sacrifice of Christ: 'we are very members incorporate in the mystical body of thy Son, which is the blessed company of all faithful people; and are heirs through hope of thy everlasting kingdom, by the merits of the most precious death and passion of thy dear Son'.

Two seventeenth-century English priest-poets were particularly gripped by the power of sacrifice. In 'The Cross' John Donne (1572–1631) echoes Peter Abelard's hymn quoted above:

> Since Christ embraced the Cross itself, dare I
> His image, the image of his Cross deny?
> Would I have profit by the sacrifice,
> And dare the chosen Altar to despise?[31]

These initial musings on the inescapability of the Cross lead to a remarkable evocation of its significance throughout creation:

> Who can deny me power, and liberty
> To stretch mine arms, and mine own Cross to be?
> Swim, and at every stroke, thou art thy Cross;
> The mast and yard make one, where seas do toss;
> Look down, thou spiest out Crosses in small things;
> Look up, thou seest birds raised on crossed wings;
> All the globes frame, and spheres, is nothing else
> But the meridians crossing parallels.[32]

Everything, then, is under the transfiguring power of the Cross. In another poem, 'Good Friday, 1613. Riding westward', written at a time when he was wrestling with the question of ordination, Donne has further recourse to cosmological imagery when he contrasts the journey westwards, following the setting sun, to death with the journey eastwards, following the rising sun, to life. It is, in fact, the journey westwards that leads to eternal life, revealing the paradoxical power of sacrifice to bring life out of death. Three hundred years before the radical theologies of John Robinson and Thomas Altizer this poem dares to speak of the death of God:

> Hence it is, that I am carried towards the West
> This day, when my Soul's form bends towards the East.
> There I should see a Sun, by rising set,

And by that setting endless day beget;
But that Christ on this Cross, did rise and fall,
Sin had eternally benighted all.
Yet dare I almost be glad, I do not see
That spectacle of too much weight for me.
Who sees God's face, that is self life*, must die;
What a death were it then to see God die?[33]

Donne's near-contemporary, George Herbert (1593–1633),
wrote a major poem, 'The Sacrifice', which describes in agonizing slow motion the crucifixion from Jesus' point of view.
Every verse ends with the refrain 'Was ever grief like mine'.
Herbert does not offer any particular theory of atonement
and presents rather a story of almost unbearable tragedy in
which Christ's work is portrayed as a sacrifice of sorrow.

> Lo, here I hang, charged with a world of sin,
> The greater world of the two; for that came in
> By words, but this by sorrow I must win.[34]

For all his image as the gentle country parson, Herbert had a
profound sense of the tragedy at the heart of all life, not least
the divine life, and of the extent to which it is the brokenness
of God that sustains us. In 'The Sacrifice' he has Christ
reflecting 'Your safety in my sickness doth subsist'. In
another poem, 'The Banquet', he begins by writing lyrically
about the sweetness of God's presence that fills our souls with
'flowers, gums and powders' so that 'as sugar we melt into
wine'. Then the mood changes as we are reminded that only
by bruising and breaking is the full perfume released.

> But as Pomanders and wood
>   Still are good,
> Yet being bruis'd are better scented:
> God, to show how far his love

---

* i.e. life itself

> Could improve,
> Here, as broken, is presented.[35]

Continental Catholicism also had its mystic artists and poets who sensed the awesome power of sacrifice. Much religious art in the sixteenth and seventeenth centuries portrayed God as the man of sorrows. It also increasingly reflected the cult of the sacred heart of Jesus which developed from the writings of Pierre de Bérulle (1575–1629), founder of the reformed Carmelites in France. For Bérulle, the wounded heart of Jesus was the effective sign of the costly love of God: 'His heart is eternally open, eternally wounded; his glory does not take this wound away. It is a wound of love'.[36]

This notion of the wound of love also featured prominently in the thought of the Spanish mystic St John of the Cross (1542–91), joint founder with St Teresa of Avila of the Discalced Carmelites. He took up and intensified St Thomas à Kempis' call on Christians to implant the Cross in their hearts: 'Unless our life consists in the imitation of Christ crucified, it is worthless'.[37] His 'Dark night of the soul' describes the way to God as that of purgation, self-denial and abasement rather than contemplation and the spiritual 'highs' of ecstasy and religious experience. 'This journey does not consist in recreations, experiences and spiritual feelings, but in the living, sensory and spiritual, exterior and interior death of the Cross.'[38]

At times St John's writings may seem to come dangerously close to glorifying suffering and suggesting that the more we suffer, the more merit we gain in the sight of God. He writes to one of his penitents, 'He gives us sufferings according to the measure of our love so that we may give Him greater sacrifices and gather more merit'.[39] His teaching can also smack of self-hatred and masochism, as in his advice to another penitent: 'Treat your body with wise severity, through hatred of yourself and prudent self-denial, and seek never to follow your own will and taste. For this self-will was the cause of His suffering and death'.[40] Yet if there is a profound consciousness of divine tragedy in the writings of this tortured mystic, there is also a great sense of divine suffering. The message of the 'dark night of the soul' is that it is when our lives are at their darkest, when we feel empty, barren, naked and without consolation that we are, in fact, closest to the God who abandoned and exposed himself. St John of the Cross understood as few others have the depth and intensity of the sacrifice of suffering, not sought out but faced and accepted in the heart of the Godhead as much as throughout the groaning and travailing creation.

6

The grand law of the universe: sacrifice in Victorian and Edwardian thought

In jumping straight from the beginning of the seventeenth century to the middle of the nineteenth, I do not wish to imply that there was no one thinking or writing in the intervening period in a way that is relevant to the theme of this book. Quite apart from anything else, that would be to exclude the hymns of Isaac Watts and the Wesley brothers which receive attention in other parts of this study. On the whole, however, neither the narrow Calvinism nor the confident deism that dominated eighteenth-century Christianity provided a very fruitful soil for the development of a theology based on the notion of the eternal sacrifice of God. Much more conducive was the religious atmosphere of the nineteenth century, that complex and paradoxical age apparently so full of faith and yet also wracked by doubts, seemingly so imperialistic and yet so imbued with the ideas of *kenosis*, socialism and service. So much so, indeed, that it is in the writings of British authors in the Victorian and Edwardian age, and of their contemporaries in other countries, that we are presented with the fullest and deepest portrayal in Christian literature of the power of sacrifice, understood as a universal principle emanating from God and animating the whole of his creation.

There has been a tendency among scholars to see this nineteenth-century concentration on sacrifice as a product of guilty consciences among the privileged sons of an imperialistic age, a phenomenon emanating almost entirely from the world of the public school chapel and the established Church. Notions of *kenosis* and self-emptying, it is suggested, appealed to men who had plenty to give up. I find this

161

interpretation too dismissive and too driven by the general tendency to debunk the Victorians: it is not wholly consistent with the facts. While it is true that public-school-educated Anglican clerics were in the van of developing a radical kenotic theology, several Nonconformists from much less privileged backgrounds also showed a strong interest in the theme of self-sacrifice. The new sacrificial theology went hand in hand with social and political radicalism and was closely associated with the birth of Christian Socialism. Nor was it an exclusively British preoccupation. As we shall see, its exponents were to be found in the United States, Denmark and most notably in Russia where it came out of a marginalized and oppressed peasant culture which was the very antithesis of privilege and imperialism.

Three important themes coalesced in mid-nineteenth-century Christian thought to produce a new interest in and a new approach to the idea of sacrifice. The first was a reconsideration of the doctrine of divine impassibility. The modern notion of the suffering God has its origins in this period. Eighteenth-century images of the divine watchmaker and the omnipotent sovereign in the sky came to be tempered by a greater sensitivity and awareness of the costliness and difficulty of God's work in bringing order out of chaos. The atonement was viewed less as a remote, mechanical transaction and more as a process by which the personal travail of God found fulfilment in both nature and humanity.

Second, there was an equally important reconsideration of the idea of the sacrifice of Christ. Growing unease about the concept of propitiation on both moral and ethical grounds led to a recovery of the biblical notion of Christ as the offering of God to humans rather than vice versa. Allied to this was a resurgence of interest in the long-neglected doctrine of the *kenosis*, or self-emptying, of Christ and in the continuous and eternal aspect of his sacrifice.

Third, the scientific theory of evolution produced a new appreciation of the extent to which all life on earth depended on struggle, surrender and self-limitation. This sense of the cosmic application of the principle of sacrifice and the dependence at every level of new life on other life dying was reinforced by the widespread experience of human death in nineteenth-century family life. Like Africans today, our Victorian ancestors regularly experienced the death of their children. There are two reactions to such loss: it leads either to a cheapening of human life or to its enhancement and a sense that death has a purpose and a role in the wider scheme of creation and redemption. The Victorian children's hymns which we now find so morbid and maudlin are part and parcel of an attempt to come to terms with the ubiquity of death and to locate it within the context of a world governed by the universal law of sacrifice and the motif of 'through death to life'.

One of the first theologians to articulate some of these new stirrings was Horace Bushnell (1802–76), a Yale graduate who became Congregational minister in Hartford, Connecticut. His *God in Christ* (1850) was written out of a determination to be rid of propitiatory and substitutionary notions of atonement and to show that suffering does not appease God but rather 'that it expresses God – displays in open history the unconquerable love of God's heart'.[1] In a later work, *The Vicarious Sacrifice* (1866), he anticipates an extremely important theme in late nineteenth- and early twentieth-century theology (particularly Anglican theology) when he remarks that 'there is a cross in God before the wood is seen upon Calvary ... a cross unseen, standing on its own undiscovered hill, far back in the ages, out of which were sounding always, just the same deep voice of suffering love and patience that was heard by mortal ears from the sacred hill of Calvary'.[2] It follows from this understanding of God as the author of all sacrifice that ritual offerings which combine 'penitence, self-mortification, homage and the tender invocation of mercy' are natural and part of the divine economy of creation and redemption: 'Sacrifices are not the mere spontaneous contrivances of men, but the contrivances of men whose contrivings are impelled and guided and fashioned by God'.[3] Seeking to get away from the notion of sacrifice as a vehicle in some process of legal substitution,

Bushnell prefers to talk in terms of a transactional liturgy which embraces a pattern of outward action signifying inner penitence, purification and acceptance with God. Sacrifice is the means that God has provided by which his creatures, self-centred and sin-laden as they are, can come back to him.

A starker and more demanding theology of sacrifice came from the pen of Søren Kierkegaard (1813–55). Attacking the comfort and complacency of late eighteenth- and early nineteenth-century Protestantism, he suggested that the true witness to Christianity did not testify by preaching in a well-endowed and socially respected pulpit but by suffering for and because of the gospel. He called for a recovery of the principle and practice of martyrdom and freely chosen sacrifice. There is a terrible bleakness about this particularly gloomy Dane's stress on suffering as the only real way for the Christian and his conviction that the life of faith is made up of endurance, patience and resignation. Yet however unappealing they are, his words authentically echo the gospel call to deny self and take up our own crosses. Couched in a less depressing form, this call was to be repeated and responded to with increasing fervency as the nineteenth century progressed.

Before turning to the very important and considerable corpus of writing on the power of sacrifice in Victorian and Edwardian Britain which will form the substance of this chapter, it is worth making one further excursion abroad to consider the strong sacrificial emphasis in both the sacred and secular literature of nineteenth-century Russia. This theme has been brilliantly explored in Nadeja Gorodetzky's book, *The Humiliated Christ in Modern Russian Thought* to which I am deeply indebted for most of the observations and extracts that follow. He points to an intuitive appreciation of *kenosis* in the Russian character, a valuing of self-abasement, voluntary poverty, humility, obedience, self-limitation, non-resistance and the acceptance of suffering and death. Deeply embedded in traditional folklore and unconsciously accepted for generations, this kenotic element to the Russian people, especially the peasantry, was rediscovered and championed in the mid-nineteenth century by political radicals and Slavo-phils who contrasted it with Western values of self-sufficiency and dominance. Some, like Feodor Tyutchev, went so far as to identify the peasantry with the figure of the humiliated Christ and to portray Russia as the suffering servant of Isaiah 53.

The power of sacrificial suffering, self-limitation and humiliation was a major theme in nineteenth-century Russian novels and poems. The writings of Gogol and Turgenev are permeated by the ideal of self-sacrifice and a positive desire for suffering and humiliation. For Fyodor Dostoyevsky (1821–81) 'all the power of Russia lies in sacrificial disin-terestedness – all her personality, so to say, and her whole future destiny'.[4] His great novel *Crime and Punishment* (1865–6) centres on the redemptive power of sacrificial suffer-ing epitomized in the utter self-giving of the prostitute Sonya which finally erases the tortured guilt of the student Raskol-nikov over the terrible crime that he has committed. The same theme of redemption through suffering and self-abasement dominates the writings of Tolstoy, particularly after his religious conversion in 1878 when he was gripped with the sense that 'he alone is superior to others who humbles himself and is the servant of all'.[5]

Given the prominence of sacrificial themes among political radicals and novelists, it is not surprising to find the idea of sacrifice in general and the doctrine of *kenosis* in particular looming large in nineteenth-century Russian Christianity. Like the Celtic Christian communities in Britain, the Russian Orthodox Church was based around monasteries where men lived according to the principles of asceticism and self-denial. Philippians 2:5–9, with its stress on the self-emptying and humiliation of the Son of God, was a favourite text for preachers. Theologians also made much of the fact that Christ had been slain from the foundation of the world and took this to indicate that God's kenotic activity of sacrificial self-giving was as much evident in the creation as in the redemp-tion of the world. For Alexis Bukharev, also known as the Archimandrite Theodor (1822–71):

God the Word was mightily creating according to the thought of his Father, but already he was dooming Himself to the immeasurable self-sacrifice in order to keep this new created world in the meaning and designation given to it.... God the Word with the Holy Ghost dwelling in Him, whilst creating the world, was already emptying Himself by the definition of the whole Blessed Trinity and by His own personal readiness and love of the world; He was coming down in the creaturely existence through the Incarnation and that, up to the offering of His flesh in sacrifice for the world which He was creating.[6]

The doctrine of *kenosis* continued to figure prominently in Russian theology through the late nineteenth and early twentieth century. It is particularly evident in the writings of Vladimir Soloviev (1853–1900), M. M. Tareev (1886–1934) and Sergej Bulgakov (1871–1944). The last of this trio also developed the theme of the continuing nature of Jesus' sacrifice: 'Christ suffers and is crucified to the world, because the sacrifice of Golgotha is still repeated in the world until He comes'.[7]

If the emphasis on sacrifice in nineteenth-century Russian thought was Christological, British writing in the same period tended to have a more universal and cosmic focus. It is epitomized in the statement by F. W. Robertson (1816–53), an Anglican clergyman in Brighton and leading preacher of his day, that 'sacrifice, conscious and unconscious for the life of others' is 'the grand law of the universe'.[8] This was to become a major theme of British theologians in the latter half of the nineteenth century. Robertson was one of the first to express it. In a sermon preached in 1849 he declared that 'it is a mysterious and fearful thing to observe how all God's universe is built upon this law, how it penetrates and pervades all Nature, so that if it were to cease, Nature would cease to exist'.[9] Significantly, he makes much of Jesus' words about the necessity of the corn of wheat falling into the ground and dying which he interprets as pointing to sacrifice as the basis of the evolution of all life:

The mountain rock must have its surface rusted into putrescence and become dead soil before the herb can grow. The destruction of the mineral is the life of the vegetable. Again the same process begins. The 'corn of wheat' dies, and out of death more abundant life is born. Out of the soil in which deciduous leaves are buried, the young tree shoots vigorously, and strikes its roots deep down into the realm of decay and death. Upon the life of the vegetable world, the myriad forms of higher life sustain themselves – still the same law: the sacrifice of life to give life.[10]

Robertson goes on to suggest that the same principle applies in the animal kingdom and in human life:

It is impossible for man to live as it is for man to be redeemed, except through vicarious suffering. The anguish of the mother is the condition of the child's life. His very being has its roots in the law of sacrifice; and from his birth onwards, instinctively this becomes the law which rules his existence.[11]

It will be noticed that Robertson speaks of 'vicarious suffering'. There is some ambiguity over how he regards this concept. In his 1849 sermon he defines vicarious sacrifice as suffering undergone in the stead of others. Yet in a later sermon he defines it slightly differently as suffering undergone for the sake of others. There is a further ambiguity over whether he sees sacrifice as voluntary or involuntary. Do we follow the grand law of the universe consciously or instinctively? At one point he says that man's true nobleness lies in the fact that he comes to follow it voluntarily and to sacrifice himself rather than others. Yet there is also an overwhelming sense of the subjection of all to the iron law of sacrifice. Even Christ does not seem to be exempt from it. 'Christ came into collision with the world's evil. . . . He approached the whirling wheel and was torn in pieces. He laid his hand upon the cockatrice's den, and its fangs pierced him. It is the law which governs the conflict with evil. It can only be crushed by suffering from it'.[12] Robertson turns specifically to the sacrifice of Christ in another sermon preached in 1850. Here he interprets the Cross as revelatory of the eternal character of God:

> The death of Christ was a representation of the life of God. To me this is the profoundest of all truths, that the whole of the life of God is the sacrifice of self. . . . Creation itself is sacrifice – the self-impartation of the divine Being. Redemption, too, is sacrifice, else it could not be love; for which reason we will not surrender one iota of the truth that the death of Christ was the sacrifice of God – the manifestation once in time of that which is the eternal law of His life.[13]

Thus understood, the Cross becomes both the supreme example and the only way for the fulfilment of human destiny. 'If man is to rise into the life of God, he must be absorbed into the spirit of that sacrifice – he must die with Christ if he would enter into his proper life'.[14] Drawing strongly on Paul's words in 2 Corinthians 5:14–15, Robertson describes the power of the Cross in terms of radical inclusivity and participation:

> The influence of that Sacrifice on man is the introduction of the principle of self-sacrifice into his nature . . . not He died that we might not die, but that in His death we might be dead, and that in His sacrifice we might become each a sacrifice to God. Moreover His death is identical with life. They who are called dead are 'they who live' . . . . Death, therefore – that is the sacrifice of self – is equivalent to life.[15]

Sacrifice is, indeed, the authentic human condition: 'Real human life is a perpetual completion and repetition of the sacrifice of Christ'.[16] There are obvious overtones here of Paul's statement in Colossians 1:24. For Robertson Christ's sacrifice is not repeated in the Eucharist but continually completed in lives of suffering and self-giving.

> This is the Christian's sacrifice. Not mechanically completed in the miserable materialism of the mass, but spiritually in the life of all in whom the Crucified lives. The sacrifice of Christ is done over again in every life which is lived, not to self but to God.[17]

Somewhat similar in tone to Robertson's sermons, though even more radical and more influential on contemporaries, were the writings of F. D. Maurice (1805–72), the Unitarian turned Anglican who was deprived of his position as Professor of Theology at King's College, London, for questioning the doctrine of everlasting punishment. He regarded sacrifice quite simply as '*the* doctrine of the Bible, *the* doctrine of the Gospel. The Bible is, from first to last, setting forth to us the meaning of Sacrifice'.[18] For him it underlay not just the Cross, though this was where it was focused most clearly, but also creation, incarnation and the whole work of the Trinitarian Godhead. Maurice saw God as the author of life through sacrifice, Christ as the demonstration of life through sacrifice and the Holy Spirit as the inner witness and inspiration of life through sacrifice.

Maurice's thoughts were spelled out in a series of sermons preached in the Chapel of Lincoln's Inn during 1854 under the general title 'The Doctrine of Sacrifice Deduced from the Scriptures'. In the preface to the book in which they were later collected together he defines true sacrifice as 'the sacrifice which manifests the mind of God, which proceeds from God, which accomplishes the purposes of God in the redemption and reconciliation of his creatures, which enables those creatures to become like their Father in Heaven by offering up themselves'. This he contrasts with 'the sacrifices which men have dreamed of in one country or another, as means of changing the purposes of God, of converting him to their mind, of procuring deliverance from the punishment of evil, while the evil still exists'.[19]

That distinction between true and false notions of sacrifice is crucial for Maurice. He emphatically wants to show that sacrifice is from God to man, not vice versa. The fallacious view of sacrifice as something done by human beings to propitiate or alter the mind of God is all too prevalent. 'There has always been a tendency in the corrupt heart of man to make Sacrifice itself the minister of man's self-will, self-indulgence, self-glorification. Instead of giving himself up to God, man seeks to make his God, or his gods, give up to him'.[20] The idea of sacrifice as in any sense propitiatory or, indeed, vicarious (and here he parts company with Robertson) he finds profoundly unbiblical.

Maurice carefully traces the development of the doctrine of sacrifice through the Old and New Testaments. He begins with the story of Cain and Abel and with seeking to understand why the latter's sacrifice is acceptable to God while the former's is not. He finds the reason to be that Abel knows his weakness and casts himself on the one whom he knows to be strong. His sacrifice is 'the mute expression of helplessness, dependence, confidence'.[21] It is the antithesis of that sense of self-sufficiency that is at the root of sin.

The sacrifice of Noah is seen as the offering of a man who feels himself to be God's instrument in furthering the divine purpose. It is a social rather than an individual sacrifice, made on behalf of the whole human race. Maurice then goes on to the key story of Abraham and Isaac which he regards as involving a total sacrifice of self in a way that makes Abraham 'free of God's universe':

for he had begun to understand the principle upon which God rules it, and the law of man's position in it. He had found sacrifice to be no one solitary act, no sudden expression of joy, no violent effort to make a return for blessings which we can only return by accepting; but that it lies at the very root of our being; that our lives stand upon it; that society is held together by it; that all power to be right, and to do right, begins with the offering up of ourselves.[22]

Moving next to the Passover, Maurice is led to consider the communal and national applications of the universal principle of self-sacrifice 'upon which all the charities and sympathies of life depend; that which is at the same time the only impulse to and security for the hard and rough work of the world'.[23] He also reaffirms his conviction that 'sacrifice cannot have this ennobling and mysterious power if it is not contemplated as flowing from the nature of God; if it is not referred to Him as its author as well as its end'.[24]

A sermon on verses 16 and 17 of Psalm 51 inevitably involves an exploration of the theme of the broken and contrite heart and the paradox that it is only by breaking man's spirit that God restores it to its true freedom and greatness. It is only when we discover our poverty and worthlessness and realize that we belong wholly to God that we begin to understand the real meaning of sacrifice. The psalmist has nothing to give but himself. He must come empty-handed and broken-hearted, to receive what God alone can give – a right and true spirit. This brings us to the 'fullest and most radical sense' of sacrifice 'as the giving up, not of something belonging to the man, but of the man himself. Till he made that oblation, he was in a wrong state. When it was made, he was in a restored state – in the state which God had intended him to be, a dependent creature, a trusting creature, capable of receiving his Maker's image'.[25] What the psalmist has learned in his shame and humiliation is the great truth that 'God is the Author of every true sacrifice; that it originates in His will, and therefore fulfils His will'.[26]

In his sermons on the New Testament Maurice naturally focuses on the Cross as the perfect expression of the true doctrine of sacrifice. Yet it is not just on the Cross that this is demonstrated but throughout the birth, life and death of Christ: 'All was self-denial, self-surrender; the love of the Father worked mightily and unresisted in the heart of the Son, till it was broken and offered with the whole body and soul as a complete sacrifice'.[27] The incarnational and revelatory aspects of Christ's sacrifice are stressed. God 'has appeared in our world, in our nature; He has sacrificed Himself. In that

171

sacrifice we see what He is – what He always has been'.[28] The crucifixion of Jesus does not represent an emergency rescue package hastily put together to deal with the unforeseen consequences of human sin: it is a revelation of the eternal character of God, 'for the mind of the Ruler of Heaven and Earth is a mind of self-sacrifice; it is revealed in the Cross of Christ'.[29]

> The Will that rules the universe, the Will that has triumphed and does triumph, is all expressed and gathered up in *the Lamb that was slain*. Beholding Him, you see whence come the peace and order of the world, whence comes its confusion. The principle of sacrifice has been ascertained once and for ever to be the principle, the divine principle; that in which God can alone fully manifest His eternal Being. His inmost character, the order which He had appointed all creatures, voluntary and involuntary, to obey.[30]

For Maurice what is revealed in the sacrifice of Christ is not just the nature of God but the law by which he rules the universe. This law is to be obeyed and followed but, more than this, it is also to be participated in. It has an inclusive corporate dimension quite apart from its legal claim on us. This derives from the headship of Christ over the whole human race. His sacrifice is not just representative; it involves us all as the body of which he is the head. It sums up and gathers in all the little acts of selflessness and dedication that we make in our lives. It is 'the very root of all sacrifices, the consummation of all'.[31] One of his sermons is entitled 'Christ's sacrifice a power to transform us after his likeness'. It is in so far as we give up self and conform to the law of sacrifice that we become like him. This is more than an exemplary theory of atonement although it has clear echoes of Abelard's approach: it couples a highly Pauline sense of our total participation in the death of Christ with a radical grasp of the liberating power of sacrifice.

Maurice develops his thinking about the law of sacrifice in

his treatment of sin. For him sin is making ourselves the
centre and attempting to be dependent on ourselves rather
than on God. It is a condition of separation both from God
and from others. He sees a battle going on between those who
try to follow the law of self-pleasing and find themselves at
war with earth and heaven and those who submit to the law of
sacrifice, who are 'consciously or unconsciously yielding to
Christ, confessing Him as their king, bearing His Cross'.[32]
There is a further internal battle being waged within human
hearts and minds between the selfish self-seeking principle
which leads to animal gratification and which is the source of
all chaos and confusion in the world and a higher principle
which is released by sacrifice and leads us to our true nature
which is, formed in the image of God, to offer ourselves as
sacrifices. It is from this natural destiny that we have been
turned away by sin:

> The sin of the world is its self-will, its self-gratification. The
> Apostle bids us behold the Lamb of God who takes away
> that sin by obedience to His Father, by emptying Himself
> of glory, by humbling himself to the likeness of the lowest
> of His creatures. By that sin-offering, He proves Himself
> to be the Lord of all. When we yield ourselves to Him as
> the Lord of our spirits, He gives us His lowly mind, and so
> gives us peace.[33]

Maurice's final sermon is entitled 'The word of God
conquering by sacrifice'. It celebrates the power of sacrifice to
deliver us from the alienation of separation and selfishness
which is the great malaise of humankind. The key to unlock-
ing this power is that Christ 'should be manifested to us, and
to the world, as the King who has vanquished by sacrifice;
that we should be His willing servants, the free children of
His Father, formed into one family and body by His blessed
Spirit'.[34] Here is the essence of Maurice's Christianity – idealistic, strongly ethical and corporate in character, founded on
the headship of Christ and centred on the great unifying and
revelatory principle of sacrifice which binds human beings to

God and to each other. For him the constant sacrificial call to renounce self was at the heart of Christian faith. 'Faith has no meaning than this', he wrote to a friend, 'that a man is converted to renunciation of self and acknowledgement of another'.[35]

How does Maurice see this life of sacrifice manifesting itself among Christians? In the offering of worship and praise, in participation in the Eucharist, in personal purity and above all in devotion to the service of others. In another letter he writes that 'self-sacrifice in everything is implied in the idea of the Eucharist, secondly in every act of confessing, hope, prayer, gentleness, kindness and forgiveness. All these are ways of acknowledging ourselves to be nothing and God to be all in all, ways by which the spirit casts off its chrysalis coat of selfishness and ascends where its Lord has himself ascended'.[36] He lists 'brotherly kindness, hospitality to strangers, the purity of the marriage bed, compassion to the afflicted' as specific examples of acceptable sacrifice.[37] The extent to which he relates both public and private morality to his underlying view of the centrality of sacrifice is highly significant and was to prove highly influential. In a lecture in Cambridge in 1869 Maurice argued that 'the Universal Sacrifice which is commemorated by the Eucharist was the deepest basis of a Human Morality'.[38] His sense that 'all right doing has its ground in sacrifice' fundamentally challenged the view that morality is ultimately based on self-interest or utilitarian considerations.[39] Alec Vidler has justly commented that 'his elevation of the principle of self-sacrifice to a level of universal moral significance ... has been of profound moral consequence for modern Christian thinking'.[40] Putting it another way one might say that what Maurice did was to add the whole realm of morality to that catalogue of human activities which are governed by the great law of sacrifice.

The influence of Maurice's views on sacrifice can be clearly traced in the development of two important and interrelated movements in mid-nineteenth-century Britain, the cult of Christian manliness and Christian Socialism. Both were driven by a heroic ideal of strenuous self-sacrifice, exemplified by moral and physical temperance and self-control and the subordination of the individual will to the cause of the common good. Thomas Arnold, the founding father of muscular Christianity, who inspired so many of his pupils at Rugby to lead lives of public service founded on the principle of self-restraint, shared Maurice's sense that the concept of sacrifice lay at the heart of the Christian gospel. For him it was only properly expressed in Protestantism. 'The great enemy' of Roman Catholicism, he wrote to a friend in 1841, had 'converted the spiritual self-sacrifice in which each man was his own priest into the carnal and lying sacrifice of the Mass'.[41]

Similarly robust Protestant sympathies characterized the writings of Charles Kingsley, another Victorian cleric for whom manliness and Socialism went hand-in-hand. Several of his longer poems and prose idylls are thinly veiled allegorical attacks on what he took to be the effeminacy and self-centredness of Catholicism and feature manly, Protestant heroes who lead lives of selfless valour and virtue, following the pattern inaugurated by Christ, the Lamb slain from the world's foundation. In his early dramatic poem *The Saints' Tragedy* (1842) he echoes Robertson in seeing the principle of self-sacrifice lying behind the whole of nature:

> Nought lives for self – All, all – from crown to
>   footstool –
> The Lamb, before the world's foundations slain –
> The angels, ministers to God's elect –
> The sun, who only shines to light a world –
> The clouds, whose glory is to die in showers –
> The fleeting streams, who in ocean-graves
> Flee the decay of stagnant self-content –
> The oak, ennobled by the shipwright's axe –
> The soil, which yields its marrow to the flower –
> The flower, which feeds a thousand velvet worms,
> Born only to be prey for every bird –
> All spend themselves for others.

Kingsley goes on to call on man to 'be what God has made him' and

> show himself the creatures' lord
> By freewill gift of that self-sacrifice
> Which they perforce by nature's law must suffer.[42]

A similar Mauricean note is struck by Thomas Hughes, who popularized Thomas Arnold's ideal of Christian manliness in the immortal *Tom Brown's Schooldays*. It was, indeed, Maurice's sermon on 'The Word of God conquering through sacrifice' which directly inspired Hughes' one and only foray into the world of hymnody, 'O God of truth, whose living word', a plea to the Almighty to slay falsehood in men's hearts so that they may fight manfully for him. Like Arnold, Hughes had a strongly Protestant sense of the Eucharist as an expression of the corporate, self-sacrificial principle at the heart of Christianity rather than as some mechanical reenactment of Calvary. One of the most powerful chapters in his great schoolboy novel recounts how the wayward Evans is persuaded by Tom to be confirmed and to take communion in the chapel. In the first edition, the chapter is headed by an extract from James Russell Lowell's poem, *Vision of Sir Launfal* which, in the words of Norman Vance, 'demonstrates a point of intersection of Tom Brown at the altar-rail, co-operative Christian socialism and Maurice's vision of church and world as Christ's family of love':

> The Holy Supper is kept indeed,
> In whatso we share with another's need – ...
> Who so bestows himself with his alms feeds three,
> Himself, his hungering neighbour, and Me.[43]

As the nineteenth century progressed the Christian element in the mid-Victorian cult of manliness became weaker and gave way to a neo-pagan athleticism which reached its height in the years leading up to the First World War. The cricket pitch rather than the chapel came to be the main training ground for learning the importance of unselfishly submitting one's individuality to the service of a common cause. The supreme expression of this more secularized concept of sacrifice is, I suppose, Henry Newbolt's well-known poem, '*Vitaï lampida*' ('There's a breathless hush in the close tonight'). Yet Newbolt was also sensitive to more specifically theological connotations of the principle of sacrifice (if not necessarily to the Christological emphasis of Maurice), as is clear from his poem 'Clifton chapel', where the chapel is portrayed as the place where the schoolboy learns not just 'to set the cause above renown' and 'love the game beyond the prize' but also the darker lesson of the life that proceeds out of death:

> My son, the oath is yours: the end
> Is His, Who built the world of strife,
> Who gave His children Pain for friend,
> And Death the surest hope of life.[44]

The Christian Socialist movement was even more directly influenced by F. D. Maurice's belief in sacrifice as the central principle of unity and brotherhood. He himself played a major role in its early stages in the 1840s and 1850s, supporting trade unions and co-operative ventures in industry and insisting that self-sacrifice rather than selfish individualism should underlie commercial and economic life as well as morality and ethics.

One of those most influenced by Maurice's writings was the idealist philosopher T. H. Green (1836–82) who came from a clerical family and had been educated at Rugby. Much taken with the writings of St Paul, he developed the notion of a perpetual renewal of the death and resurrection of Christ taking place within the individual soul: 'As the primary Christian idea is that of a moral death into life, as wrought for us and in us by God, so its realisation, which is the evidence of its truth, lies in Christian love – a realisation never complete, because for ever embracing new matter, yet constantly gaining in fullness'.[45] Faith for Green, as for Maurice, is a perpetual process of dying to self. Each person has to reenact

the eternal act of God – a death to life and a life out of death –
in order to be conformed to the being of God. This rather
than any creed or dogma is the essence of Christianity.

If the influence of St Paul is clear in Green's thought, then
so is that of Greek philosophy. He felt that God was to be
found neither 'up there' in the heavens, nor 'out there' in
nature but in the higher self possessed by every human being.
The way of realizing that higher self, and therefore of reaching God, lay through self-sacrifice and self-denial. Above all,
it was a way of action, and specifically of throwing oneself
into public service and espousing what Green called Christian
citizenship. He saw this call to social action as the feature
which most clearly distinguished Christianity from the Eastern religions with their stress on detachment, passivity and
disengagement from the world.

Through his writings and more directly through the pupils
who passed through his hands during twenty years as a philosophy lecturer at Balliol College, Oxford, Green exerted a
considerable influence on social and political thought in Britain in the latter part of the nineteenth century. Opinions differ
as to the orthodoxy of his Christian faith and some have
accused him of preaching mere morality rather than a full
gospel of repentance. It is true that he lent towards Pelagian-
ism in seeing sin in terms of selfishness which could be eradi-
cated by intense discipline and devotion to a noble cause.
There is no doubt, however, of the clear Christian roots of his
conviction that social policy and reform should rest on the
principle of self-sacrifice rather than on Marxist rhetoric or
mere utilitarianism. In the words of one of his pupils, Henry
Scott Holland, 'he gave us back the language of self-sacrifice,
and taught us how we belonged to one another in the one life
of organic humanity'.[46] Melvin Richter, author of a fine study
on Green and his disciples, sees his distinctiveness lying in his
belief 'that the philosopher who sought reform should provide not directions on how to use the felicific calculus but a
doctrine of self-sacrifice in the interest of altruism'.[47]

Green's gospel of social reform grounded in sacrifice bore
fruit in a host of ameliorative projects set up by his pupils in

the closing decades of the nineteenth century. They included the Charity Organisation Society, designed to co-ordinate voluntary philanthropy among the poor and destitute, Toynbee Hall, the university settlement in the East End of London which was to become a laboratory for social policy research, and the Passmore Edwards Settlement founded by Mrs Humphrey Ward to educate crippled children unable to attend school. Green's evangelical call was enthusiastically taken up in the new London School of Economics, among socialist intellectuals in the Fabian Society and by many of the younger members of the Liberal Party. Among his pupils who went out from Balliol determined to put his teaching into practice were H. H. Asquith, who was to preside over the great reforming Liberal government of 1908–14, and William Beveridge, architect of the post-war welfare state.

The vision put forward by F. D. Maurice and T. H. Green of a society ordered on the principle of self-sacrifice for the sake of others helped to create an ethos of obligation, responsibility and duty among a substantial section of the better-off members of late Victorian and Edwardian society. It was an important element in forging those notions of the corporate and moral worth of the state and the value of public services which were to guide British politicians and administrators for most of the twentieth century and which have been so brutally discarded in the last fifteen years. It is true that the vision became increasingly secularized – in the words of Beatrice Webb, 'the impulse of self-subordinating sacrifice was transferred, consciously and overtly, from God to man'.[48] Yet the religious inspiration behind the teaching of Green and the activities of many of his disciples cannot be denied. The British welfare state was built not on the basis of denouncing the Christian virtues of charity, justice and sacrificial giving but rather by affirming them.

While many of Green's followers were drawn from the liberal Broad Church fold, there was an important group of High Church Anglican disciples who found that his views strengthened their own incarnational and sacramental theology. In 1889 a group of his former students, most of whom were now theologians teaching in Oxford, published *Lux Mundi: A Series of Studies in the Religion of the Incarnation*, a tract that was to be highly influential in awakening the Church of England in general, and the High Church movement in particular, to the importance of practical action in the areas of social and economic reform. Another impetus came from the Christian Social Union, founded in the same year to 'claim for the Christian law the ultimate authority to rule social practice' and 'to present Christ in practical life as the living Master and King, the enemy of wrong and selfishness, the power of righteousness and love'.[49]

The theme of sacrifice bulked large in both *Lux Mundi* and the Christian Social Union as the writings of the three men who were the prime movers in both ventures clearly demonstrate. Their strong emphasis on the doctrine of *kenosis* and their insistence that sacrifice is as much at the root of incarnation as of atonement is particularly evident in the work of Charles Gore, the first principal of Pusey House, Oxford, and later the first Bishop of Birmingham. 'The Incarnation', he wrote, 'is the supreme act of self-sacrificing sympathy, by which one whose nature is divine was enabled to enter into human experience. He emptied himself of divine prerogative in so far as he was involved in really becoming a man, and growing, feeling and suffering as a man'.[50] Gore also stressed the eternal nature of the sacrifice being offered by Christ as the high priest in heaven. For him this was linked to the presentation of Christ in our midst in the Eucharist where 'God has united the offerings of the church to the ever-living sacrifice of the great High Priest in the heavenly sanctuary'.[51]

The eternal nature of Christ's sacrifice was also a major theme in the books and sermons of the second leading member of the *Lux Mundi* group, Robert Campbell Moberley:

Christ's offering in Heaven is a perpetual ever-present offering of life, whereof 'to have died' is an ever-present and perpetual attribute. If 'Calvary' were the sufficient statement of the nature of the sacrifice of Christ, then the sacrifice would be simply done and past, which is in truth both now and ever present. He is a Priest for ever, not as it were by a perpetual series of acts of memory, not by multiplied and ever remoter acts of commemoration of a death that is past, but by the eternal presentation of a life which is eternally 'the life that died'.[52]

Perhaps the most radical and comprehensive treatment of the whole theme of sacrifice in late nineteenth-century Anglicanism came from the pen of the third leading figure in the *Lux Mundi* movement, Henry Scott Holland, author of the hymn 'Judge eternal, throned in splendour', Precentor of St Paul's Cathedral and a strong Christian Socialist. In 1876 he preached a sermon which Michael Ramsey has described as 'one of the greatest of all time'.[53] Entitled 'Christ, the justification of a suffering world', it is in many ways reminiscent of the first sermon of F. W. Robertson quoted above and shows the impact on a powerful theological mind of discoveries in geological science and the theory of evolution. Holland begins by asking what nature reveals to us of God's primary plan. He finds the answer in terms of a consistent pattern of order coming out of chaos, progress out of surrender and struggle and life out of death. It is through the cooling down of the primeval fireball that the earth's crust is formed. In the 'death and decay of this first life of fire . . . the law of surrender, of self-sacrifice, has already begun to work'.[54] That law continues to be the guiding principle of evolutionary creation with the emergence of life on earth:

> Hidden swarms of living things in silent seas perish for myriads of generations, and yet the very constancy, the very unchangeableness of their waste lays the even layers of man's home. It is not that there is one law of death and quite another of life, but that the very principle of death is turned into being the principle of a fuller and richer life.[55]

With the appearance of human life, the apparent crown of creation, there is in fact no sense of perfection or completion.

Rather the sacrifice, the struggle, the toiling and the labour continue unabated. 'Still our civilisation rests on this vast under-world of terrible ruin: still, alas! it fails to win its way forward from an evil state to a better, except by the old familiar road of war'.[56] Human beings across the world cry out to God and ask him what can be worth this tremendous cost in pain and suffering: 'Man cannot find in himself the worth of all this age-long sacrifice'.[57]

One nation alone in history has kept its head clear and grasped the answer to this age-old question of suffering and struggle. Israel saw that it was worth the cost because God would bring something out of it. So Israel lived by hope and promise. It is the one nation that has ever discovered a permanent purpose of God for his creatures in and through history. That purpose is the attainment of holiness – the union of his creatures with God. Yet, paradoxically, the path by which that can be achieved was not open to Israel. It is only possible because of the sacrifice of Christ, the justification of a suffering world. He takes all the pain and suffering on himself, 'dying the death which justifies all death, in that it turns death itself, by the honourable way of sacrifice, into the instrument of the higher inheritance, into the sacrament of righteousness, into the mystery of holiness, into the pledge of perfect peace; this, and this only, makes a consummation by which the effort of God's creation achieves an end'.[58] It is Christ's sacrifice, and it alone, that makes sense of, and even makes worthwhile, all the suffering and pain in the world and which makes Holland want to pray, 'fill us with sorrow, if so only Thou canst fill us with Thyself'.[59]

When this sermon was published in 1882 it was in a volume entitled *Logic and Life* which included four other sermons on the theme of sacrifice. In them Henry Scott Holland takes further his argument that this is not just the supreme revelatory principle in Christianity but that it is also at the root of the whole religious instinct:

Religion is man's recognition that he himself, with all that he possesses, is entirely and absolutely the possession of

God. Hence religion is, primarily, an act of homage, an act of dedication, a sacrifice – not of blood, or agony, or overwhelming dismay, but the sacrifice of a delighted and exultant confession in the glad lordship of God. . . . The root spring of all religion lies in the intense joy of the discovery: 'I am not mine own. I have nothing of myself. O my God, I am altogether Thine!'. . . . Sacrifice in this sense carries us back behind and beyond all pain, and sin, and suffering. It is, in its primary premiss, not the sad means of recovering a lost state, but the delightful recognition of what actually is, and has never ceased to be. It is the symbolic act of a discovery; the discovery by the creature of its Creator.[60]

The human impulse to sacrifice is implanted in us by God. 'He has made man that he may offer up the sacrifice of a true heart to Him.'[61] Yet coming as we do from a state of alienation and finding ourselves outside rather than within God, what do we bring to the altar of sacrifice? 'Surely one offering and one only – the offering of that very sense of death, which loads and drags downward into ruin all his life.'[62] That is the offering that we can make by being drawn into the sacrifice of Christ through our participation in the Eucharist, our actions of selfless service and through daily dying with him to self and rising again to new life.

It was not just High Church Anglicans who dwelt on the centrality of sacrifice in the closing decades of the nineteenth century. This theme also appealed to writers and preachers of other theological and other denominational persuasions, the most significant of whom were a quartet of Scottish ministers, two of whom were Congregationalists and two Presbyterians. Andrew Fairbairn, who became the first principal of Mansfield College, Oxford, had a strong sense both of the passibility of God and the kenotic nature of Jesus Christ. His book, *The Place of Christ in Modern Theology* (1893), presented an atonement theory worked out in terms of a sacrifice made by God the Father in giving up his Son to die for the sins of the world. P. T. Forsyth, the Aberdeen-born and educated Congregational minister who spent all his ministry in England, has already been quoted in the opening chapter of this book (p. 11–12). His insistence that sacrifice comes from God to us and not vice versa is accompanied by a strongly developed sense of the *kenosis* of both the Father and Son. Christ's 'sacrifice began before He came into the world, and His Cross was that of a lamb slain before the world's foundation. There was a Calvary above which was the mother of it all'.[63] In a way that is strongly reminiscent of the kabbalistic Jewish concept of *zimsum* and the creation theology of Jürgen Moltmann in the late twentieth century, Forsyth explores God's sacrificial nature in terms of the notion of self-limitation: 'The omniscience of God does not mean that it is incapable of limitation, but rather that, with more power than finitude has, it is also more capable of limitation. Only it is self-limitation. He limits Himself in the freedom of holiness for the purposes of His own end of infinite love'.[64] This is a difficult concept to grasp. I hope that I am doing justice to it by suggesting that rather as process theology has developed the notion of God as the self-surpassing surpasser to explain the continuing change and evolution of one who is always ahead of his creatures, so Forsyth sees God as 'the self-limiting limiter' who subjects himself to the self-sacrificial principle while also calling us to lives of sacrifice and self-denial.

Although there are clear affinities between Forsyth's sacrificial theology and that of the *Lux Mundi* group, there are also major differences. His stress is much more on atonement than incarnation and he is very uneasy about seeing Christ's sacrifice as in some way a summation of human offerings. In his important book, *The Work of Christ* (1910), he takes considerable pains to point up the differences between divine and human sacrifice and to show that the purpose of the Cross is 'to effect God's holiness and not to concentrate man's self-sacrifice'.[65] For him the great work of sacrifice wrought by God in Christ is the objective restoration of a disordered relationship with his creatures caused by their sinfulness. He has no time for the more subjective and exemplary atonement theory associated with Aberlard or with Mauricean notions of human participation in Christ's sacrifice through acts of selfless service. Not that Forsyth is indifferent to the rule of the law of sacrifice in human relations. Writing about marriage, for example, he declares that 'a complete humanity rests on men and women who do not simply fuse in passion, but who grow into each other in sacrifice as only souls can'.[66] For him, however, such self-sacrificial behaviour among human beings, laudable and essential as it is to social order, should not be compared with or regarded as somehow contributing to God's own sacrifice of himself through Christ.

The two leading Church of Scotland ministers who wrote about sacrifice in the late nineteenth century were closer in their approach to the Anglicans in the *Lux Mundi* movement. This was particularly the case with William Milligan, a parish minister in Fife who later became Professor of Biblical Criticism at Aberdeen University. Insisting that Jesus' work was not completed by his death, resurrection or ascension, he developed a 'high' doctrine of the eternal priesthood of Christ who makes a continuous offering to his father in heaven. For Milligan the element of blood is all-important to the concept of sacrifice, establishing it as a process which is centred on life rather than death. As the blood of a sacrificial animal is poured out and liberated to effect a union between the offerer and God, so the blood of Christ is liberated on the Cross in order that our lives may be united in him to the Father. Christ's offering, begun on the Cross and continued in heaven, included and embraces all humanity as he himself predicts when he says 'I, if I be lifted up on high out of the earth, will draw all men unto Myself' (John 12:32). The living sacrifice which Jesus presents to the Father is of his humanity as well as his divinity.

Like Maurice, Milligan makes much of the headship of Christ and sees him as representative of all humanity who are involved and included in his eternal offering of life, passing through death on the cross and perfected in heaven: 'One with Him, we die in Him, rise in Him, reign in Him. We are in Him from the beginning to the end of our spiritual experience'.[67] What is particularly important for Milligan about Christ's offering, and what makes it the fulfilment of the whole sacrificial system, is its present reality and efficacy:

> As an offering of life it possesses the power of a present offering, not merely of an offering made and accepted for us nineteen centuries ago, but one which ascends even now for us before God, as much an offering as it ever was.... As an offering continually presented to the Father, it has a present sacrificial efficacy as powerful always as it was at the very first. The present becomes the past in vividness. The Mount on which the Redeemer died can never be removed, and we are ourselves on Calvary.[68]

Milligan's stress on the present and eternal character of Christ's sacrifice leads him to a strongly catholic and sacramental view of the Church as the representative of this heavenly priesthood on earth. He finds the communion table, 'more than any other spot', to be 'the meeting-place of heaven and earth' and notes that 'in the sacrament of the Supper the Church realises to a greater extent than in any other of her ordinances both her own deepest, that is her sacrificial life in her glorified Lord, and His peculiar presence with her as her nourishment and strength and joy'.[69]

Equally catholic, though more mystical and poetic in its expression, is the sacrificial theology of George Matheson (1842–1906) who is now best remembered as the author of the haunting hymn 'O love that wilt not let me go'. A parish minister throughout his working life, he was totally blind from his late teens, an affliction which plunged him into periods of profound loneliness and near-despair but also gave him an intensified sense of the reality and power of suffering. Trusting where he could not see, faith and imagination became his two eyes and his prolific output of theological and devotional writings displays a striking depth and originality.

Matheson's Christology, like that of P. T. Forsyth, was deeply kenotic and gives the lie to the argument that the emphasis on *kenosis* in late nineteenth-century British theology was simply an expression of guilt on the part of public-school and Oxbridge-educated Anglicans in privileged positions. For this Glasgow-born parish minister the key feature of Jesus' life was that it represented 'a ladder of descent that goes systematically from the top to the bottom ... its progress has been a descending progress – from the hill to the plain, from the plain to the valley. Each step has been a step in sacrifice'.[70] This motif of descent was purposed by God. It fitted with the fact that it is in the depths rather than the heights that we meet Christ and each other. It also fitted with Matheson's essentially exemplary theory of atonement in which Christ died not to propitiate or appease an angry God but to show us the way to follow so that we might pray, 'Inspire me with Thy power to descend the ladder of human experience. Let me come after Thee in the downward steps of sacrifice'.[71]

For Matheson the essence of Christianity is 'the belief in the power of the Cross – the belief in the survival of that which is the opposite of selfishness and the crucifier of the selfish man'.[72] He takes the sacrificial nature of the Son as being revelatory of the nature of the Father and goes beyond Maurice in seeing God not simply as the author of life through sacrifice but as the personification of the sacrificial spirit. He wrestles with this notion in one of his prayers: 'If Thou art love, then, Thy best gift must be sacrifice; in that light let me search Thy world. It has pains wrapped up in every pleasure, and who can explain them? Only Thyself – the Spirit of sacrificial love'.[73] That spirit is nothing less than the engine which is driving the world towards its destiny – the gathering of all things together into Christ and the creation of a new heaven and a new earth of inconceivable beauty and splendour.

Like the Russian Orthodox theologians mentioned above, Matheson was particularly fond of preaching on 'the lamb slain from the foundation of the world' (Revelaton 13:8). He held that Christ's death was purposed by God from the beginning of time and supremely signified the power of sacrifice as the central animating principle in the life of the universe. 'All things shine by passing into the life of others:

the seed into the flower, the sun into nature, the sea into the reflections of light. Each stage of human life expands by sacrifice of the self-will'.[74] This conviction of the centrality of sacrifice is powerfully expressed in a poem entitled 'The divine plan of creation' which has come to haunt me almost as much as the text about the corn of wheat falling into the ground and which has been another major stimulus behind the study which has led to this book:

> Thou hast, O Lord, a wondrous plan,
>   To build a tower to reach the skies;
> Its base is earth, its progress man,
>   Its summit sacrifice.
>
> 'Tis only for the summit's sake
>   Thou layest the foundation-stone;
> The mornings of creation break
>   For sacrifice alone.
>
> Thou wouldst not have prepared one star
>   To float upon the azure main,
> Hadst Thou not witnessed from afar
>   The Lamb that would be slain.
>
> Thou wouldst not have infused Thy life
>   Into the insect of an hour,
> Hadst Thou not seen 'neath nature's strife
>   Thy sacrificial flower.
>
> To Him that wears the cross of pain
>   Thou leadest all Thine ages on;
> Through cloud and storm, through wind and rain,
>   Through sense of glories gone.
>
> Through kingdoms lost, through pride displaced,
>   Through systems tried and cast away,
> Through hopes dispelled, through stars effaced,
>   Thou leadest to the day.[75]

In common with F. W. Robertson and Henry Scott Holland, George Matheson found the Christian message of life through death and progress through sacrifice and suffering reinforced by the new scientific theory of evolution. In a remarkable book published in 1885, *Can the Old Faith Live with the New?* he proposes a synthesis between Christianity and evolution on the basis of the theme of sacrifice. A key feature of Christianity, he argues, is the way in which it unites the concepts of sacrifice and royalty. In all other religions kingship is associated with independence and self-reliance. Christianity links it rather with suffering and humility and establishes the idea of an 'empire of sacrificial service'.[76] The theory of evolution posits a similar kind of empire in which species survive and evolve only through suffering and surrender.

> The providential law of God's government in the system of evolution is identical with the providential law of God's government in the sphere of the old faith – the principle of perfection through suffering. The providential place of suffering in the world is more vindicated in the doctrine of evolution than in any other view of nature, except that embraced in the direct teaching of Christianity. The very nature of an evolution from the imperfect to the perfect type of existence demands the presence and the experience of suffering, and demands that the suffering shall be most present and most experienced precisely in those beings whose evolution towards the higher type is most marked and unmistakable.[77]

In developing this argument Matheson seems to me to anticipate in an extraordinary way the thinking of certain scientists and theologians in the late twentieth century. In particular, I am thinking of the conception of evolution developed by Charles Birch, Professor of Biology at the University of Sydney and John Cobb, Professor of Theology at Claremont, California in their seminal book, *The liberation of life*. They use the phrase 'the fall upward' with its significant theological connotations as a way of identifying the occurrence of new and higher levels of order and freedom which are bought at the price of increased pain and suffering. 'In this sense', they write, 'the coming of animal life was a fall upward. Until animal life came there was no suffering, but also there was little value. Animal life introduced greatly increased instability into an otherwise regular world. But the instability was transcendence. The emergence of the distinctively human was another fall upward ... each new liberation in technology, politics, education and sex, produces new forms of enslavement'.[78]

Matheson has the same sense of the equivocal and ambiguous nature of the benefits conferred by evolution. Each step up the evolutionary ladder brings greater liberation and potential but also a greater capacity for suffering. For him the whole process centres on the operation of the sacrificial principle.

> With the entrance of life upon the scene there begins to emerge that type of being which is best described by the name of sacrificial. The moment life is planted on the globe there is planted the necessity for sacrifice. The process of evolution thenceforth progresses by the one surrendering its life for the many, and the many for the more. The life of sacrifice, like every other form of creation, is itself a development, and is progressively unfolded. At first it is involuntary; the surrender is made as the result of compulsion, and in submission to the necessity of things. But with the development of instinct there comes the beginning of something like a sacrificial spirit.[79]

While the first stirrings of this spirit can be discerned in the animal kingdom, it finds its fullest expression with the arrival of *homo sapiens*:

> At last there comes upon the scene a creature capable of a form of sacrifice higher than either of the two foregoing, and with the birth of the spirit of man the gradation is potentially complete. In the spirit of man the life of sacri-

fice is no longer involuntary and compulsory, nor is it any longer the result of an instinctive impulse; it becomes for the first time a deliberate and voluntary act. For the first time in the evolutionary history of the world there appears a being who, without any dynamical compulsion either from without or from within, has the ability to choose the path of sacrifice, and to surrender his personal joy through the simple motive of impersonal love.[80]

Matheson goes on to explain the Christian doctrine of the Fall and redemption in terms of this potential for sacrifice and its failure to be realized. It is Adam's failure to attain this ideal type of sacrificial being and his descent to the lower animal type that constitutes sin. Another Adam is required to complete and fulfil human potential. In totally sacrificing himself he epitomizes the highest point in human evolution.

The very nature of an evolution from the imperfect to the perfect type of existence demands the presence and experience of suffering, and demands that the suffering shall be most present and most experienced precisely in those beings whose evolution towards the higher type is most marked and unmistakable. . . . The doctrine of evolution coincides with the doctrine of the old faith in holding that the perfect man must be a man of sorrows.[81]

This fascinating restatement of St Paul's Second Adam Christology in terms of the theory of evolution is accompanied by a broader sense of the workings of providence revealed in the gradual progress of the world. Matheson posits three successive stages in evolution: first, the dominance of the animal world where physical strength predominates and might is right; second, the battle between animal and human instincts; and finally the age which he sees as dawning where the spirit of sacrifice triumphs.

There has come into the world a new ideal of heroism, – an ideal which consists, not in self-aggrandisement, but in

191

self-surrender for the sake of others; not in the abundance of the things a man possesses, but in the abundance of the things he can bestow. There is no man who does not in his heart believe that the life of sacrifice for the universal good is nobler than the life of struggle for individual gain, more like a hero, more worthy of a human soul. This state of mind is a transformation in the belief of the world, and it is a transformation which virtually amounts to the selection of a new order of being on which to bestow the gift of survival.[82]

I have quoted at some length from Matheson's attempt to produce a synthesis between Christianity and evolution because I find it both fascinating and also largely convincing. In many ways it fits very closely with my own understanding of the centrality of the principle of sacrifice in the natural world in the light of recent research in the biological sciences (see Chapter 8). It is also a profoundly hopeful approach which stands in welcome contrast to the great despair and pessimism that gripped so many Victorians when they tried to come to terms with the implications of the theory of evolution. That despair is epitomized in Tennyson's great poem, *In Memoriam*, the supreme literary expression of the mid-Victorian crisis of faith, where the poet rages at the apparent waste, futility and destruction of nature red in tooth and claw. An even greater sense of a world abandoned by God, or ruled by a God who doesn't care about his creation, underlies the poems of Thomas Hardy. Matheson counters this bleak nihilism with his insistence that there is a purpose and pattern behind all creation – the principle of sacrifice. We may find his view of the impending dawning of a new age of self-sacrificial heroism hopelessly over-optimistic at the tail end of a century that has seen so much human suffering and slaughter often for seemingly so little cause. There is no naive optimism in Matheson's position, however; it is informed by the very different quality of genuine Christian hopefulness born out of suffering and touched by a deep sense of the tragedy at the heart of all life. Above all, it is the expression of a highly

192

personal faith and an overwhelming sense that his own life, like every life, is an offering which has its origin in God and is to be given up to him in gratitude and surrender. This is the message of the closing lines of 'O love that wilt not let me go':

> I lay in dust life's glory dead,
> And from the ground there blossoms red
> Life that shall endless be.

Explaining this somewhat puzzling imagery, he wrote, 'I took red as the symbol of that sacrificial life which blooms by shedding itself'.[83]

George Matheson never claimed that he had found an explanation for the world's suffering but he did feel that the universal principle of sacrifice at least pointed towards a purpose for it. A parishioner recalled that one of the most common themes for his sermons was 'the perfection of man through suffering. He shed many a ray of light on the mystery of pain. He taught us that God meant us to overcome the pains of life, not by avoiding them, but by taking them to our hearts and passing them through our souls. We were to conquer all enemies by conquering all our enmity to them. Man was made by God to become perfect through sufferings, not to be made perfectly free from sufferings'.[84] In practical terms, this meant not just the acceptance of pain and adversity but also a total surrender of self to God and to fellow human beings.

The image which Matheson uses most often to express his ideal of sacrificial self-abandonment is that of the sea. Perhaps it was because its sound was his only companion during long, lonely evenings in his manse at Innellan on the Clyde coast. One of his most original meditations is based on the statement in Revelation 21:1: 'and there was no more sea'.

> Human life below has more sea than land. It is not a con-
> nected continent – a brotherhood of souls; it is a multitude
> of little islands divided by stormy waves. There is a great
> gulf fixed between my life and the life of my brother –

the gulf of self-interest; I cannot pass over to him and he cannot pass over to me. . . . But in that higher life which the seer of Patmos saw the gulfs were all dried up, and the separation of land from land appeared no more. Human nature became to his gaze a continent. Men lost their isolation and ran together in unity. . . . There was perfect self-forgetfulness, therefore there was no more sea.[85]

Many religious traditions have employed the image of the sea to express their beliefs about death. Buddhism and Hinduism in particular have likened human souls to rivers merging into the infinity of the ocean. Matheson paints what at first sight seems a similar picture in the first verse of 'O love that wilt not let me go' (quoted on p. 26) when he speaks of the individual's life being given back to God 'that in thine ocean depths its flow may richer, fuller be'. In contrast to the teaching of Eastern religions, however, he wants to stress the survival of the individual personality after death, while at the same time insisting that this is only achieved through the surrender of self:

Thou speakest of losing thyself in the ocean of His love, but this is only poetically true. Love is an ocean where no man permanently loses himself; he regains himself in richer, nobler form. The only ocean in which a man loses himself is self-love; God's love gives him back his life that he may keep it unto life eternal.[86]

We are back to the paradox in Jesus' statement to his disciples that whoever wants to save his life must first lose it.

By the end of the nineteenth century the theme of sacrifice was spreading beyond the confines of theological treatises and sermons. Several poets writing in the 1890s and 1900s picked up its prevalence in the world of nature and related it to Christ's sacrifice on Calvary. Alfred Noyes' poem 'Art, the herald', was inspired by the text 'the voice of one crying in the wilderness':

> Come; come and see the secret of the sun;
> The sorrow that holds the warring worlds in one;
> The pain that holds Eternity in an hour;
> One God in every seed self-sacrificed,
> One star-eyed, star-crowned universal Christ,
> Re-crucified in every wayside flower.[87]

The Irish poet Joseph Plunkett found an even more direct echo of Christ's sacrifice in the natural world:

> I see his blood upon the rose
>   And in the stars and glory of His eyes
> His body gleams amid eternal snows,
>   His tears fall from the skies.
>
> All pathways by His feet are worn,
>   His strong heart stirs the ever-beating sea;
> His crown of thorns is twined with every thorn;
>   His cross in every tree.[88]

The end of the century also saw the language of sacrifice being applied increasingly to the service of nation and empire. Where F. D. Maurice and T. H. Green had called for selfless devotion to the causes of domestic social reform and economic justice, Rudyard Kipling and Henry Newbolt were inciting their countrymen to 'take up the white man's burden' and 'play up, play up and play the game'. This new emphasis did not necessarily betoken a narrow xenophobic jingoism nor an abandonment of the principles of social justice at home. Indeed, for many Fabians and New Liberals a commitment to socialism and imperialism went hand in hand, both driven by a strong urge to sacrifice self for the sake of a greater cause. Nor was it simply a sign of growing secularization. The revived cult of martyrdom which dates from this period, and which was to reach its apogee in the early years of the First World War, owed less to the classical Greek ideal of laying down one's life for one's country than to the recovery by late Victorian Evangelicals of the ideology which sustained the early Church. General George Gordon believed that 'the thousands who fall in battle are thousands liberated from prison to see the effulgent God'.[89] When he himself died a martyr's death in Khartoum in 1885, defending the British garrison from heathen rebels, he became an icon of heroic Christian chivalry, immortalized in statues and stained-glass windows as the embodiment of Christ-like self-sacrifice.

Perhaps the main reason for this shift of emphasis by both churchmen and secular writers lay in a *fin-de-siècle* sense of national decadence and self-indulgence. In the midst of the celebrations in 1897 to mark Queen Victoria's Diamond Jubilee Kipling felt compelled to warn his countrymen of the dangers of hubris and excessive pride and to remind them of the need for sacrifice:

> The tumult and the shouting dies,
> The captains and the kings depart;
> Still stands Thine ancient sacrifice,
> An humble and a contrite heart.
> Lord God of Hosts, be with us yet,
> Lest we forget – lest we forget![90]

A sermon preached in 1901 by Brooke Fosse Westcott, Bishop of Durham and the first president of the Christian Social Union, provides a striking statement of this new mood. It combines a clarion call for social and economic justice and reform at home with a fervent patriotism and imperialism. The dominant and unifying theme of the sermon is the importance of practising self-sacrifice, both at the level of individual behaviour – 'everyone that striveth in the games is temperate – self-controlled in all things' – and in the life of the nation – 'imperial duty corresponds with national sacrifice.... The love of country, like all love, is sustained, not by gaining, but by giving'.[91] There is also an undeniable whiff of élitism: 'Great men stir the enthusiasm, and direct the movements and administer the resources of the multitude which, for the most part, is inclined to acquiesce in things as they are. Their labours most commonly become fruitful through sacrifice'.[92]

The idea of national regeneration through temperance and self-sacrifice was taken up by a number of writers in the 1900s. *The Christ that is to Be*, written in 1905 by the Fabian intellectual Philip Snowden with the object of converting Christians to socialism, looked forward to an earthly paradise in which the values of Christ's Kingdom had been established through sacrifice. In 1906 Rudyard Kipling stressed the virtues of temperance in his patriotic hymn 'Land of our birth, we pledge to thee':

> Teach us to rule ourselves alway,
> Controlled and cleanly night and day, –
> That we may bring, if need arise,
> No maimed or worthless sacrifice.[93]

Eight years later, on the outbreak of the First World War, Kipling was sounding a grimmer and more determined note and calling on his countrymen to make 'the iron sacrifice of body, will and soul'.[94] No period in history has seen the language of sacrifice so nobly evoked, nor so shamefully abused, as the years between 1914 and 1918. Few conflicts have been entered into with such high ideals of self-sacrifice and ended with such widespread disillusionment with the whole notion of lives being lain down for a cause.

In his superb study, *The Church of England and the First World War*, to which I am indebted for many of the extracts that follow, Alan Wilkinson has shown how enthusiastically the concept of sacrifice was invoked by churchmen as well as politicians at the outset of hostilities. David Lloyd George spoke melodramatically of the 'great pinnacle of sacrifice ... clad in glittering white and pointing like a rugged finger to heaven'.[95] R. J. Campbell, a leading London Congregationalist minister, looked forward to the cleansing and purging effect of the coming conflict on human souls: 'As humanity has been constituted up to the present, war has been the means, more than any other agency, of bringing out on the grand scale that truth of sacrifice without which flesh can never be made to serve the ends of the spirit and the kingdom of the soul be won'.[96]

A leading article in *The Observer* on the day war broke out shared this sense of the cleansing and redemptive power of sacrifice and expressed the hope that 'after a rain of blood, there may be set the greater rainbow in the Heavens before the visions of the souls of men'.[97] In similar vein, the young Rupert Brooke wrote in sacramental terms of the pouring out of 'the sweet wine of youth' and looked forward to having his inner rottenness and self-centredness purged by sacrificial service. The idea that the shedding of blood would somehow purify and purge a nation that had become lazy, selfish and enfeebled has roots that go back beyond Christianity into primal sacrificial ritual. It had widespread currency in the 1910s, appealing not just to patriots and enthusiasts for the great war for civilization but also to more radical groups at odds with the establishment. Emily Davison, the suffragette who threw herself in front of the king's horse at the Derby in June 1913, spoke of the need to make a 'grim holocaust to Liberty' and said that she must 'drink the cup of anguish' like Christ and reenact Calvary for generations yet unborn.[98] The necessity and nobility of blood sacrifice is also a significant theme in the writings and speeches of many of those involved in the 1916 Easter Rising in Ireland. It underlies much of the poetry of Joseph Plunkett whose execution for his part in the rising helped to establish a cult of martyrdom within the Irish nationalist movement. James Connolly, another Irish 'martyr' quoted St Paul's words in Hebrews 9:22: 'without the shedding of blood there is no redemption' on the eve of his execution.[99]

This sense of the positive redemptive power of sacrifice did not diminish once the terrible reality of war was experienced, even if it was now expressed in less triumphalist terms. In his contribution to a 1915 symposium on 'The War and the Kingdom of God', Henry Scott Holland admitted that for him the carnage in the trenches meant that 'all chivalry, all generosity, all the glory of strife has gone. . . . It is insane'. Yet

'Right in the heart of hell, men have found a strange heaven. They have been nearer to the mind and heart of Christ than they had ever attained to in the life of peace. They have known what it was to give away their hope of life out of love of others . . . they have been initiated into the secret of sacrifice, into the inner meaning of life through death'.[100]

Many military chaplains turned to the language of sacrifice in their efforts to come to terms with the horrendous loss of life in the early years of the war, relate it to their Christian faith and console bereaved relatives. In a letter to a father to tell him of the death of his son in France in October 1915 a Wesleyan minister wrote, 'I pray that the heavy weight of sorrow may be eased by the knowledge that he was a true Christian and a true soldier and such sacrifice as his has made us all nobler'.[101] Paul Bull, a High Anglican priest serving in France, was overwhelmed with sadness by the death of so many fit young men. God rebuked him with the words, 'Nay, they are lambs for the sacrifice' and in July 1915 he preached at St Paul's Cathedral on Hebrews 12:1 and asserted 'after a year of crucifixion our Nation answers with unflinching resolution, "To the last drop of our blood" '.[102]

Other chaplains were moved by what they saw at the front to espouse a profound patripassianism. In a poem entitled 'The suffering God' Geoffrey Studdert Kennedy, better known as 'Woodbine Willie' for the cigarettes he handed out to the troops, expressed his sense that those who fell in the trenches were re-enacting Christ's passion:

> I was crucified in Cambrai,
> And again outside Bapaume;
> I was scourged for miles along the Albert Road,
> I was driven, pierced and bleeding,
> With a million maggots feeding
> On the body that I carried as my load,[103]

There was a widespread conviction that those who suffered or died fighting for their country and for freedom could be compared to Christ and were somehow sharing in his great sacrifice to save the world. The Christmas 1914 issue of *The Graphic* carried an engraving which was destined to become one of the great icons of the First World War. Entitled 'The great sacrifice' it portrays a dead soldier in a field, his uniform neat and tidy, his only wound a small round bullet hole in his head. He lies with one hand on the feet of a spectral crucified Christ. Beneath is the text, 'Greater love hath no man than this'. In an Advent sermon in 1916 Arthur Winnington Ingram, Bishop of London, spoke of those who had lost sons in the war: 'the precious blood of their dearest boy mingles with the precious blood which flowed in Calvary; again the world is being redeemed by precious blood. "CHRIST did what my boy did; my boy imitated what CHRIST did" they say'.[104] Neville Figgis, an Anglican priest and historian, reflected in a sermon in 1917: 'When the Cross of Christ is held before us, it is not as a strange, unique phenomenon. It is the inner meaning of all our struggles, the symbol of all sacrifice for distant ends'.[105]

Perhaps the most powerful and suggestive attempt to link the surrender of human life in war with the sacrifice of Christ on Calvary was made by Sir John Arkwright in his great hymn 'O valiant hearts who to your glory came', generally sung to a tune appropriately named 'The supreme sacrifice'.

> Long years ago, as earth lay dark and still,
> Rose a loud cry upon a lonely hill,
> While in the frailty of our human clay
> Christ, our Redeemer, passed the self-same way.
>
> Still stands his Cross from that dread hour to this
> Like some bright star above the dark abyss;
> Still, through the veil, the Victor's pitying eyes
> Look down to bless our lesser Calvaries.
>
> These were His servants, in His steps they trod,
> Following through death the martyr'd Son of God.
> Victor He rose; victorious too shall rise
> They who have drunk His cup of Sacrifice.

Many people now feel uneasy with these words, not just because of their apparent glorification of war but because they seem to detract from the uniqueness and all-sufficiency of Christ's sacrifice and put human suffering and self-giving almost on a level with it. Yet this hymn is not suggesting that 'our lesser Calvaries' in any sense equate with or rival Christ's death in their efficacy or significance but that they manifest our discipleship in following the way of the Cross and involve our participation in his eternal sacrifice. As we have seen, the New Testament itself portrays Calvary as the beginning rather than the end of Christ's sacrifice. It suggests an ongoing redemptive process of offering and self-giving which involves all who follow Christ and drink his cup of sacrifice.

A rather more serious objection to Arkwright's hymn and to the tenor of the sermons quoted immediately above it is that they grossly distort and misrepresent the reality of war by talking in terms of Christlike self-sacrifice. The fact is, of course, that for the most part the soldiers who perished in the trenches of Flanders and northern France were not so much willing volunteers as victims sacrificed by commanders prepared to write off the loss of thousands of men in order to hold a few yards of ground. The altar on which they perished was not that of king and country, even less of freedom and civilization but military incompetence and foolish pride. Yet in a strange way does not this make them even closer to Christ, who was himself a passive victim as much as a willing actor in the events that led up to the crucifixion and whose death has about it as much tragedy as nobility? When the men who were actually stuck in the trenches reflected on their fate it was in rather less exalted and pious terms than those who wrote hymns and sermons from the comfort of the home front. After a Passiontide service one soldier was heard to say to another, 'And now they're going to crucify us'. Another commented of Jesus, 'Who was he anyway? I bet I've suffered more than ever he did'.[106] It would be hard to find a more authentic echo of the Son's cry from the Cross that his Father has forsaken him.

Perhaps what makes us most uneasy now about the way in

which the theme of sacrifice was treated in the First World War is the extent to which it was hijacked for purely militaristic and nationalistic purposes. Another great hymn of the period, written like 'O valiant hearts' by someone who never himself experienced the horror of the trenches, seems to sum up this tendency and express the pagan ideal, *'Dulce et decorum est pro patria mori'*, rather than any Christian notion of sacrifice:

I vow to thee, my country – all earthly things above –
Entire and whole and perfect, the service of my love:
The love that asks no questions, the love that stands the test
That lays upon the altar the dearest and the best;
The love that never falters, the love that pays the price,
The love that makes undaunted the final sacrifice.

This hymn appears on the face of it to be a wholly secular expression of the virtue of patriotism which dangerously abuses the religious language of sacrifice. The notion of laying 'the dearest and the best' on the national altar and pursuing 'the love that asks no questions' suggests a blind adherence to the ideal of 'my country, right or wrong'. Its author, Cecil Spring Rice, was British ambassador to Washington throughout the First World War and did much to coax the United States out of its neutrality. The original version, which he had written before the outbreak of war, was in fact, more belligerently nationalistic and militaristic. Following the war, he toned it down to produce the version quoted above and familiar to generations of school pupils in twentieth-century Britain. He sent the poem to an American friend with an accompanying note, 'The greatest object of all – at the most terrific cost and the most tremendous sacrifice – will, I hope, at last be permanently established, Peace'.[107]

There is, of course, a second verse to Cecil Spring Rice's hymn which points to another country which claims the loyalty of Christians. It is interesting that while he delineates the special qualities of this other realm – 'her fortress is a faithful heart, her pride is suffering' – he does not specifically invoke the concept of sacrifice in writing about it. Yet it is clear that like Sir John Arkwright he saw the surrender of those who fell for their country as intimately linked to and somehow subsumed in the one great sacrifice of Christ. Speaking in Canada a few days after completing the revision of his poem, he said: 'The Cross is a sign of patience under suffering, but not patience under wrong. The Cross is the banner under which we fight – the Cross of St George, the Cross of St Andrew, the Cross of St Patrick; different in form, colour, in history, yes, but the same spirit, the spirit of sacrifice'.[108]

Perhaps at the tail end of the twentieth century, after so much destructive iconclasm and debunking of ideals, we are now more ready to respect and respond to some of the values that prevailed in its opening years. Reflecting on contemporary unease over 'I vow to thee my country' Hugh Montefiore, the former Bishop of Birmingham, has recently written: 'Real patriotism, in the sense of discriminating love for one's country, is beautiful when it leads to service and self-sacrifice for a just cause. . . . It is also beneficial. It motivates people to work together for the common good'.[109] The same could be said of other Victorian and Edwardian values that we are now inclined to scoff at. The coinage of sacrifice may have been debased between 1914 and 1918 through its association with nationalistic jingoism and the glorification of needless slaughter. Yet the First World War also brought many to a deeper sense of the suffering which is at the heart of the life of the world and its creator. It is both a fitting postlude to a century which was gripped by the mysterious creative power of sacrifice throughout the universe and a fitting prelude to one which was to wrestle with the problem of suffering and develop the notion of the crucified God.

7

Sharing in God's suffering: sacrificial theology in the twentieth century

A week after the signing of the armistice which brought the First World War to an end the *Daily Mirror* reported over three million casualties among British and imperial forces and commented that, 'the people of the Empire see figures that will cause them to bow their heads in proud grief at the Noble Sacrifice of the Great Dead'.[1] For many of those who survived such language seemed inappropriate. They shared the sentiments of one of the characters in Ernest Hemingway's novel *A Farewell to Arms*, who wrote that following the war he felt unable to cope with words like 'sacred', 'glorious' and 'sacrifice': 'I had seen nothing sacred, and the things that were glorious had no glory and the sacrifices were like the stockyards of Chicago if nothing was done to the meat except to bury it'.[2] The widespread and wholly understandable existence of such feelings in the aftermath of two world wars has led to a distinct unease over the concept of sacrifice in the twentieth century. There has been considerably less enthusiasm than in earlier periods to find it a heroic or helpful ideal. At the same time attempts to come to terms with the sheer horror and extent of suffering in the modern world have given rise to an intense patripassianism which has been one of the most distinctive hallmarks of twentieth-century theology. If there has been a good deal of reticence about acknowledging the validity and worth of human sacrifice, there has also been much more readiness to acknowledge the cost and pain to God of his eternal sacrifice of self-giving love.

One of the first expressions of this idea which has been so important to contemporary theologians is to be found in a book by Clarence Rolt published in 1913 and entitled *The World's Redemption*. Although it was hailed as an important work at the time, inspiring an article by Burnett Streeter on 'The suffering of God', it has been curiously neglected since. It receives no mention, for example, in either Michael Ramsey's magisterial survey of British theology from Gore to Temple or the recent collection of essays on sacrifice and redemption edited by Stephen Sykes. It is, in fact, the contemporary German theologian Jürgen Moltmann who has pointed to its significance in the development both of the specifically and distinctively Anglican idea of God's passibility and of patripassian theology more generally.[3]

In many ways what Rolt does in his book is to bring together and take forward the ideas expressed in the later nineteenth century by the likes of F. D. Maurice, William Milligan and George Matheson. For him the character of God is to be understood in terms of what is revealed to us in Jesus Christ. This means that the sole omnipotence which he possesses is the power of suffering love, the love displayed by Christ which is perfected through suffering, dies in meekness and humility on the Cross and yet which saves and reveals the world. What Christ did in time, God does in eternity. He suffers in weakness and humility. His nature is the eternal self-sacrifice of love. His suffering love is at the root of all evolution and all redemption, constantly transforming brute force and deadly violence into vital energy.

The idea that God suffers as much as, if not more than, his creatures on earth was taken up in the aftermath of the First World War. In his book, *The Hardest Part*, written for those who had been through the war and published in 1918, Geoffrey Studdert Kennedy speaks of God as the greatest sufferer of all. Drawing on his own experiences as a slum priest and a chaplain in the trenches, he dismisses the conventional religious picture of an almighty and omnipotent ruler as the projection of human power fantasies. The true God is the suffering, crucified servant who comes to us vulnerable and naked. A poem written shortly after the end of the war by Edward Shillito, 'Jesus of the scars', makes the same point:

> The other gods were strong; but Thou wast weak;
> They rode, but Thou didst stumble on a throne;
> But to our wounds only God's wounds can speak,
> And not a god has wounds, but Thou alone.[4]

Patripassianism was not the only doctrine to grip Anglican theologians in the aftermath of the First World War. There was a more general feeling that the theme of sacrifice had an important ecumenical dimension and was worth pursuing for this reason as well as for its own sake. Laurence Grensted's *A Short History of the Doctrine of the Atonement*, published in 1920, pointed to 'the supreme mystical value' of the 'conception of sacrifice' as a basis for fruitful dialogue between Roman Catholics and Protestants.[5] There was a widespread hope that sacrifice might turn out to be 'the long-searched-for common denominator of doctrine, liturgy and Christian life in and between the Churches'.[6] This was the rationale behind a number of studies of the subject published in the 1920s which culminated in Nugent Hicks' important book, *The Fullness of Sacrifice*, which appeared in 1930.

Hicks' great concern is to reconcile Roman Catholic and Protestant ideas about sacrifice in the context of the Eucharist. He is anxious to avoid any hint of propitiation and for this reason plays down the significance of the Cross *per se*. For him Christ's sacrifice is something much bigger than the death at Calvary: it takes in his whole life and also our continuing participation through self-surrender and perfect obedience. Drawing on the evidence from evolution, he also relates it to the much wider process in which all created life is drawn towards God:

What we have learned to see, in the discoveries of the development of created life, in biology, in anthropology, in every other branch of science, in the history of the upward movement of the human individual and of society, is indeed the picture of the ceaseless stream of created life towards God who gave it. When that movement becomes conscious, wherever there is a deliberate choice of the better and the higher instead of the worse and the lower, we call it self-dedication. When it is fully self-conscious in the Christian sense it becomes a part of the offering of the Christian sacrifice.[7]

Hicks' language is still very much that of late nineteenth-century ethical idealism. Sacrifice for him involves 'the pursuit of an ideal', doing one's duty, setting one's face towards God and moving towards the Cross of self-surrender. He is at pains to argue that this has no necessary connection with institutional religion: 'indeed, it could be begun and continued in a character actually but not in any sense consciously Christian'.[8] It may be 'nothing more explicit than a general idea of self-denial and self-discipline'.[9] The role of the Church is to make its own conscious offering include the unconscious offering of the many outside it. In this way, the dedicated and moral lives of many can be brought within the great Christian economy of sacrifice.

Hicks' sense of the inclusiveness and comprehensiveness of the Christian doctrine of sacrifice is to some extent echoed, albeit in a less idealistic and more Christocentric form, by the Russian philosopher and spiritual thinker, Nikolai Berdiaev in his great book, *Freedom and the Spirit*, published in 1935. Equally determined to eschew such concepts as propitiation and satisfaction, and deeply troubled like his hero Dostoyevsky by the extent and intensity of suffering in the world, Berdiaev sees sacrifice in terms of transfiguration. In living out the cycle of birth, suffering, death and resurrection which is the experience of all created beings, Jesus points to the submission of all life to sacrifice. His death on the Cross as the Lamb slain from the foundation of the world both signifies and focuses the mysterious sacrificial power of suffering to transfigure sin and death. Like Matheson, he expresses this in terms of a Second Adam Christology:

In Christ, as Man in the absolute sense, summing up in Himself the whole of spiritual humanity, man makes a heroic effort to overcome by sacrifice and suffering both sin and death, which is the consequence of sin. And this he does in order to respond to the love of God. In Christ human nature co-operates with the work of Redemption. Sacrifice is the law of spiritual ascent and with the birth of Christ a new era in the life of creation begins ... Christ, the New Adam, makes this response to the love of God and thereby points out the way to this response to all who are spiritually His.[10]

The heroic note struck by both Berdiaev and Hicks sounded ever more faintly as the 1930s progressed. In the face of the Great Depression, the failure of internationalism and the rise of fascism, sacrifice and particularly self-sacrifice came to look at best an unaffordable luxury and at worst rank hypocrisy. The high-minded idealism forged in the late Victorian and Edwardian period and already sorely tested by the First World War finally evaporated and a more cynical mood overtook Christians as well as the secular-minded majority.

This gradual loss of confidence in the power of sacrifice can be traced very clearly in the life and thought of William Temple (1881–1944), the great Anglican social reformer who was to become Archbishop of Canterbury during the Second World War. Educated at Rugby, where he imbibed the Arnoldian ethic of strenuous public service and at Balliol, which was still under the influence of T. H. Green's gospel of self-sacrifice, he began his ministry a firm believer in the benefits of self-denial and devotion to others. Like so many of his contemporaries, he had a spell in a university settlement in the East End of London and along with older churchmen like Henry Scott Holland he threw himself into Christian Socialist projects such as the Industrial Christian Fellowship, the Life and Liberty movement and the Workers' Educational Association. His strong sense of the need for sacrifice was strengthened rather than diminished by the First World War which left him with the conviction that those who survived owed it to the fallen to strive at whatever cost to themselves to create a better world.

In his many writings on social and political issues in the 1920s Temple constantly holds up sacrifice as the only power strong enough to overcome injustice and aggression in an evil world. Not just individuals but sectional groups, classes and nations must put others before themselves in a kind of heedless altruism. This is the key to ending the increasingly bitter clash between capital and labour and the rise of narrow nationalism. He develops this argument most fully in *Christus Veritas* published in 1924. Here he lays down four principles for the actualization of the Kingdom of God: political liberty which respects the sacredness of personality; a sense of membership of a community which promotes the spirit of co-operation rather than competition; the duty of service; and the power of sacrifice. This last is the most distinctively Christian of the four. It is also the driving engine of progress and the force that links eternity to history: 'Sacrifice is the root principle of Reality because it is the characteristic activity of God'. It is 'the noblest of spiritual qualities, the highest of human joys . . . and the open secret of the heart of God'.[11]

Temple comes close to espousing patripassianism, writing in *Christus Veritas* that 'all that we can suffer of physical or mental anguish is written within the divine experience; He has known it all Himself', although he prefers the formula 'there is suffering in God' to the phrase 'God suffers'.[12] He also strikingly anticipates the writings of Moltmann and other late twentieth-century theologians in pointing to a relationship based on self-giving love within the Trinity: 'God loves; God answers with love; and the love wherewith God loves and answers is God'.[13] Love is for him the defining characteristic of sacrifice and this is what makes suffering for the sake of others so potentially joyful an experience. It is selfishness which makes the substitution of love for self painful, 'but the essential sacrifice need not be painful at all; it can be the most intense delight. All who have loved know this. Whenever a man chooses to do or to suffer, because of his care for others, what apart from that care he would not choose to do or suffer, that is the essence of self-sacrifice'.[14] There is an unmistakeable echo of late nineteenth-century idealism in his stirring conviction that the human task is to participate in Christ's sacrifice through strenuous service and work for the coming of the Kingdom:

> The sacrifice of Christ is potentially but most really the sacrifice of Humanity. Our task is, by his Spirit, to take our place in that sacrifice. In the strict sense there is only one sacrifice – the obedience of the Son to the Father, and of Humanity to the Father in the Son. This was manifest in actual achievement on Calvary; it is represented in the breaking of the Bread; it is reproduced in our self-dedication and resultant service; it is consummated in the final coming of the kingdom'.[15]

The seemingly unstoppable tide of selfishness, narrow sectional interest and nationalism that swept over Europe in the 1930s caused Temple to lose his faith in the power of sacrifice. In an article in the religious weekly, *The Guardian*, in November 1939, two months after the outbreak of the Second World War, he admitted that he no longer believed in preaching the gospel of corporate self-sacrifice: 'I used to preach it once; I thereby gained much applause, which I very much enjoyed; but I have long been convinced that such talk is only 'uplift'; it does not affect anything which actually happens'.[16] In his final major work, *Christianity and Social Order* (1942), sacrifice has disappeared as a social principle. It is too exacting, he declares, to force on societies. The most that one can hope for is individual repentance and self-restraint.[17]

The note of pessimism and disillusionment that enters into William Temple's thought around 1940 is by no means unique to him. It exemplifies a widespread Christian reaction to a world where ethical idealism and human altruism seemed to be powerless in the face of unprecedented organized human brutality and evil. In many ways the Second World War and the events that led up to it had more significant and damaging effects on orthodox Christian belief than the First. The 1914–18 war had resulted in an unease about invoking the concept of sacrifice as a heroic virtue although, as we have seen, it was by no means extinguished in the 1920s and 1930s. Indeed, this spirit continued to animate those fighting in the 1939–45 conflict, as evidenced by Enoch Powell's comment when asked in a radio interview how he would like to be remembered, 'I would like to have been killed in the war. . . . An act of abandonment for a cause, total abandon for a cause, is something that accompanies me through life'.[18] The horror of the holocaust and other Nazi atrocities posed an altogether bigger challenge to faith – where was God in this systematic genocide and massacre of the innocents? Human suffering rather than human self-sacrifice came to be the dominant moral and ethical issue for Christians – and has remained so throughout the latter half of the twentieth century. Attempts to come to terms with it have focused in varying degrees on the notion of the God who himself suffers, the tragic dimension at the heart of creation and the reworking of primal sacrificial ideas concerning the necessity to society of victims and scapegoats.

For one theologian in particular the experience of the Second World War forced a radical reassessment of the churches' traditional image of God and a stark sense of divine passibility. In a series of letters written from his German prison cell just months before his execution by the Nazis for involvement in the Confessing Church and alleged complicity in the plot to assassinate Hitler, Dietrich Bonhoeffer hammered out a theology for a godless world which was to prove highly influential. Humanity's coming of age, he argued, involved discarding our traditional and fallacious notion of the strong and omnipotent God and returning instead to 'the God of the Bible who wins power and space in the world by his weakness'.[19] In our distress we look in vain for a powerful God when in fact God is weak and vulnerable and has forsaken us because only in that way can he help us. 'Before God and with God we live without God. God lets himself be pushed out of the world on to the cross.'[20] That is the stark and unavoidable meaning of God's supreme revelation of himself through Christ on Calvary.

Bonhoeffer goes on to spell out what this means in terms of human life and Christian discipleship. 'Man is summoned to share in God's sufferings at the hands of a godless world.'[21] Being a Christian does not mean being a religious person but quite simply participating in the sufferings of God in ordinary life. This involves a constant and costly discipleship but even more it involves a total abandonment of self: 'One must completely abandon any attempt to make something of oneself . . . and live unreservedly in life's duties, problems, successes and failures, experiences and perplexities. In so doing we throw ourselves completely into the arms of God, taking seriously, not our own sufferings, but those of God in the world – watching with Christ in Gethsemane. That, I think, is faith'.[22]

There is more than a hint here of Kierkegaardian gloom. Karl Barth discerned in Bonhoeffer 'the melancholy theology of the north German plains' while others have accused him of preaching a 'moral masochism'.[23] Yet his sacrificial ethic of self-abandonment does not amount to a nihilistic doctrine of self-immolation. It is neither gloomy nor introspective. On the contrary, it calls for a total identification with and involvement in the world with all its joys as well as its sorrows. It does not make a virtue of suffering. Bonhoeffer was most insistent that he should not be seen as a martyr. He did not court death but when he knew that it was coming he accepted it as part of sharing in the divine suffering and in the great sacrificial work of bringing life out of death. His last recorded utterance was 'This is the end – for me it is the beginning of life'.

Rather more masochistic, at least on the face of it, was the sacrificial theology developed by Simone Weil, the French mystic and philosopher who died of tuberculosis in a Kent sanatorium in 1943. Like Bonhoeffer, she was gripped by a sense of God's absence and by a conviction that suffering is the essential and authentic quality of human existence. For her it is also profoundly redemptive, transforming evil and always impregnated by love. Human separation from God can only be ended by what she calls 'de-creation' involving a surrender of the illusory existence known as 'I'.[24] Simone Weil lived her own life on the principle that truth and fulfilment could only be attained on the basis of total sacrifice. She longed to be involved in the war, conceiving reckless schemes for being parachuted into Czechoslovakia to support anti-Nazi risings and leading a group of nurses working among soldiers on the front lines. Her neglect of her own health similarly suggests a self-destructive urge in keeping with her frighteningly physical conception of divine and human sacrifice with its echoes of primeval pagan rituals:

> God has not only made himself flesh once; every day he makes himself matter in order to give himself to man and be consumed by him. Conversely, through fatigue, affliction, death, man is made matter and consumed by God. How refuse this reciprocity?
>
> Sacrifice is a gift to God, and giving to God is destroying. It is right, therefore, to think that God abdicated in order to create and that by destroying we are making restitution to him. God's sacrifice is creation: man's sacrifice is destruction.[25]

The essentially destructive aspect of the sacrifice which human beings must make if they are to achieve their destiny is also stressed in a book which came out in the year of Simone Weil's death. Reinhold Niebuhr's *The Nature and Destiny of Man* is an important text for later twentieth-century theology because it takes up the modern psychological concept of the tyranny of the self and finds it supported by biblical teaching. The great human malaise is self-preoccupation: the self in this state must be shattered and broken, or in Paul's words 'crucified'. Man cannot be rescued from the debilitating constriction of self-possession in any other way – 'the self must be possessed from beyond itself'.[26] Like Weil, Niebuhr sees an inevitable element of tragedy at the heart of the human condition, even in its liberated state. The heedless, uncalculating self-sacrificial *agape* which replaces the selfish love of *eros* as the self is destroyed is not able to maintain itself in historical society and is itself doomed to destruction. This is perhaps what it means to live under the perpetual shadow of the Cross, to be crucified with Christ so that, in Paul's words, 'it is no longer I who live, but Christ who lives in me' (Galatians 2:20). Significantly, this same text also inspired one of the most important British theological works of the 1940s, Donald Baillie's *God was in Christ* (1948) which argued for an expiatory theory of atonement based on 'the sacrifice that God is continually making, because he is infinite love confronted with human sin'.[27]

Perhaps the most remarkable piece of writing on the theme of sacrifice to come out of the experience of the Second World War is Ulrich Simon's *A Theology of Auschwitz*. Seeking to find some positive meaning in the holocaust, the author, a German-born Anglican priest, sees it as standing in the great Israelite tradition of ritual sacrificial atonement. 'This holocaust is no less a sacrifice than that prefigured in the Scriptures. Here again the circle closes, and the lives of the many are given for the sins of the world'.[28] He goes so far as to call Auschwitz an altar of sacrificial atonement. Speaking of the Jewish victims of the Nazi extermination camps as representing 'a new type of corporate martyrdom', he compares their death to that of Jesus, the suffering servant:

> Christ died to save mankind from its pagan madness. The victims of Auschwitz died because pagan madness wished to extirpate the light and to rule the world in dark, ecstatic nihilism. The cause of passing over from darkness into light is theirs, and they have consecrated it afresh in the modern struggle against the destroying forces and their dark works.[29]

In highlighting the Passover theme, Simon points to the role of the victims of the deathcamps as scapegoats. They are accused of precisely those sins of which the Nazis know themselves to be guilty. A whole people must die for the sins of another people. 'It does not absolve the guilty of killing, but it accepts the place of the innocent in an act of universal

214

identification. From the blood of Abel to the present day there runs a red thread of meaningful sacrifice through the history of men.'[30]

A similar emphasis on the importance of scapegoats characterizes the writings of the French anthropologist, René Girard, and his disciples. For Girard sacrifice has an extremely important function in primitive society as the means of neutralizing and averting violence. It acts as a kind of safety valve or escape conduit directing the aggressive tendencies within the community towards a surrogate victim. Modern advanced societies with judicial systems have abandoned this method of dealing with violence, thinking that they do not need it but Girard argues that the collapse of a sacrificial system has led to increased physical violence and social and cultural disintegration. Girard's thesis, stated most clearly in his book *Violence and the Sacred*, first published in English in 1977, has prompted a new interest in primal sacrificial ritual and in the role of the sacrificial altar as the sacred space which marks the dividing point between order and confusion. It has also been taken up by a number of Christian theologians, notably James Williams, who has stressed the extent to which it applies to the sacrifice of Jesus:

> God has entered into human existence and his fate must necessarily be that of expulsion and death, for human darkness and deceit, the prevalence of mimetic desire and rivalry, cannot tolerate the presence of One who does not distinguish people and values according to structures that control and validate violence. But his fate is not the same as that of the tragic hero or the dying and rising god, for his death on the cross is not a necessary sacrifice of man to God but God's self-giving gift of love to his creatures. It reveals the violent origins of sacrifice and the complicity of us all in victimization which makes our world go round.[31]

This emphasis on the darker side of human nature and the necessity of sacrifice as a mechanism for neutralizing and containing violence and aggression is to some extent paralleled by the so-called 'death of God' theology associated particularly with the 1960s. This extreme form of patripassianism is perhaps most clearly expressed in Thomas Altizer's *The Gospel of Christian Atheism* (1967) which portrays God as expending himself in love and sacrificing his own essence to meet the needs of humanity. In this process of 'kenotic metamorphosis' he annihilates himself as an objective deity leaving us to hope in our faithful waiting that he may reappear. There is a clear Hegelian strain in this view of God losing himself into the world for the sake of humanity. There are also distinct echoes of the God of Bonhoeffer who lets himself be pushed out of the world. Something of the same sense underlies Eberhard Jüngel's description of the death of the living God on the grounds that God has used death to define his own being, revealing himself as the crucified Christ.

While some of the more extreme pronouncements of the 'death of God' theology of the 1960s have been moderated and quietly discarded over the last twenty-five years, their emphasis on divine suffering and sacrifice has, if anything, been strengthened by more recent works. Thanks both to the influence of those mentioned above and others within the mainstream European theological tradition and also to influences from further afield, patripassianism has been the dominant theme of late twentieth-century theology. Christians from Asia interacting with and reflecting on Eastern religious traditions have made a significant contribution here. In *Third Eye Theology* (1979) and *The Compassionate God* the Taiwanese theologian, C. S. Song, has pointed to the strong common motif of divine suffering that runs through Christianity and Buddhism and portrayed God as the One who discloses himself in pain-love. In similar vein, Raymond Panikkar's *The Unknown Christ of Hinduism* (1964) finds the theme of self-sacrifice linking Hinduism and Christianity. From a rather different perspective, process theologians have sought to strip away alien attributes applied to the God of Christianity via Hebrew legalism, Greek philosophy and Roman imperialism, leaving the vulnerable and infinitely passible figure of the wandering Galilean in whom he chose to incarnate himself.

This trend has left an increasing problem for Christians in reconciling the notions of divine suffering and divine omnipotence. For Arnold Toynbee, who grasped the universal power of sacrifice in history as clearly as anyone has in the twentieth century, it was the major stumbling block to belief. At the basis of his great *Study of History* published in ten volumes between 1934 and 1954, was the thesis that the whole story of human progress is based on suffering and sacrifice.

> Christ, Socrates and Lycurgus died that others might live ... civilizations must die that new civilizations may be born. There is a profound intimation here of a broad moral and psychological truth to which empirical facts are almost irrelevant. Does not every creative act involve both violence and suffering? Must we not *payer de nos personnes*, if not harm others, in everything we do? Do we not see everywhere in animal life and in plant life, as much as in human life, perhaps even also in the inanimate world of physics, a constant dissolution and transcendence?[32]

Toynbee recognized that this was also the message of the Cross. He saw in Christianity the universal principle of sacrifice, and the power of self-sacrificing love, acknowledged and actualized in the person of Jesus Christ. Yet he also found in Christianity an insistence on divine omnipotence which he felt contradicted this great truth and which he could not accept:

> The Christian belief that, in the crucifixion of Jesus, God was sacrificing himself for mankind's sake seems to me to be incompatible with the Christian doctrine that God is omnipotent, but to be reconcilable with my own unorthodox belief that God's love is unlimited but that his power is not.[33]

In fact, what Toynbee described in 1969 as his 'unorthodox

belief' would now be shared by many mainstream Christian theologians. The notion of divine omnipotence has been quietly dropped as has the allied doctrine of divine impassibility, itself the product of Greek philosophical influences on the early Church rather than biblical teaching. In its place has come a recognition that there is some kind of limitation operating both upon and within God. This is variously interpreted, being seen by some as entirely self-imposed and therefore in some sense voluntary and by others as unavoidable. Process theologians to some extent get round this dilemma by talking about God's capacity to surpass himself and constantly to grow and develop in a reciprocal relationship with his creation. In somewhat similar terms Karl Rahner, arguably the leading Roman Catholic theologian of the late twentieth century, speaks of God surpassing himself by overflowing into self-dispossession and giving himself away. Others prefer to see the limitations imposed on God's power in terms of the risk which he takes in creating other beings (see p. 32).

The most detailed and systematic treatment of this whole theme over the last twenty-five years has come from the writings of Jürgen Moltmann. Rejecting the atheistic and nihilistic tendencies of the 'death of God' approach, he prefers to think in terms of death *in* God. The keystone of his theology of divine passibility is the concept of the Trinity understood as a relationship grounded in mutual self-giving between Father, Son and Spirit. Indeed, the essence of his whole argument can be summed up in a statement which he quotes from an earlier twentieth-century German theologian, Bernhard Steffen: 'The most concise expression of the Trinity is the divine act of the Cross in which the Father lets the Son sacrifice himself through the Spirit'.[34]

The earliest and perhaps still the most powerful statement of this profoundly sacrificial theology is to be found in *The Crucified God* (English translation 1974). Much is made here of the παραδιδόναι theme found throughout Paul's epistles, suggesting the giving up by God of his Son to the world. Moltmann expresses the agony of the Cross in terms of what he calls a 'patricompassianism' within the Trinity. The Son

218

suffers death in dereliction; the Father suffers the death of his Son in the pain of his love. Each is forsaken and given up by the other. Yet they are also brought together by the Cross in their common sacrifice. In surrendering his Son, the Father surrenders himself. He is both forsaking and forsaken.

This theme of divine surrender is further pursued in Moltmann's subsequent books. In *The Trinity and the Kingdom of God* (English translation 1981) he develops a patripassian theology rooted in the Christian revelation of God in the person of the suffering Christ. In place of the pervasive notion of divine apathy based on the Greek ideal of the unmoved mover he proposes a theopathy, or sense of the pathos of God, drawing on the notion of the *Shekinah* in rabbinic and kabbalistic Judaism, the stress within the Anglican tradition on the sacrifice of eternal love, the emphasis on the pain of God in Spanish mysticism and the image of the humiliated and tragic Christ in Russian orthodoxy. He also pursues his argument that what Jesus reveals in history is the character of God in eternity. 'If we follow through the idea that the historical passion of Christ reveals the eternal passion of God, then the self-sacrifice of love is God's eternal nature.'[35] It is not simply a reaction to human sin, nor is it a free decision of will on God's part – it is an essential, necessary, inescapable part of his being. Indeed it is his being. God is nothing other than love, construed not in terms of benign benevolence but of infinitely costly and painful self-giving.

In both *The Trinity and the Kingdom of God* and *God in Creation* (1985) Moltmann draws on the doctrine of *kenosis* and the notion of God's self-limitation. As we have already noted (pp. 75–6), he is particularly attracted to the concept of *zimsum* found in kabbalistic Judaism and applies it to suggest that God withdraws into himself in order to create the world. Wrestling with the central paradox at the heart of Christianity, which points to the power of weakness, he argues that while God's humiliation of himself in Christ represents a limitation of his omnipotence, it represents a de-limitation in terms of his goodness: 'God is nowhere greater than in his humiliation. God is nowhere more glorious than in his impotence. God is nowhere more divine than when he becomes man.'[36] The theme of *kenosis* also underlies *The Way of Jesus Christ* (1990) where he seeks to relate the agony of the crucified Christ to the sufferings of the whole creation and to develop a theology of surrender which cuts through the trite sentimentality of the phrase 'God is love' to an awareness of 'the path that leads to that definition: Jesus' forsakenness on the Cross, the surrender of the Son, and the love of the Father, which does everything, gives everything and suffers everything for lost men and women'.[37]

Moltmann makes much in *The Way of Jesus Christ* of the fellowship of Christ's suffering and comments approvingly on the wave of Christian martyrdom in the late twentieth century. This marks a significant shift in contemporary Christian thinking. Much of the theological writing in the twentieth century has sought to establish the idea that God suffers. We are now at the more challenging stage of working out what it means for us to share in that suffering. Significantly, the lead here, both in theory and in practice, has come not from Christians in Europe and North America but from those in areas where the Church faces persecution, and where it is also growing, notably South America, Africa and Asia. It is from the liberation theologians of these lands that the power of the Cross to evoke a response is being most clearly articulated, and most obviously obeyed. In the words of one of them: 'The cross does not offer us any explanatory model that would make us understand what salvation is and how it might itself be salvation. Instead it invites us to participate in a process within which we can actually experience history as salvation'.[38]

One of the most important tasks for theologians in the so-called developed world in coming years will be to work out how Christians living in the midst of relatively affluent, if declining and increasingly angst-ridden, societies can participate in this salvation history and meaningfully share in God's suffering. Some are already turning to this question and finding the answer in terms of a notion of self-transcendence through self-giving. Karl Rahner sees human salvation lying in our capacity 'to be given away and to be handed over, to be that being who realizes himself and finds himself by losing himself once and for all in the incomprehensible'.[39] In similar vein, John Taylor proposes a pattern for human fulfilment in imitation of his Trinitarian understanding of God as the self-giving Father, the given Son and the 'in-othered' Spirit:

> In our self-giving is our own self-transcendence. The mother living for her children, the scientist committed to a particular search, the liberator dedicated to an oppressed people, the artist giving form to an inner vision, the devotee pursuing the vision of God – each of them is simultaneously in three distinct states of self-awareness though only fully conscious of one of them at a time. There is the self-giver absorbed in willing the welfare of the children, the discovery of the truth, and so on, fulfilled in pure *generosity*. There is the given self, conscious of the imperative 'I must', fulfilled in *obedience* to it. And there is the 'in-othering' self that is so identified with the child, the work of art, the victims, the presence of God, as to know them from the inside and be fulfilled only in *their fulfilment*.[40]

My aim in the last three chapters of this book is twofold: to explore how this insight into the cosmic power of sacrifice that we have gained in the twentieth century fits with current scientific understanding of the processes behind life and to sketch out ways in which we can both come to terms with and respond to this call to share in the suffering of God. First, however, by way of a brief postscript to this chapter, I want to offer some poetic musings into the themes that we have so far treated from a rigorously theological perspective. Poets have always been among the most helpful interpreters and guides to the mysteries of faith. It seems to me that their role will be even more important in a culture which increasingly relies on fleeting impressions and glancing allusions and where there is neither the patience nor the inclination to clamber up mountains of dense theological prose. The present century, for all its supposed secularism, has produced a remarkable company of Christian poets who have illuminated the power of sacrifice, dare I suggest, more sharply and certainly more concisely than many a theologian.

The theme of the suffering God who spends and empties himself in self-giving love is explored in a number of modern hymns. W. H. Vanstone's 'Morning glory, starlit sky' speaks of the hidden agony of God's love:

> Love that gives, gives ever more,
>> Gives with zeal, with eager hands,
> Spares not, keeps not, all outpours,
>> Ventures all, its all expends.

Brian Wren portrays the kenotic Christ in 'Here hangs a man discarded':

> Life emptied of all meaning,
> Drained out in bleak distress,
> Can share in broken silence
> My deepest emptiness;
>
> And love that freely entered
> The pit of life's despair
> Can name our hidden darkness
> And suffer with us there.

He also expresses the idea of Christ's continual suffering in and through the sufferings of the world in 'Christ is alive! Let Christians sing':

> In every insult, rift, and war
> Where colour, scorn or wealth divide
> He suffers still, yet loves the more,
> And lives, though ever crucified.

This theme also inspired T. S. Eliot:

The Son of Man is not crucified once for always.
The blood of martyrs is not shed once for always.
But the Son of Man is crucified always
And there shall be martyrs and sinners.[41]

For Eliot, indeed, with his sense, so memorably expressed in the *Four Quartets* that 'time present and time past are both perhaps present in time future', all moments of renunciation and sacrifice are linked to the crucifixion at Calvary and take us to the brink of eternity:

Men's curiosity searches past and future
And clings to that dimension. But to apprehend
The point of intersection of the timeless
With time, is an occupation for the saint –
No occupation either, but something given
And taken, in a lifetime's death in love,
Ardour and selflessness and self-surrender.[42]

The key sacrificial motif of the life that comes out of death has been a major theme in twentieth-century poetry, especially in the Celtic tradition. It underlies Dylan Thomas' 'No man believes' which postulates a sacrificial assumption of created things after their deaths so that they return to the world. To believe, argues Thomas, is to 'make a wound in faith' and accept that life is death. A similar sense of the sacrificial power of death and resurrection is to be found in many of the poems of Euros Bowen, the Welsh priest and bard who died in 1988, and it is the central theme of Alan Llwyd's recent poem, 'Rebirth' with its opening line 'The beginning of the journey is death'.[43] The specific imagery of the corn of wheat buried in the ground has inspired the Gaelic poet and minister Roderick Macdonald:

But swiftly there arises
From the grave of death each seed that has been sown
With the expectation of a heavy crop
In the joyous autumn

And from the dustiness of the grave will arise also
Our perfect home.[44]

This image has been more explicitly applied to the sacrifice of
Christ by the Irish poet Thomas Kinsella:

> Garden and gardener He made
> And then for seed Himself He laid
>   To rectify our loss.
> O red the Spring on the cruel blade
> And lily-white His body splayed
>   In pity on the cross.
>
> Haunting our harvest like a thief
> He hides His flesh in every sheaf,
>   His blood in every fruit,
> But rank the weed – Our Saviour's Grief –
> We nourish into thorn and leaf
>   To live by the sour root.[45]

Another Irishman, Joseph Plunkett, intermingling pagan and
Christian imagery, writes of how he has seen 'the sun at midnight, rising red, deep-hued yet glowing, heavy with the stain
of blood compassion' and felt moved to call out:

> O Sun, O Christ, O bleeding Heart of flame!
> Thou giv'st Thine agony as our life's worth.[46]

Perhaps the most powerful piece of writing on the theme of
sacrifice in the late twentieth century comes from the Orcad-
ian poet, George Mackay Brown. His novel, *Magnus*, which
is set in Orkney in the early days of Christianity, contains a
vivid description of the pagan sacrifices that would have
occurred on the island 4,000 years earlier when the whole
tribe ritually washed itself clean of its blemishes with the
blood of slaughtered beasts.

At the moment of sacrifice on the wine-dark moor, inside

the stone circle, the god and the tribe and the slain beast share in each other's life. A man eats a dripping sliver of ox imbued with divinity and thereby he (the wayward one) takes into himself both the sweetness and wisdom of the god (in so far as his being can bear such intensities) and also a draught of the dark primitive power of the earth. The whole tribe kneels with reddened mouths. It knows then what it truly is, a dedicated people, one with the stars and sun and with the fruitful fires at the centre of the earth.[47]

Brown goes on to speak of other more terrible altar-stones to which beautiful young men were led to be sacrificed to the sun god. This leads him to a more general consideration of the evolution of sacrifice in which the biblical image of the corn of wheat buried in the ground plays a central part.

A festival, a shared meal, a song of praise, a death and a renewal, a dancing together: every sacrifice has these elements in it. Who first tore long wounds in the earth and sowed in it the seeds of wild corn nobody knows, but it was one of the great discoveries. The winter after that the women laid on the tables circles of bread beside the baked fish and the sirloin, and a new taste entered the world: an earth food that was altogether lighter and pleasanter in the mouth and the stomach, and was even more nourishing.

We know the name of the first priest who offered bread and wine on the altar instead of a slain beast: Melchisedec the Israelite. This was a thrilling moment in the spiritual history of mankind. Nor was the pattern altered in the concert of god and man and the animals: for the earth had to be wounded in order to contain the seed, and the ripening corn drew its sustenance from the same deep sources that nourished the animals. Moreover it was a clean sacrifice, not the deluge of blood over the altar and the desperate flailing of hooves. Instead bread shone on the tongues of the worshippers, and the redness that stained the brim of the chalice was wine. Also the god of the tribe, it seemed, was well pleased with the silence and the immaculateness of

ffering made by Melchisedec. Men uttered new
⌐ ⌐o one another – 'pity', 'mercy', 'love', 'patience',
'peace', – as if this new food in some sense quickened their
minds and hearts . . .

. . . What if the god himself were to come to the altar-
stone, himself the deity and the priest and the victim? The
tribe must have fallen into a deep dark pit to require such
unique assistance. Yet to bring this about a man and a
woman and a hidden one stood one night at an innkeeper's
door in a village. And in the fulness of time the same
hidden one endured gladly the fourteen stations of his
death-going.

That was the one only central sacrifice of history. *I am
the bread of life*. All previous rituals had been a foreshadowing of this; all subsequent rituals a re-enactment.
The fires at the centre of the earth, the sun above, all divine
essences and ecstacies, come to this silence at last – a circle
of bread and a cup of wine on an altar.

Out of earth darkness men set the bread on their everyday tables. It is the seal and substance of all their work;
their very nature is kneaded into the substance of the bread;
it is, in an ultimate sense, their life. They bring a tithe
of this earth-gold to the holy table. At the moment of
consecration, the bread – that is to say, man and his work,
his pains, his joys and his hopes – is utterly suffused and
irradiated with the divine. *Hic est enim corpus meum*.[48]

In that description of the Christian Eucharist there is a
real meeting of the two meanings of sacrifice which we must
somehow hold together – the giving up and the making holy.
There is a real sense too of sacrifice as the essential work of
humanity, not in the sense of something done to gain merit or
curry favour, but a self-offering which springs from some
deep, primeval, necessary urge. Devout Christian though he
is, however, George Mackay Brown acknowledges the persistence in our supposedly enlightened and civilized society of
a much darker pagan sacrificial urge which expresses itself in a
lust for scapegoats and victims. Here more than anywhere he

speaks in the authentic accent of our frightened and dislocated age.

At certain times and in certain circumstances men still crave spectacular sacrifice. When there is trouble in the dockyards and there is no sound from the weaver's shed; when theologians brood over the meaning of such words as 'justification' and 'penance' beside dribbling waxflames; when the frontier tower becomes a strewment of stones; when black horsemen and red horsemen ride through the hills and the heavy heraldic coat is riven; when the deep sources are seemingly hopelessly polluted – then bread and wine seem to certain men to be too mild a sacrifice. They root about everywhere for a victim and a scapegoat to stand between the tribe and the anger of inexorable Fate.[49]

8

Unselfish genes and suicidal cells: towards a new natural theology of sacrifice

Scientists and religious believers have generally been cast as adversaries. Their guiding principles – detached observation and demand for proof on the one hand; total commitment and blind faith on the other – seem mutually antagonistic. It is therefore particularly significant that we are at present witnessing a recovery of the tradition of natural theology in which the main initiative is coming not from theologians but from practitioners in the physical sciences. The statements of some of those involved in this exciting new movement echo the old 'design' argument which found a proof for the existence of God in the wonderful symmetry and order of the world of nature. Astronomers and physicists point to a mysterious buzz of energy and a marvellous harmony of patterns, even in the midst of chaos, which they are unable to explain in the scientific language of theorems and equations. Instead, many are increasingly having recourse to religious and poetic metaphors to describe what they find at the extremities of space and at the basis of matter. More generally, there is an awareness that science is not as clear-cut and objective as was once thought. Quantum physics has shown that the observer can never be totally detached but is always a participant and player in the process being studied and may significantly affect its outcome. It has also shattered the closed, mechanistic, deterministic world picture of Isaac Newton and the 'old' physics. We now know that we live in a world which is open-ended and uncertain, a world where there is, in fact, more room for God, seen not as a divine watchmaker or a rigidly deterministic law-maker but as one who suffers and labours to bring order out of the underlying chaos.

228

This new natural theology is not necessarily Christian. Indeed, two pioneering studies, Fritjof Capra's *The Tao of Physics* (1975) and Gary Zukav's *The Dancing Wu Li Masters: An Overview of the New Physics* (1979), find the world revealed by modern physics to be closer to the cosmology of Eastern religions. However, a strong Christian orientation has been given to it by a number of scientist-theologians, notably John Polkinghorne, a theoretical physicist ordained into the Anglican priesthood in 1982 and now president of Queen's College, Cambridge, Paul Davies, professor of mathematical physics at the University of Adelaide and author of *God and the New Physics*, Robert Jastrow, an American nuclear physicist and astronomer who is author of *God and the Astronomers* and Arthur Peacocke, a biochemist ordained in 1971 who is now warden of the society of ordained scientists. It is interesting that apart from Peacocke these leading Christian exponents of the new natural theology are all physicists. There has, so far at least, been less interest in this area among those working in the life sciences of zoology, biology and microbiology. It does indeed seem, as Lewis Wolpert, author of the recently published *The Unnatural Nature of Science*, has observed, that modern physicists are much more likely to be religious than modern biologists.[1] Yet there is a very important religious message conveyed by recent discoveries in the life sciences. They point very clearly to the centrality of the sacrificial principle and the dependence of life at every level on surrender, self-limitation and death.

This is a very different picture of the world and its workings from that held in the heyday of the old natural theology. For the eighteenth-century scholar parsons who pursued natural history in their spacious rectory gardens, nature was essentially beautiful, ordered and benevolent. Their outlook is perfectly summed up in William Paley's *Natural Theology, or Evidences of the Existence and Attributes of the Deity*, published in 1802: 'It is a happy world after all. The air, the earth, the water, teem with delighted existence. In a spring noon, or a summer evening, on whichever side I turn my eyes, myriads of happy beings crowd upon my view'.[2]

Nowadays we cannot take such a benign view of the natural world. We are too conscious of the violence, waste, suffering and death which permeate it at every level. Darwin and his successors have made us painfully aware of the high cost of evolutionary progress, achieved by one species dying out to make room for another and by individuals surrendering themselves for the good of the species. It seems very difficult to reconcile what scientists tell us of the evolution of life with what the Bible says about a creator who cares for each individual to the extent that he numbers the hairs on our heads and knows of every sparrow that falls from the sky. Do we not find ourselves echoing the terrible doubts and fears of Tennyson's *In Memoriam*?

> Are God and Nature then at strife,
>   That Nature lends such evil dreams?
>   So careful of the type she seems,
> So careless of the single life;
>
> That I, considering everywhere
>   Her secret meaning in her deeds,
>   And finding that of fifty seeds
> She often brings but one to bear,
>
> I falter where I firmly trod . . .
>
> 'So careful of the type?' but no,
>   From scarped cliff and quarried stone
>   She cries, 'A thousand types are gone:
> I care for nothing, all shall go.
>
> 'Thou makest thine appeal to me:
>   I bring to life, I bring to death:
>   The spirit does but mean the breath:
> I know no more.' And he, shall he,
>
> Man, her last work, who seemed so fair,
>   Such splendid purpose in his eyes,

Who rolled the psalm to wintry skies,
Who built him fanes of fruitless prayer,

Who trusted God was love indeed
And love Creation's final law –
Though Nature, red in tooth and claw
With ravine, shrieked against his creed –

Who loved, who suffered countless ills,
Who battled for the True, the Just,
Be blown about the desert dust,
Or sealed within the iron hills?

If anything, this fear haunts and troubles us more now than it did in Tennyson's time. The possibility of forms of artificial intelligence which may match or even outstrip the capabilities of the human brain and developments in the field of genetic engineering and *in vitro* fertilization threaten to destroy the sanctity and integrity of human life. At the same time we are plunged into a kind of helpless pessimism by the horrendous suffering of the millions who starve in Africa and the ever-growing threat to our global environment from depletion of the ozone layer, acid rain, deforestation and chemical pollution of the land, sea and air.

It is all too easy to fall into a kind of gloomy fatalism and believe that the world is nothing more than a gigantic structure subjected to a perpetual cycle of pointless suffering. There is, of course, nothing new in this view. It is found in many ancient religions. At the heart of the Vedic tradition is the conviction that 'suffering is the essence of the universe, since the universe is a chain of killing and being killed, of devouring and being devoured. The whole world is just food and the eater of food'.[3] A similar sense of the apparent futility and purposelessness of creation is to be found in the Hebrew scriptures:

Vanity of vanities, says the Preacher,
vanity of vanities! All is vanity,
What does man gain by all the toil

at which he toils under the sun?
A generation goes, and a generation comes,
    but the earth remains for ever.
The sun rises and the sun goes down,
    and hastens to the place where it rises.
The wind blows to the south,
    and goes round to the north;
Round and round goes the wind,
    and on its circuits the wind returns.
All streams run to the sea,
    but the sea is not full;
To the place where the streams flow,
    there they flow again.
All things are full of weariness (Ecclesiastes 1:2–8).

There is, in fact, both pattern and progress in all life on earth and in the very universe itself but it is not to be found in Paley's notion of a 'happy world' teeming with 'delighted existence'. It is, rather, a darker pattern of evolution through self-limitation and surrender and progress and perfection through suffering. At its root is the seeming paradox that life depends on and proceeds from death. This is apparent in the physical world – astronomers have found that it is the process of star death in galaxies that releases energy vital to the creation of new matter – but it is preeminently the case in the world of living creatures and organisms. It is, indeed, in the recent work of life scientists working in the fields of animal behaviour and cell biology that we find the clearest illustration of the extraordinary power and ubiquity of the principle of sacrifice.

Charles Darwin's theory of evolution by natural selection was based on the observation that the number of offspring in an interbreeding community exceeds the number that will ultimately survive and breed. There has been much debate among zoologists as to the level at which the processes of self-limitation and surrender operate which allow those best fittest to their environment to survive. Some favour individual, kin or gene selection while others are more inclined to see selection operating at the group level. It is the advocates of group selection who have particularly stressed the importance of altruistic or sacrificial behaviour in the evolutionary process. The leading exponent of this position has been Professor Vero Wynne-Edwards and it has been popularized by Robert Ardrey in his book, *The Social Contract*. Their argument, in a nutshell, is that 'a group, such as a species or a population within a species, whose individual members are prepared to sacrifice themselves for the welfare of the group, may be less likely to go extinct than a rival group whose individual members place their own selfish interests first. Therefore the world becomes populated mainly by groups consisting of self-sacrificing individuals'.[4]

Wynne-Edwards has been particularly struck by the way in which animals and birds reduce their birth rates and avoid over-exploiting their food resources for the good of the population as a whole. This kind of behaviour, he asserts, 'could not exist in a world where individuals were set against each other, all against all, in an unregulated scramble for food and still more progeny'.[5] His main evidence for the incidence of this altruistic behaviour has come through studying red grouse. He has found that around 60 per cent of the grouse population sacrifice their own personal fitness for the sake of the remaining 40 per cent. He believes that this sacrificial tendency, which is found in other species as well, cannot be explained in terms of a process of natural selection based on gene selfishness or competitive struggle among individuals. On the contrary, it suggests a selection process where the good of the group takes precedence over self-interest and where 'attributes are wholly dependent on mutual co-operation for the achievement of beneficial effects and require that individuals conform to rule in order to promote the common good'.[6] Indeed, as evolution progresses so this sacrificial or altruistic trait is favoured and becomes stronger.

There are many other examples in the natural world of apparent altruism involving self-destructive behaviour performed for the benefit of others. After giving birth, the mother octopus devotes herself entirely and unsparingly to the care of her young, even to the extent of going without food herself. In the words of Frank Lake, author of a standard work on the species, 'the female's devotion to the eggs is such that her health often suffers. Quite frequently when her maternal duties are finished she dies'.[7] Similar behaviour is exhibited by the female sea-louse whose energies are totally consumed by the mass of babies hatched within her shell and who dies exhausted as the last one leaves. The female Pacific salmon dies after laying her eggs, utterly exhausted by the effort of swimming up river to find a safe place for the young to be born. Among Florida scrub jays it is is common for adult birds to help parental pairs raise their offspring by contributing food and defending the nest from predators instead of setting up breeding territories of their own. Worker bees commit suicide by stinging potential robbers of the colony's honey supplies. It is relatively common for birds to give off an alarm call to alert others when they see a predator. The bird who gives out the call puts itself in greater danger of attack by drawing attention to itself. It is also well known for adult birds to feign injury in order to draw off a predator and protect their young. Other altruistic traits which would seem clearly to reduce personal fitness and survival chances have apparently been favoured through evolution. An example which is often cited is the rabbit's white tail which does not help the hapless individual being chased by a fox but helps other rabbits by alerting them to the danger.

Two questions need to be asked here. First, are these examples of apparently altruistic behaviour really what they seem, or are they in fact motivated by a genetic selfishness? Second, even if they do seem to us to be altruistic, are we justified in applying the term 'sacrificial' to the actions of birds, bees and invertebrates like crustaceons and cecaphods?

The first of these questions is hotly debated among zoologists and animal behaviourists. Against the advocates of group selection and inherited altruism are those who favour a theory of individual selection based on the principle of gene selfishness. They point to the fact that the beneficiaries of the apparently altruistic behaviour are almost always very closely

234

related to those displaying it. Indeed, 'most of the acts of altruistic self-sacrifice that are observed in nature are performed by parents towards their young'.[8] What is really happening here is that parents, or other close relatives, are ensuring the perpetuation of their own genes. This is equally true in the case of the suicidal behaviour of the worker bees who, as sterile females, have no offspring. The *hymenoptera*, to give this species its proper name, are, in fact, very closely related to each other and carry a large proportion of identical genes. So what appears like self-sacrificial altruism when they kill themselves in the act of stinging predators is in fact gene selfishness, increasing the chances of their genes surviving in future generations.

The key proponent of this view is the Oxford zoologist Richard Dawkins, author of the highly influential book, *The Selfish Gene*. For him all living creatures, including humans, are basically 'survival machines ... guided by selfish genes' and all behaviour can be explained by the principle of gene selfishness.[9] He utterly rejects Vero Wynne-Edwards' theory of group selection on the basis of an inherited altruistic trait. Instead, he proposes a system of individual or gene selection in which selfishness is the driving force of evolution:

> Even in the group of altruists, there will almost certainly be a dissenting minority who refuse to make any sacrifice. If there is just one selfish rebel, prepared to exploit the altruism of the rest, then he, by definition, is more likely than they are to survive and have children. Each of these children will tend to inherit his selfish traits. After several generations of this natural selection, the 'altruistic group' will be over-run by selfish individuals, and will be indistinguishable from the selfish group.[10]

Dawkins explains away the examples of apparent altruism cited above as manifestations of a system of kin selection designed to maximize the survival of the gene. What is happening in the case of the octopus, he would argue, is that the genetic characteristics of the mother are being preserved in the population through her offspring. The same drive for gene replication explains the rabbit's white tail. It is a fallacy that living creatures ever do anything for the good of the group or the species. We like to think that they do because such behaviour fits in with our moral and political ideas but this is mere wishful thinking and has no scientific basis. The stark truth is that the individual is nothing more than 'a selfish machine'.[11]

This depressingly reductionist and mechanistic view of life is put forward in the context of a rigid neo-Darwinism which Dr Dawkins espouses with evangelical fervour and which has led him to mount a concerted attack on Christianity in general and the academic study of theology in particular. I suppose that his insistence that it is selfishness rather than sacrifice that makes the world go round could be seen as confirming the Christian doctrine of the Fall and the pervasiveness of original sin, although I am sure that he would not see it that way. His theory of gene selfishness, which is presented with great clarity and forcefulness, certainly needs to be taken seriously by those, like me, who would prefer to believe in the rival theory of group selection and inherited altruism and who see human beings and all other living creatures as something more than mere 'gene machines'. Indeed, it has become the new orthodoxy although the biological materialism which he has so eloquently championed is now being challenged in favour of a more open-ended and interdependent view of life similar to that which has replaced the mechanistic determinism of the old physics.[12]

Yet even if we reject Dawkins' position and persist in seeing the behaviour of animals, birds and bees as altruistic, can we go on and apply the epithet 'sacrificial' to it? It has to be said that several scientists are happy to use this term. In the *Collins Encyclopaedia of Animal Behaviour*, for example, Paul Greenwood writes of worker bees committing 'the ultimate sacrifice'.[13] In *Animal Behaviour: Ecology and Evolution* C. J. Barnard notes with respect to the same species that 'individuals may even sacrifice their lives defending the interests of others' and goes on to comment that 'these females sacrifice their own reproductive potential and devote their time and energy to raising the progeny of the colony queen'.[14] Discussing the 'true altruism' shown in the stomping of a Thompson's gazelle and the defiance of the head of a troop of gorillas to ward off predators, E. J. Ambrose, declares that 'love and sacrifice in the sense that we understand them are beginning to flower in the higher animals'.[15] Many scientists, however, are profoundly unhappy with applying such an anthropic concept as sacrifice to the behaviour of non-human creatures. For them it implies volition in a way that self-preservation, for example, does not. To ascribe self-sacrificing love to the octopus is as fallacious as to attribute happiness to shrimps as William Paley did. We simply do not know enough of the invertebrate mind to make this kind of statement. Perhaps there is a case for attributing some kind of volition and conscious moral choice to the higher primates, as Professor Ambrose does, but even this is a matter of considerable debate.

Two questions seem to me to be relevant here. First, if it is wrong to describe the behaviour of non-human creatures as sacrificial, then is it not equally wrong to call it selfish? Both terms seem to me to have equally anthropomorphic connotations. It is interesting that Richard Dawkins seems to have no qualms about applying both of them to animal behaviour. Indeed, in an article arguing for the word 'altruism' to be dropped from the technical vocabulary of animal behaviour and suggesting that what appears to be altruism at the individual level is simply a manifestation of selfishness at the gene level, he still feels able to write that 'a bee sacrifices herself by using her barbed sting'.[16] Those who share his preference for kin selection over group selection are happy to talk about individuals sacrificing their own lives in order to save the lives of other individuals with a similar genetic make-up. Seen from one perspective, this may be a matter of gene selfishness, but could it not equally well be interpreted as a sign of the prevalence and power of sacrifice in the natural world?

The second and much bigger question which needs to be

considered is whether the notion of sacrificial behaviour necessarily implies an element of volition and conscious choice. I am not at all sure that it does. It can arise from a kind of compulsion as much as from a free and conscious act of will. This is surely what George Matheson had in mind when he talked about the inner necessity which comes to compel sacrifice among animals at a certain stage in the evolutionary process.

> The instinct of self-preservation ceases to be sole master of the field, and is compelled to share its empire with another and a higher instinct – that which impels the animal to provide for its offspring. This is no doubt still a species of compulsion, but it is no longer a compulsion of the old sort. If the animal is compelled to sacrifice, it is no more compelled from without but purely from within; its necessity has ceased to be a necessity imposed by the nature of its own being.[17]

There is a parallel here, it seems to me, with the sacrifice of Jesus which, as we have seen, is presented in the gospels as having a certain inevitability and necessity. While there is undoubtedly a voluntary element in Jesus' surrender and death, there is also a very clear sense of inner compulsion. Jesus is presented in the gospels as a man who is destined for sacrifice, the Lamb who is slain from the foundation of the world. He accepts that destiny but can hardly be said to will it – indeed he prays that the cup may be taken away from him. Can we say something similar of Wynne-Edwards' grouse – that they are somehow programmed to limit their population numbers and their food intake? Their self-limitation is not a conscious voluntary act but a programmed response to the fact that a larger number of ill-fed offspring are going to have a poorer chance of survival than a smaller number of well fed ones. Is there, indeed, an unselfish gene in the make-up of living beings which triggers sacrificial and even suicidal acts of self-limitation and surrender in the interests of the survival and propagation of the gene pool, the kin group or the species?

This is not as far-fetched as it may seem. Even Richard Dawkins has conceded the possibility that there could be a 'gene for altruistic behaviour'.[18] Biologists have, in fact, recently revealed the existence of a 'sacrificial' gene which is programmed for its own self-destruction. It has long been known that cells are constantly dying in all living creatures. Within the human body every cell is replaced over a period of six to seven years, giving rise to the question as to how far we really remain the same person during the course of our lives. Until recently it was thought that cells died because they were 'murdered', either by other cells or by invading micro-organisms. Now, however, as a result of work done in a number of countries it is clear that cell death is programmed and depends on 'suicide' genes which kill cells by causing them to shrink, chew up their DNA and feed themselves to their neighbours.

This programmed cell death is essential to the creation and maintenance of life. It controls the sculpting of the human body during foetal development. As a hand forms, the fingers grow and the web of tissue between them dies. The same process takes place during the formation of many other features of the developing foetus, including the skin, brain and components of the immune system. In the words of one science writer: 'Cells must die to allow new features to evolve. In other words, death becomes us'.[19] Suicide genes are also vital in the prevention of cancer. Individual tumour cells are constantly springing up but are generally nipped in the bud by programmed cell death. It is when the suicide mechanism fails that cancers develop and spread. Scientists have discovered that white blood cells taken from patients suffering from leukemia have an over-active gene called bcl-2. In leukemia the body is flooded with mutant white blood cells that divide uncontrollably and cannot kill themselves. When normal 'suicidal' white blood cells are given extra doses of bcl-2 they can no longer kill themselves and behave as if they were leukaemic cells. There is now an urgent hunt on in laboratories around the world to find a drug which will 'switch on' the cell death mechanism in rogue cells where it has failed to operate. This is regarded as one of the best hopes for the treatment of cancer.

Two very important facts about death are revealed in these recent findings. The first is that it can be programmed and orderly as well as accidental and random. It has a purpose and a function. This is true both at the level of the cell and at the level of the individual human life where a similar programmed process of self-destruction operates for the benefit of the species as a whole:

> At a genetically determined age, senile decay and death are imposed on individuals that have hitherto escaped mortality. It ensures that longevity will not be extended indefinitely for personal advantage, and that generation-time will be brought to an optimal long-term compromise instead. Programmed mortality . . . plays an essential part in the perpetuation of variation.[20]

Closely allied to this is the revelation that death is not the opposite of life but rather an essential aspect of it – in the words of one scientist, 'its guardian, saviour and companion'.[21] Indeed, death is in many ways the chief begetter of life. This has important implications for medicine. Scientists working on programmed cell death are already talking of death as therapeutic. Much of modern medicine is geared to prolonging life at almost any cost and staving off physical death. The hospice movement has shown an alternative and much more holistic approach that treats death as an inevitable process to be prepared for and worked through. It has already done much to show that the concept of 'the good death' is just as important and as valid as that of 'the good life'. Maybe we can now come to see death more as a friend and less as an enemy, more as a beginning and less as an end.

There are also, of course, profound theological implications in this new view of death. If death is, indeed, at the root of life then there is a fundamental coincidence between the principles of Christianity and the laws that govern the natural world. St Augustine wrote that 'in the natural order things rise into being and then die; in Christianity they die and rise into being'.[22] If, in fact, it comes to be shown that in some sense death also precedes and paves the way for life in nature, then the central Christian motif of death and resurrection, which 'grounds life by being destroyed' is not so contrary to the ways of the world as we have long been taught.[23] Christianity is distinguished from most other religions in taking death as its starting point. It is based not on the hope of surviving or avoiding death through some kind of immortality but of dying and rising again. Modern science seems to be suggesting that this is also the way of nature and that it is indeed the case that in the midst of death we are in life.

So we are brought back to the mysterious and universal power of sacrifice with its underlying motif of 'through death to life'. In the words of John Moses, 'sacrifice recognises intuitively the necessity of the *death* – the giving up, the offering, the handing-over, the destruction – that leads to *life*'.[24] This is the principle supremely embodied and actualized in human history in the death and resurrection of Jesus Christ. It is also 'the grand law of the universe'. The discovery of the importance of programmed cell death to human life and health and the more general revelation that biology has given us of the extent to which all life depends on self-destruction and surrender indicate that there is indeed a purpose and pattern in creation and evolution. It is not simply a matter of pure blind chance as Jacques Monod in *Chance and Necessity* and Richard Dawkins in *The Blind Watchmaker* have argued. Pierre Teilhard de Chardin was right to see 'the majestic unfolding of a programme woven into the very fabric of the universe'. That programme is sacrifice.

This is the new natural theology to which recent advances in the life sciences seem to me to be leading us, although it has to be said that so far, unlike several of those involved in the new physics, most biologists and zoologists do not see a religious dimension to their work. Theologians need to wrestle with the question of what it means for our view of God and our understanding of our own role in the world. Let me offer some very brief and preliminary observations on these two points. With regard to God, there is an extent to which the new biology reinforces the image associated with the old funeral service of the one who gives and who takes away:

Thou takest away their breath, they die,
And return to their dust.
Thou sendest forth thy spirit, they are created:
And thou renewest the face of the earth (Psalm 104:29–30).

This is not, however, a callous and remote deity who creates and destroys randomly and wantonly. Tennyson was right to go on trusting that love was creation's final law. So it is: but it is hard, costly, sacrificial love rather than the soft and sentimental kind. The new natural theology gives us a very different image of God from the benign but detached figure portrayed by the old one. It suggests a God who is involved and takes risks, who spends himself and suffers in his continuous activity of creation. Arthur Peacocke has rightly commented that new scientific perspectives encourage the development of a patripassian theology 'by showing how the world processes inevitably involve death, pain and suffering if self-conscious sentient creatures are to emerge in a physical universe. An immanent Creator cannot but be regarded as creating through such a process and so as suffering in, with and under it'.[25]

If sacrifice is, indeed, the principle at the heart of the being of God and the power driving the universe which he has created and continues to sustain, then it must also guide our lives and our interaction with the rest of creation. For our supposedly primitive ancestors sacrifice was, as John Bowker has put it, 'an identification with the inherent process of creation'.[26] It involved both a recognition of the surrender, destruction and death that is at the heart of all life and a participation in those processes in solidarity and harmony with the rest of nature. Significantly, this understanding of the centrality of sacrifice went alongside a reluctance to dominate or exploit the natural world. Surviving primal peoples like the native American Indians and Australian aborigines still combine the performance of complex sacrificial rituals with reverence and respect for nature. Modern 'advanced' humanity has all but lost that sacrificial sense of its relationship with the rest of creation. The magnitude of the environmental crisis that we are now facing may yet bring us back to the principles of self-limitation and self-restraint which still guide most of the other species on the planet. If so, we will have fused the two great strands in sacrifice as in giving up our greed, our materialism and our pride we proclaim and celebrate the holiness and sanctity of God's creation.

9

Sin, suffering and salvation

At various points so far in this book I have alluded to the subjects of sin and suffering. In this chapter I want to explore further their relationship with our overall theme of sacrifice. Neither is an easy nor a congenial concept to deal with yet both are fundamental to an understanding of the salvific power of sacrifice. Indeed, they are at the root of all religion. The world is full of evil and suffering; likewise the human condition. It is a sense that things are not as they should be and that there is another and better way which inspires humanity's spiritual quest as Nikolai Berdiaev has observed:

> It is pessimism and not optimism which lies at the bottom of religious experience and the religious consciousness. Our natural world is apparently in the victorious grip of the inane; for it is dominated by corruptibility and death, animosity and hatred, egoism and discord. Man is overwhelmed by the meaningless evil of the whole of life. In religion and in faith he turns towards the world of meaning, and receives strength from that world where love triumphs over hatred, union over division, and eternal life over death.[1]

From the beginning of human religious consciousness sacrifice has been regarded as a major means of dealing with and negating the power of sin and evil. The precise mechanisms involved are complex and varied but they can be broadly summarized under three heads: the propitiation of a righteous deity made angry by sin through the offering of costly gifts; the off-loading of the sins of a community on to a victim or

244

scapegoat who somehow takes them away with him when he is put to death or banished; and the expiatory blotting out or covering over of sin which is effected through the blood and smoke of the sacrificial holocaust.

Of these three ways of understanding the power of sacrifice as a remedy for sin the last seems to me the most relevant and helpful to us today. The principle of expiatory atonement is based on the fact that, in the words of F. D. Maurice, 'sin and sacrifice are the eternal opposites'.[2] At the root of sin is selfishness. If the world can be flooded with the sacrificial spirit, would this not drown out sin and evil? This idea is, of course, at the root of the Christian understanding of the power of the Cross and of prayers for the coming of Christ's kingdom.

Flow, river, flow, flood the nations with grace and mercy;
Send forth your word, Lord, and let there be light![3]

The power of Jesus' sacrifice to blot out and cover over sin is reflected and manifested in our own lesser Calvaries. Consider the healing power of real forgiveness, one of the most difficult and costly forms of sacrifice, which can blot out long-harboured resentments and bitterness both in individuals and communities. Then there is the less tangible but no less real expiatory effect of the gratuitous love and care lavished on the handicapped, the insane, the frail elderly and the dying in hospitals, nursing homes, hospices and homes up and down the land. Does not this exquisite care and costly devotion for those who are in the world's terms useless somehow overshadow and outshine the numerous acts of gratuitous violence and vandalism committed in our society? This expiatory process can work at a national level as well. Can it be that the sacrificial giving of millions of people to Third World charities, such as Oxfam and Christian Aid, in some sense atones for the paucity of our government's commitment to overseas aid? The effect of sacrificial behaviour on sin and evil can be likened to that of a shower of pure water on a stagnant and polluted puddle. Sadly with the decline of the sacrificial ethic and the modern mass media's heavy bias in favour of reporting the negative and the trivial, it often seems nowadays as if the polluted streams are becoming dominant and steadily contaminating the few pools of pure water that are left.

There is another way in which we can think positively and relevantly today of sacrifice as a remedy for sin. It is by returning to the classic definition of Augustine and Luther which sees sin as a state of being turned in on oneself, or *incurvatus in se*. If this is indeed the case, and our own experience surely confirms it to be so, then the salvific power of sacrifice lies in its ability to free us from the tyranny of self and the *angst* of introspection and self-obsession by directing our thoughts and energies outwards towards God and others. Seen in another way, sin represents the gap between what we could be and what we are and the extent to which we have fallen short of the mark. The notion that we achieve our full human destiny only by being saved from ourselves and turning from self-centredness to sacrificial self-giving is, of course, at the heart of Christ's teaching and is expressed in some of the best-known and most beautiful prayers in the Christian tradition.

O Lord, who has taught us that to gain the whole world and to lose our souls is a great folly, grant us the grace so to lose ourselves that we may truly find ourselves anew in the life of grace, and so to forget ourselves that we may be remembered in your kingdom.[4]

Teach us, good Lord, to serve thee as thou deservest, to give and not to count the cost; to fight and not to heed the wounds; to toil and not to seek for rest; to labour and not to ask for any reward save the joy of knowing that we do thy will.[5]

O divine Master, grant that we may not so much seek to be consoled as to console; to be understood, as to understand; to be loved, as to love; for it is in giving that we receive; it is in pardoning that we are pardoned; it is in dying that we are born to eternal life.[6]

Thanks to their beautiful language and their familiarity these are easy prayers to say and sing but they are extraordinarily difficult prayers to live. The discipleship to which we commit ourselves when we use them is costly and hard.

A life which is intended to be sacrificial, a life dedicated to the service of others because in that way Christ himself is served, is a life which really will be characterised by personal disadvantage. The brutal truth is that those who are self-publicists are the ones who come to occupy positions of power and influence, and those who try to be humble end up at the bottom of the stack if they are truly effective at it. Humility is achieved at high cost. It can mean a life which to the world's judgment may appear unsuccessful; it can also mean the loss of self-esteem through the dispiriting fact of marginalisation. Humility is conventionally praised in our culture and almost universally not practised. We are, nevertheless, called to be fools for Christ's sake, and turning down personal advantage and worldly advancement as dimensions of spiritual formation will inevitably look foolish.[7]

How far should this pursuit of the path of sacrifice go? We need to be mindful of the boundary between sacrificial behaviour and destructive self-hatred and self-annihilation and to remember the affirmation of individual worth and self-esteem which is also at the heart of Christianity. Yet there is no doubt that Christ demands a high level of personal sacrifice from those who follow him and that many Christians have taken this to mean not just embracing but positively seeking out lives of suffering and martyrdom. 'To suffer patiently is not specifically Christian at all', wrote Søren Kierkegaard, 'but freely to choose the suffering which one could also avoid, freely to choose it in the interest of a good cause –

this is Christian.'[8] The notion that Christians are specifically called on to suffer is clearly expressed in the Bible:

> For one is approved if, mindful of God, he endures pain while suffering unjustly. For what credit is it, if when you do wrong and are beaten for it you take it patiently? But if when you do right and suffer for it you take it patiently, you have God's approval. For to this you have been called, because Christ also suffered for you, leaving you an example, that you should follow in his steps (1 Peter 2:19–21).

Unjust suffering may be praiseworthy in Christian terms if it is sought out and endured in imitation of Christ but does it also carry the further value of having redemptive and salvific efficacy in respect of either individual or communal sin? Is suffering, in fact, sacrificial? This was the basis of the doctrine of martyrdom first clearly worked out in Judaism in the second century BC. Those who accepted suffering and death rather than betray God are described in the Books of Maccabees in sacrificial terms as expiating the sins of the community and giving it life through their deaths. As we have already seen, this notion was taken up in the early Church (see p. 143). A more general concept of suffering as an atoning sacrifice for sin pervaded Rabbinic Judaism in the period up to AD 500. It was seen as a gift of God, provided alongside prayer, the Torah and other sacrifices as a means not just of chastising his people but also of drawing them towards him. 'Beloved are sufferings' begins one of the most often quoted rabbinic sayings, 'for they appease like offerings; yea, they are more beloved than offerings, for guilt and sin offerings atone only for particular sins, but suffering for all sins.'[9] Another saying portrays suffering as a means of grace not just for the individual enduring it but also for the community as a whole: 'He who gladly bears the sufferings that befall him brings salvation to the world.'[10]

There are clear parallels here with the suffering servant passage in Isiah 52:13—53:12 and with the Christian understanding of Jesus as the one who has taken away the sins of the world through his own suffering. Much Christian teaching has, indeed, followed Rabbinic Judaism in seeing suffering as a condition to be sought out and welcomed for its atoning sacrificial efficacy as well as for its role in perfecting sinful souls. I have already discussed the principle of perfection through suffering, which is clearly put forward in the Epistle to the Hebrews and which has found its way into the corpus of Christian doctrine (see pp. 120–1). It seems monstrous to suggest that God wills and ordains suffering for his creatures as a way of chastening and perfecting them, particularly when so much pain falls on the most innocent and vulnerable. The abducted or abused child, the rape victim, the teenage passenger maimed in a car crash and the aid worker crippled by a sniper's bullet while seeking to bring relief in one of the world's trouble spots can hardly be said to be made better people though being victims of human evil and stupidity. Suffering disproportionately afflicts the weakest and most harmless members of society while crooks and cheats of every kind sail through life unscathed and unchastened.

I have no intention here of attempting to solve the problem of theodicy and offering an explanation as to why there is so much evil and suffering in the world. Dark forces of disorder and chaos confront us all, including God. Suffering is a terrible mystery before which all we can do is bow down. We certainly cannot explain it or mitigate its cruelty and pain through mere words and rational analysis. What we can legitimately ask, however, is whether suffering can be transfigured and made into sacrifice. I am thinking here not of martyrdom and the pain or disadvantage which is consciously courted for the sake of a cause, but rather of the kind of suffering with which most of us are much more familiar – the suffering that we do not seek out, indeed that we do our best to avoid, but which comes upon us and from which we cannot see any escape. This can take many forms: the birth and growth of a child with a physical or mental handicap, the torture of physical abuse, domestic violence, bullying and cruelty, the terrible scourge of schizophrenia and mental illness, the progressive debilitation of a slowly advancing illness, the numb trauma of bereavement and loss or the tension, anxiety and stress that come as a result of difficult relationships, problems at work or simply coping with life.

It is hard to find anything intrinsically redemptive or sacrificial about these kinds of suffering. Far from perfecting those who are afflicted and making them more holy, it more often diminishes them, cramping and narrowing their horizons as they are turned more and more in on themselves. Saints like Dietrich Bonhoeffer may be able to turn their suffering to some spiritual benefit but for most of us it is destructive rather than supportive of faith.

Various attempts have been made to suggest how this unsought-for suffering can in fact have a sacrificial and redemptive purpose. In her book *Sharing the Darkness* Sheila Cassidy, medical director of St Luke's hospice in Plymouth, powerfully describes her conviction that all suffering is taken up by God and used in the Divine economy:

> I believe
> no pain is lost.
> No tear unmarked,
> no cry of anguish
> dies unheard,
> lost in the hail of gunfire
> or blanked out by the padded cell.
> I believe that pain
> and prayer
> are somehow saved,
> processed,
> stored,
> used in the Divine Economy.
> The blood
> shed in Salvador
> will irrigate the heart
> of some financier
> a million miles away.
> The terror,

pain,
swamped
by lava, flood or earthquake
will be caught up
like mist and fall again,
a gentle rain
on arid hearts
or souls despairing
in the back streets
of Brooklyn.[11]

This is the personal credo of someone who has been intimately involved with human suffering throughout her
working life and who has a strong sense of God as the One
who suffers and shares the darkness with us. I find it both
fascinating and moving that it should so clearly acknowledge
the power of sacrifice even to the extent of echoing the stress
found in primal religious ritual on the regenerative power of
spilt blood. There is a real acknowledgement here of the dark
and mysterious power of sacrifice to transform and transfigure suffering and turn it into life-giving energy.

Another way of expressing the redemptive power of suffering is to stress its power to evoke a response in others. In
The Christlike God John Taylor argues that it is only in an
atmosphere of suffering and pain that 'responsive self-giving
love, to say nothing of courage, compassion or self-sacrifice,
could have evolved'.[12] God embarked on his 'huge adventure
of making this universe of accident and freedom and pain as
the only environment in which love could one day emerge to
receive and delight in and respond to his joyous love'.[13] It is
certainly true that countless self-sacrificial acts and numerous
lives devoted to the selfless care of others are directly and
wholly inspired by suffering. Group Captain Leonard
Cheshire was much struck by this when he reflected on his
experience of setting up and running homes for the incurably
ill: 'In my own opinion the great mission of those who suffer
and are in want is to draw out the inherent goodwill that is in

all of us, and so to make us forget ourselves and draw closer to one another in our common journey through life'.[14]

But what of those who suffer? Are they only to have the consolation of knowing that they may be inspiring others to self-giving love and contributing to some divine store of pain and prayer which will one day be used for good? In fact, they may well experience for themselves the redemptive power of sacrifice through their participation in that deepest form of human companionship, the fellowship of suffering. One of the few positive things to come out of the whole tragedy of AIDS is the level of support that fellow sufferers give one another. It is particularly noticeable among those in groups which are already to some extent marginalized and rejected, such as drug users, homosexuals and prostitutes. My own experience of the selfless behaviour of a very close friend who exhausted his own meagre reserves of strength caring for another afflicted by the disease is confirmed by this account by a journalist of a visit to Milestone House, Edinburgh, Scotland's only hospice for HIV/AIDS sufferers:

> There was a complete absence of the selfishness, alienation, withdrawal from and contempt for others I had expected to find. The people around that table showed more care for each other than you would find in almost any church prayer meeting. . . . Workers in other hospices have long since noticed how the terminally ill become more considerate of other people's feelings: they literally have no time for pettiness or pretence. People with AIDS are no different, except that perhaps the bond between them is even stronger.[15]

This is also the message of Scott McPherson, author of the play 'Marvin's Room', written shortly before his death in November 1992:

> Now I am 31 and my lover has AIDS. Our friends have AIDS. And we all take care of each other, the less sick caring for the more sick. At times, an unbelievably harsh

fate is transcended by a simple act of love, by caring for another. By most, we are thought of as 'dying'. But as dying becomes a way of life, the meaning of the word blurs.[16]

In an interesting way McPherson's remarks echo the findings of scientists discussed in the last chapter which suggest that dying should be thought of more as a beginning than an end of life. They also emphasize the power of compassion, the love which is itself born out of suffering and which shares the pain and anguish of another. This is the strongest kind of love and it is, of course, the kind that is displayed on the Cross. The message of Christianity is that it is the love that suffers which is the love that saves. It is one thing to say that suffering love is salvific and sacrificial, however, but quite another to apply these epithets to suffering itself. Can the experience of suffering, in all its depressing and boring self-centredness, be conceived of as a sacrificial offering with a redemptive value? Certainly so in the view of Brother Edward (Edward Bulstrode), Anglican Franciscan and co-founder of the movement known as the Village Evangelists:

I do seriously believe that all suffering patiently endured is linked with the one suffering of Christ in redeeming the world. I believe that if I can suffer bravely and put faith and courage and love into it, that suffering of mine will count towards the world's salvation. I believe that actually those who suffer in the Spirit are, under Christ, our greatest and most generous benefactors. They do more for us than the busiest who bustle round in service.[17]

Ten years as a hospital chaplain gave F. D. Maurice a similar conviction:

Sufferers have a wonderful appointment and ordination. No men give me the notion of the privilege of being priests unto God so much as they; and, kings, too, they are in a sense, though a less obvious one. . . . We shall know more about it hereafter, but I suspect the cross will be found to have been the great *power* of the world, both in the members and the head . . . suffering does more than doing.[18]

I think the key to understanding how the experience of suffering with all its passivity and apparent uselessness can, in fact, be redemptive and sacrificial lies in returning to the argument of W. H. Vanstone in his book *The Stature of Waiting*. 'What glory is there', he asks, 'what trace of the divine image, in that figure who, through no choice of his own, lies helpless upon a hospital bed, monitored by machines, assessed by doctors, attended by nurses, visited or neglected by friends?'[19] For him the answer is to be found in the sufferer's state of need and receptivity to the world. It is this which links him, helpless and dependent as he is, with the suffering God:

> He is one who, like God, is handed over to the world, to wait upon it, to receive its power of meaning: to be the one upon whom the world bears in all its variety and intensity of meaning: to receive upon his transforming consciousness no mere photographic imprint of the world but its wonder and terror, its vastness and delicacy, its beauty and squalor, its good and evil. It is in this dimension – the dimension of meaning – that man receives the world; and as he does so, a figure exposed and waiting, he appears no diminished or degraded figure but a figure of enormous dignity.[20]

Vanstone reminds us here that sacrifice can be passive as well as active. There is a sacrificial redemptive quality in patient suffering and utter dependence just as there is in the broken heart and the contrite spirit. This message is articulated in a beautiful prayer which I heard in a broadcast of choral evensong from Lichfield Cathedral. It asks that all who are handicapped in the race of life for whatever reason may 'learn the mystery of the road of suffering which Christ has trodden and saints have followed, and bring thee this gift which angels cannot bring, a heart that trusts thee even in the dark'.

What, however, of those who find their trust ebbing away, who do not suffer patiently but rage and rail at their pain and refuse to go gently into the night? Can their sufferings, borne with protest and ill grace, also be sacrificial? It is here that Christ's last words on the Cross as recorded in St Mark's Gospel become supremely relevant in all their anger and desolation. The experience of Calvary shows how all suffering, however unwillingly shouldered, can be sacrificial and salvific. As we have already seen, there is a strong element of inevitability and inescapability about Jesus' passion and death as described in the Gospels. He is a passive victim of circumstances as much as an active arbiter of his own fate, a reluctant hero who prays that the cup of suffering may be taken away from him rather than a martyr who seeks death.

This understanding of the Cross and what led up to it is crucial in establishing that there can be a sacrificial dimension to unsought for suffering. Many modern theologians, especially of a feminist persuasion, are uneasy about this. A recent report by a taskforce on violence against women set up by the Anglican Church of Canada, for example, asserts that 'Jesus' voluntary suffering and death on the cross cannot and must not be paralleled with the involuntary suffering of women, children or other victims of violence'.[21] In similar vein, Mercy Oduyoye, a Ghanaian theologian writing about 'An African woman's Christ', insists that 'the Christ for me is the Jesus of Nazareth who agreed to be God's sacrificial lamb, thus teaching that true and living sacrifice is *that which is freely and consciously made* . . . noble and lovely, loving and motivated by love and gratitude'.[22] The fact is, however, that Jesus' sacrifice was not entirely voluntary or freely made. It had elements of inevitability, inescapability and dark necessity. His status as victim was something that happened to him rather than one that he willed. His suffering was wholly undeserved and in certain respects unmeditated. To that extent, his passion and death can indeed be paralleled and linked with the involuntary suffering of innocent victims everywhere, though it can certainly never be used to justify or glorify their situation in any way.

The Cross points to the ubiquity and unavoidability of suffering. Like the first of the noble truths delivered by the Buddha it proclaims that 'birth is suffering; death is suffering; presence of the hated is suffering; age is suffering; sickness is suffering; absence of the loved is suffering; to wish and not to get is suffering; briefly, the fivefold nature by which all things cling to existence is suffering'.[23] In marked contrast to the Buddha, however, the Cross teaches that there is no escape from suffering. If anyone could have avoided its pain and agony, that person was surely the Son of God. Yet he, more than anyone else, faces and bears it. Unlike most of the world's great religions, Christianity does not offer a way of avoiding the suffering to which all living creatures are subjected. It points rather to the total involvement in suffering of God himself and its transfiguration through the miraculous principle of resurrection.

At the centre of that process of involvement and transfiguration is Jesus' passion and death on the Cross understood as a sacrifice for suffering as much as a sacrifice for sin. This is very important. Jesus dies not just for sinners but for all who suffer. He takes upon himself all the world's agony and pain as well as all its evil and offers it to God to be redeemed, transfigured and used in the Divine economy. We should remember how much of Jesus' teaching is directed towards those who suffer rather than to those who sin. This is the whole thrust of the Beastitudes with their specific blessing of the meek, the poor in spirit, those who mourn and those who are persecuted and reviled. It is also, as the Old Testament scholar, Claus Westermann, has eloquently pointed out, the clear message of the words of desolation which Jesus speaks on the Cross:

> If the Gospel story of the passion is presented in the words of Psalm 22, the authors wanted to say that Christ had taken up the lament of those people who suffer, that he too had entered into suffering. . . . His suffering is a part of the history of those who have suffered, who have found their language in the Psalms of lament. With his suffering and

dying, therefore, Jesus could not have had only the sinner in mind; he must also have been thinking of those who suffer. If, as in the New Testament, the work of Christ is described as salvation from sin and death, then (following the Old Testament understanding) by 'death' we mean not only the cessation of life but the power of death at work within life which people experience in all types of suffering.[24]

Westermann goes on to make a timely plea for the recovery in worship of the great Hebrew Psalms of lament to correct the idea that Christ died for sin alone. Several liturgists, led by John Bell of the Church of Scotland's Panel on Worship, are now stressing the importance of communal singing of the songs of lament and protest from the psalter as well as the praise psalms with which we are more familiar in church worship. Jürgen Moltmann has also stressed the significance of Christ's quotation from Psalm 22 on the Cross and the extent to which it speaks to all who find themselves the victims of needless suffering:

> Anyone who suffers without cause first thinks that he has been forsaken by God. God seems to him to be the mysterious, incomprehensible God who destroys the good fortune that he gave. But anyone who cries out to God in his suffering echoes the death-cry of the dying Christ, the Son of God. In that case God is not just a hidden someone set over against him, to whom he cries, but in a profound sense the human God, who cries with him and intercedes for him with his Cross, where man in his torment is dumb.[25]

This brings us back to the compassion that is at the heart of Christianity and the fact that, far from being the author of suffering, the Christian God is rather to be counted among its victims. This is why Moltmann talks about the crucified God. Suffering befalls God as it befalls us. He himself is caught up in the great cosmic tragedy which is both grounded in and ultimately resolved by the power of sacrifice. In the words of Paul Fiddes, 'God the Father reconciles himself not by making the Son suffer, but by opening his triune being to a situation in which suffering *befalls* him as he accepts into himself the consequences which flow from sin and natural disorder . . . if we affirm that God truly suffers with his world this must mean that suffering *happens* to him'.[26]

Perhaps the most moving way in which the Bible expresses the anguish and compassion of both the Father and Son in their suffering is by alluding to the tears which they shed. The Old Testament speaks of God watering his people with his tears (Isaiah 16:9) while in the New Testament Jesus is portrayed as weeping when he beheld Jerusalem (Luke 19:41). 'Jesus wept' (John 11:35) is the shortest verse in the Bible. It is also one of the most poignant and significant. It points to the sacrificial and salvific power of tears – to heal and redeem, to express our deepest angers, frustrations and sorrows when words alone fail us, and to make us one with God through Christ the weeper.

This particular image of Jesus is not as prominent in Christian theology as it should be. It is interesting that it is one of the features that has most attracted followers of Eastern religions to Christianity. In the tears which are shed by both God and his Son they find a passion and anguish which is missing from their largely impassive deities. This is why K. C. S. Paniker, a prominent Hindu artist, chose to paint a picture of 'The sorrow of Christ': 'I felt attracted by the anguish of Christ. We talk about joy and peace. We do meditation, we fast strictly. But we have nothing to do with physical anguish. However, in Christ I encounter the man who made his love recognizable by giving his own blood'.[27]

We do not cry enough nowadays. I am not just thinking of times of mourning and funerals when we are too often concerned with trying to keep a stiff upper lip and not showing our emotions, although we can certainly learn from the more spontaneous and less inhibited grief displayed by those in other supposedly more 'primitive' cultures and by our own ancestors. There are also other occasions, when we are full of anger and sorrow and pent-up emotion, when we need to let the tears flow and do their redemptive and sacrificial work. By offering up tears to God we are not simply signalling our helplessness and dependence; we are also linking ourselves with him through the depth of our feelings and compassion for his suffering creation. Weeping over the sorrows and evils of the world is not just a profoundly sacrificial act, it is also one which often leads to practical action in the cause of peace and justice. As the Taiwanese theologian, Choan-Sen Song, puts it in his book, *The Tears of Lady Meng*: 'The tears of the people are the source and power of our political theology'.[28]

We need to recover that sense of the redemptive and sacrificial power of shedding tears which lay at the heart of the medieval cult of the *mater dolorosa*. Virtually every European church in the late Middle Ages had a picture of Mary weeping beside her crucified son, as described in that great Passiontide hymn from the thirteenth century, *Stabat Mater Dolorosa*:

> At the Cross her station keeping,
> Stood the mournful Mother weeping,
> Close to Jesus at the last,
> Through her soul, of joy bereaved,
> Bowed with anguish, deeply grieved,
> Now at length the sword hath passed.
>
> O, that blessed one, grief-laden,
> Blessed Mother, blessed Maiden,
> Mother of the all-holy One;
> O that silent, ceaseless mourning,
> O those dim eyes, never turning
> From that wondrous, suffering Son.
>
> Who on Christ's dear Mother gazing,
> In her trouble so amazing,
> Born of woman, would not weep?
> Who on Christ's dear Mother thinking,
> Such a cup of sorrow drinking,
> Would not share her sorrow deep?[29]

Mary's tears became the paradigm for the Christian response

259

both to the suffering of Jesus and to all pain and anguish. The gift of tears, like the sacrifice of a broken heart, came to be seen as a precious offering which brought those who shed them closer to the suffering Christ.

> Drop, drop, slow tears,
> And bathe those beateous feet,
> Which brought from heaven
> The news and Prince of peace.[30]

There is a very important message in these late medieval hymns. It is that those whose hearts are broken and full of sorrow stand closest to the crucified and risen Saviour, the one whose healing and redeeming power is directed as much to the suffering as to the sinful. As the *mater dolorosa* Mary becomes the entry point for approaching Jesus through our compassion and brokenness and also the agent who liberates us from the tyranny of self. It is by sharing her sorrows that we break our own hard hearts:

> O come and mourn with me awhile;
> See Mary calls us to her side;
> O come and let us mourn with her:
> Jesus, our Love, is crucified.
>
> O break, O break, hard heart of mine;
> Thy weak self-love and guilty pride
> His Pilate and His Judas were:
> Jesus, our Love, is crucified.
>
> A broken heart, a fount of tears,
> Ask, and they will not be denied;
> A broken heart love's cradle is:
> Jesus, our Love, is crucified.[31]

This compassionate theology is not found at all in the writings of the early Church fathers. Their stress is rather on the virtue of *apatheia* and on showing that grief is not consistent with faith. The patristic Mary, like the patristic Christ and the patristic God, is almost entirely passionless. Interestingly, recognition of the positive redemptive value of tears occurs in just two parts of the Church before the rise of the cult of the *mater dolorosa* in eleventh-century Europe. It is found in the hymns of the Syrian Church and in some of the poems written by Irish monks in the heyday of Celtic Christianity. Gilbert Màrkus, a Dominican priest based in Edinburgh, has pointed to the prominence of this theme in a poem dating from around AD 750 and attributed to an Irish monk named Blathmac. It takes up the notion of keening – that extravagant display of grief involving weeping and wailing, beating and possibly even smearing the body with the blood of the deceased that characterized the mourning rituals of the Celts and is practised today by many African tribes. Anticipating Julian of Norwich, Blathmac pictures the whole of creation keening its Saviour.

> A stream of blood gushed forth – severe excess! –
> so that the bark of every tree was red;
> there was blood on the breasts of the world,
> in the tree-tops of every great forest.[32]

All suffering is in some way an experience of dying, whether to strength, health, vitality, independence and self-sufficiency or to peace and calmness of mind. In a wider sense, all life is a constant process of dying, not just in the physical sense as cells and tissue die and wear out but in terms of hopes and expectations dashed and unfulfilled, relationships soured and spoiled and old habits and attachments constantly having to be surrendered and given up. This is true even of the most positive experiences in life such as falling in love. As Thomas Merton has observed, 'We have to become, in some sense, the person we love. And this involves a kind of death of our own being, our own self'.[33]

At the heart of this constant process of dying in order to allow new life in is the liberating power of sacrifice which is released through surrender and letting go. This power can be felt by those undergoing the experience of unwanted suffering, as Paul Fiddes has discerned. 'The suffering that befalls us can be embraced as a means of dying to ourselves and our selfish preoccupations, of detaching ourselves from the possessions of life, and letting ourselves go into the "calm" of being.'[34] The liberation that comes from letting go, whether of attachments and feelings that have become encumbrances or of life itself when it has ceased to have purpose and meaning, is well described in a prayer by John Taylor, former Bishop of Winchester:

> Father,
> if the hour has come
> to make the break,
> help me not to cling,
> even though it feels like death.
> Give me the inward strength
> of my Redeemer, Jesus Christ,
> to lay down this bit of life
> and let it go,
> So that I and others may be free
> to take up whatever new and fuller life
> you have prepared for us,
> now and hereafter.[35]

Seen in these terms, any kind of dying, including the ultimate experience of death itself, assumes the essential sacrificial role of bringing us to our destination and leading us home to God. Thomas Merton was surely right to characterize Christian hope as 'the acceptance of life in the midst of death, not because we have courage, or light, or wisdom to accept, but because by some miracle the God of life Himself accepts to live in us at the very moment we descend into death'.[36] In a similar way St Francis of Assisi, tormented by blindness and physical suffering, looks forward to death as a homecoming:

> And thou most kind and gentle death,
> Waiting to hush our latest breath,
> O praise him, Alleluia!

Thou leadest home the child of God,
And Christ our Lord the way hath trod.
O praise him, O praise him,
Alleluia! Alleluia! Alleluia![37]

For Christians the Cross is, of course, the key to under-standing death in these positive terms. It is through Christ's experience of passion, crucifixion and resurrection that the central sacrificial motif of suffering, dying and being reborn is both revealed and released in all its life-giving power. The Cross defies the wisdom of the world which is that death must be defied, cheated and kept at bay. On Calvary Jesus embraces and accepts death so that he may transfigure it through his resurrection. Herein lies the uniqueness of Christianity.

Christianity, alone among the religions and philosophies of the world, succeeds in eliciting from death, i.e. from the actuality of dying, a unique value, so that it is found to make a positive and necessary contribution to the perfec-tion of created life. Other philosophies of immortality sug-gest either that death is in some way unreal, or that it constitutes merely a release for the spirit through the drop-ping off of the material body. Not so Christianity. To it dying is an essential part or moment in that act through which love accomplishes the self-sacrifice which issues in eternal life. And thus physical death, in all its terrible uni-versality, becomes for the Christian a sacrament of the spiritual truth that, because it is love which saves, life must be lost before it can be fully won.[38]

Of all the Christian authors and theologians who have sought to elucidate the mystery at the heart of this paradox, St Paul surely stands out with his intense personal experience of entering into the dying and rising of Christ. It is significant that he makes his clearest statement on the subject in the context of a discussion of baptism, that most misunderstood

Christian sacrament which is as much about dying to old life as rising to new.

> Do you not know that all of us who have been baptized into Christ Jesus were baptized into his death? We were buried therefore with him by baptism into death, so that as Christ was raised from the dead by the glory of the Father, we too might walk in newness of life (Romans 6:3–4).

It is striking that the image Paul uses to describe our baptism into Christ is that of burial rather than the more usual one of drowning. We are brought back yet again to Jesus' own words about the need for the grain of wheat to fall into the ground and die if it is to bear fruit. Here we find not an explanation for the terrible mystery of suffering and pain but an affirmation of its sacrificial and redemptive value when transfigured and taken up in the double salvation event of the crucifixion and resurrection. The dying of suffering is integral to the living of the resurrection life.

> Cold as a tomb is the silent earth
> In which the Christ-seed is sown.
> There must it lie,
> There must it die,
> Before it sprouts and is grown.
>
> Lonely and dark are the dreadful depths
> To which our souls can descend.
> There must we lie,
> There must we die,
> Before we rise in the end.[39]

10

Making the sacrifice complete

The theme of this book has been the power and centrality of the principle of sacrifice which lies at the very heart of the being of God and animates the entire created world. I have tried to show the fundamental fallacy and heresy of the view still evident in much church teaching and thinking which regards sacrifice primarily as something done by humans to God in an attempt to placate, persuade or propitiate him. In order to rid ourselves of this heresy we need to return to the scriptures of the Old and New Testaments and draw on the writings of that great pantheon of Christian thinkers down the ages who have understood the God-given and God-centred power of sacrifice. We can also learn much from the findings of modern science that evolution depends on surrender and self-limitation and that life proceeds from death. I have argued that creation as much as redemption is a work of sacrifice for God and that his whole nature is not just to suffer in compassion with his creatures but continually to offer himself to them in costly self-giving. More radically, I have suggested that divine omnipotence is limited and constrained by the power of sacrifice and that the supreme salvific event of Jesus' passion and death has both an inevitability and a necessity that link it with all the unwanted suffering in the world.

Throughout this book I have drawn extensively on insights and concepts from other religious traditions, most notably, perhaps, from the Vedic scriptures of Hinduism. Its central thesis, however, derives first and foremost from an understanding of the Cross of Christ as the supreme expression of the awesome power of sacrifice both in the heart of the

Trinitarian Godhead and in the world in which Jesus lived and which he continues to perfect and redeem. The Cross reveals sacrificial love, with all its cost and pain, as the dynamic which moves and powers the Trinity. This eternal offering of mutual love within the Godhead is reciprocated and echoed in the ceaseless process of sacrifice which gives order and purpose to creation, constantly bringing wholeness out of brokenness, strength out of suffering and life out of death. With its unique power to evoke a response, the Cross both calls and draws us into a heedless participation in that process.

All this is very well in theory but what does it mean for us in practice as Christians (or, for that matter, as Hindus, Jews, Buddhists or adherents to other faiths which have a sense of the centrality and power of sacrifice) living in a culture which is not just indifferent but positively inimical to the sacrificial principle? The values of Western society, and increasingly also of the so-called developing world, at the tail end of the twentieth century are the antithesis of those which were preached by Jesus and proclaimed so starkly and so clearly on the Cross. We regard surrender and letting go as signs of weakness rather than strength. We laud freedom of choice and individual rights and shun notions of limitation, restraint and obligation. In the words of Robert Jeffery, 'Our world is brought up on the language of self-fulfilment, of avoidance of repression and the need for personal satisfaction. It is a consumers' world where everyone tells us we should have what we want.... We are encouraged to think that competition is a good thing and that all that really matters is effective productivity. This is not the hidden life of Christ'.[1]

It is all too easy to produce a catalogue of indicators which show how far both the principle and practice of sacrifice have disappeared from contemporary British life. Many charities and voluntary bodies struggle to find helpers as the ethic of gratuitous service for the common good has increasingly come to be replaced by the notion that there is a price for everything and you should never do something for nothing. Independent television companies have recently abandoned their 'telethons' to raise money for good causes because of reduced giving in recent years as a result of the modern phenomenon known as 'compassion fatigue'. Faced with a growing gap between rich and poor, most politicians refuse to contemplate a more redistributive tax regime, prompting one newspaper editorial to ask 'Has the concept of self-sacrifice to help the less advantaged, or to promote common good, really passed into quaint antiquity?'[2]

Yet there are also signs that the mood may be changing. We are increasingly aware of the human and social cost of the new ethic of self-gratification and fulfilment in terms of the breakdown of the family as an institution, rising levels of alcohol and drug dependency and increasing instances of greed and corruption in business and public life. We are also becoming more and more conscious of the harm that our refusal to practise the kind of self-limitation and restraint found in other species is doing to the environment. Far from making us happier and more fulfilled, abandonment of the principle of sacrifice in order to live primarily for ourselves seems to have made us more neurotic and dissatisfied with life. We find ourselves looking with growing envy at the relative social harmony and lack of stress in supposedly more primitive societies where the sacrificial principle is still taken very seriously.

Recognizing the benefits of self-limitation and restraint is one thing: radically altering our expectations and lifestyles so that they are in line with the great sacrificial principle which derives from God and which drives the world is quite another matter. It will certainly not be easy. There is nothing very attractive about sacrificial behaviour – nor, if we are honest, is there often anything very noble about it either. For the most part it is demanding, frustrating, boring and unrewarding, however holy it may also be in the eyes of the saint or the theologian. It means almost always taking the more difficult option and the one that we would often rather avoid: as a parent, for example, giving our children our time rather than another video, an ethic of self-restraint rather than a packet of condoms. A life which is lived sacrificially will be characterized by personal disadvantage and marginalization.

Are we then driven back to William Temple's conclusion that there is no point in talking about sacrifice because it is altogether too demanding? Maybe the times are now, in fact, more auspicious for an awakening to both its power and necessity at individual, national and international level. It is true that the message is more likely to be conveyed through social dislocation or environmental catastrophe than through the words of any preacher or prophet. We live in troubled times when the forces of disorder and chaos in the physical and the moral sphere seem to be particularly near the surface. There is a sense of living in a world that is spinning out of control. We no longer feel that we have the answer to every question and the mastery over every other part of creation. Gradually we are conceding that the world is full of mysteries and wonders that we cannot entirely fathom and reduce to scientific formulae. We are increasingly conscious of our interdependence with the rest of life on the planet and perhaps even of our dependence on something outside of ourselves if we are to survive and continue.

This shattering of our sense of self-sufficiency and ability to master and dominate every situation is the crucial first step towards recovering a conviction of the power and centrality of sacrifice. More basically, of course, it is the key to regaining the religious faith that we have largely discarded. In her book, *Sacrifice and the Death of Christ*, Frances Young identifies the growth of a spirit of self-sufficiency as the main reason for the loss of religious faith in the Western world over the last 150 years. In fact, as she points out, our highly complex technology and differentiated forms of social organization make us much more dependent on others than is the case in simpler, more self-sufficient societies. Yet we do not feel dependent on any divine or unseen powers. It is, of course, such a sense of dependence that lies behind the human practice of sacrifice, whether it be primitive tribes making an offering to the nature deities in the hope of securing good weather or Christians worshipping God as the creator and sustainer of all.

The twenty years since Frances Young wrote her book have, I think, witnessed a considerable weakening in that sense of self-sufficiency that she rightly sees as fundamentally inimical to the spirit of sacrifice and the practice of worship. We are less certain now about our ability to dominate and control everything unaided and about our mastery over our own lives and the physical environment in which we live. We perhaps have more sense of our frailty and dependence – certainly we have much more sense of the frailty and interdependence of life on our planet. Of course, there is a terrible danger that this can lead us simply to nihilism and despair and to a kind of paralysis in the face of seemingly inevitable disaster. This is one side of feeling dependent, but there is another much more positive side which expresses itself in a sense of wonder and awe in the face of the marvels and mysteries of the world in which we live and a profound sense of thanksgiving and gratitude for it. For all the brutalizing reductionism of video arcades and the gameboy culture, children still respond to the message of modern worship songs like 'Who put the colours in the rainbow' and 'Carpenter, carpenter, make me a tree, that's the work of somebody far greater than me'. Maybe, as scientists point increasingly to the extraordinary fragility and beautiful complexity of matter, all of us are more inclined to look at the world with childlike eyes and to see it as an enchanted place.

This sense of the sacramentality of the universe is, of course, intimately bound up with an understanding of the transfiguring power of sacrifice. It is by appreciating the sacredness of physical matter that we can begin to understand the creative and redeeming power centred in God and transmitted throughout his world to make holy through offering and giving up. Then perhaps we will recover the natural religious sense of our ancestors which led them to offer sacrifices of praise and thanksgiving to divine and unseen powers, not primarily to curry favour but as a spontaneous human response to the wonderful gifts of someone greater than themselves. In so doing, we will have rediscovered worship as a primary human activity.

It is often said that modern 'advanced' societies have lost the ability to worship. In some ways, of course, we worship too much – money, possessions, status, leisure and so many other selfish gods. What we do not worship any longer, at least as far as the majority is concerned, is anything or anybody outside ourselves, a being or power on whom we acknowledge our utter dependence and whose gratuitous and unceasing love and care fills us with an overwhelming desire to offer praise and thanksgiving. Yet here again there has been a discernible shift of emphasis in the last few decades. There is a much greater sense of the numinous, the spiritual dimension of life and the presence of an unseen power in our midst. This has found expression in many different forms of worship, among them techniques of meditation and other practices from Eastern religions and more sinisterly in an upsurge of Satanism and black magic. Perhaps its most widespread and significant manifestation in the West, however, has been an enormous movement of liturgical and spiritual revival within Christianity, both inside and outside the institutional churches. The rise of the charismatic movement, the huge influence of the meditative chants and incarnational songs of the Taizé and Iona communities, the boom in retreats and quiet days and the explosion of new liturgical material for children and all-age groups point to the great revival in worship that is currently taking place in the life of Christian communities everywhere.

A revival of interest in worship could well betoken a reawakened appreciation of the importance of the idea of sacrifice. For, as Stephen Sykes has pointed out, it is only in the context of worship that sacrifice assumes its theological significance: 'The only adequate reason for recognizing in sacrifice the central notion, or one of the central notions, of a systematic Christian theology lies in the centrality of worship for the Christian tradition. A theology of sacrifice will be, therefore, a theology in which worship plays a central role'.[3]

At the heart of any new sacrificial theology which is to come out of the current reinvigoration of Christian worship must be a recovery of the notion of the sacrifice of praise. This is the work to which Christians are clearly called in the Bible: 'Through him [Jesus] then let us continually offer up a sacrifice of praise to God that is the fruit of lips that acknowledge his name' (Hebrews 13:15–16). Hand in hand with this offering of praise goes a more physical offering of self-sacrificial behaviour: 'Do not neglect to do good and to share what you have, for such sacrifices are pleasing to God' (Hebrews 13:17). It is significant, however, that it is the spiritual offering that comes first. So it has long been regarded by writers on spirituality and devotion. For James Sibbald, minister of St Nicholas Church in Aberdeen in the 1630s, 'The proper sacrifice of Christians is the sacrifice of praise and thanksgiving, everywhere vehemently urged in the New Testament. . . . By the right performance of this duty, we begin our heaven on earth, for the proper exercise of heaven is praise'.[4]

The portrayal of Christian worship as a sacrifice of praise offered to God has been a favourite theme of hymnwriters. It is the inspiration for the much-loved morning hymn penned by James Sibbald's near-contemporary, Thomas Ken, for the boys of Winchester College:

> Awake, my soul, and with the sun
> Thy daily stage of duty run,
> Shake off dull sloth and joyful rise
> To pay thy morning sacrifice.

Robert Bridges' marvellously uplifting adaptation of the seventeenth-century German hymn *'Meine hoffnung stehet feste'* ends with the ringing affirmation:

> Still from man to God eternal
> Sacrifice of praise be done,
> High above all praises praising
> For the gift of Christ his Son.

A modern hymn by G. B. Timms, found in the *New English Hymnal* and based on lines by an eighteenth-century author, William Drennan, picks up the primal theme of the sacrificial altar as the place where heaven and earth meet:

> Where the appointed sacrifice
> Of worship, praise and fervent prayer,
> Ascends from earth unto the skies,
> The very gate of heaven is there.

Perhaps the finest hymnic evocation of the concept is to be found in Folliott Sandford Pierpoint's simple call to give thanks to God for the beauties of the world:

> For the beauty of the earth,
> For the beauty of the skies,
> For the love which from our birth
> Over and around us lies;
> Christ, our God, to thee we raise
> This our sacrifice of praise.

It is a sign of the extreme unease felt by some Christians over the whole notion of sacrifice that the compilers of *Hymns Ancient and Modern* felt compelled to change the last two lines of this hymn to:

> Lord of all, to thee we raise
> This our grateful hymn of praise.

As with so many other aspects of spirituality, we can usefully draw on our Celtic Christian heritage to help us recover the notion of the sacrifice of praise. In his book, *Praise Above All*, Donald Allchin has identified the offering up of praise as lying at the heart of the Celtic tradition in general and Welsh poetry in particular. From the early Christian centuries right up to the present day he finds a distinctive genre of Welsh praise poems, conceived as sacrificial offerings of thanksgiving to God for the world which is his gift. As Allchin comments, pure praise is something that we find difficult to handle in our society where reductionism is so prevalent and the writer's task is so often to belittle or explain away. Our problem, he suggests, is that we no longer see praise in a religious context – as an aspect of worship in which we refer all things back to their creator and see them again lit up by the light of his glory. Praise is a recognition and celebration of the goodness of God's world and its essential sacramentality.

> Seen in this perspective the task of the priest and the task of the poet are very closely allied. Both are called, in different ways, to bless; and to bless (*benedicere*) in its original meaning is to speak good things, to declare the goodness which is latent in the world around us, when that world is seen and known as the world of God. Both are called to offer up a sacrifice of praise and thanksgiving and, as Augustine makes plain, a sacrifice is any action in which things are made over to God, restored to him, so that from his uncreated holiness their own created holiness may be made manifest and renewed.[5]

Recovering this notion of the sacrifice of praise, not as a mere man-made work but as a reciprocal giving back to God in mutual love what he has already given to his creation, is vital to the reinvigoration of Christian worship. It is also fundamental to the renewal of the Church. Colin Gunton is right to suggest that 'the church's primary way of embodying the sacrifice of Jesus is – consistently with the early metaphorical use of the word sacrifice in the Psalms – as a community of praise'.[6] This does not mean a self-indulgent and inward looking approach. Quite the reverse, in fact. 'Worship is enjoying God. In worship our attention is directed away from ourselves, to God and to our neighbour. We do not "enjoy ourselves" in worship, indeed the very opposite; at the start we look at ourselves honestly and confess our sins; *then* as forgiven sinners we can cease to be absorbed by self and open out to God and His glory, and our neighbour and his needs'.[7]

The notion of the 'sacrifice of praise' is not, of course, foreign to those who worship in most mainstream churches today. The phrase occurs in the great thanksgiving prayer in most contemporary eucharistic liturgies. The first eucharistic prayer in the Rite A Order for Holy Communion in the Church of England Alternative Service Book (hereafter referred to as the ASB), for example, asks God to accept through Christ, our great high priest, 'this our sacrifice of thanks and praise'. The second prayer makes the same plea in more truncated form, 'through him accept our sacrifice of praise', while the third contains the words: 'We pray you to accept this our duty and service, a spiritual sacrifice of praise and thanksgiving'.[8] The prayer after the unveiling of the elements in the first order for Holy Communion in the Church of Scotland's 1994 Book of Common Order uses a slightly different formula, asking God that 'We, approaching you with pure heart and cleansed conscience, may offer you a sacrifice of righteousness'. The second and third orders contain the more familiar plea 'Most gracious God, accept this our sacrifice of praise and thanksgiving'.[9] Virtually identical phraseology is to be found in the great thanksgiving prayer in the Church in Wales' order for the Holy Eucharist in modern language: 'We ask you to accept our sacrifice of thanks and praise'.[10]

The communion service is, indeed, the one place where the language of sacrifice is still regularly employed by virtually all churches. In a way this is surprising given the terrible controversy which the use of the word in the context of eucharistic theology has caused among Christians over the last five hundred years and more. A brief survey of communion hymns indicates both the ubiquity of the concept and also the wide range of meanings and applications which it has been given. Several speak directly of Christ in sacrificial terms. Thus Arthur Wotherspoon's 'O Christ, who sinless art alone' describes Jesus as 'our sacrifice and priest' and James Montgomery's 'According to thy gracious word' is addressed to 'Lamb of God, my sacrifice'. Authors of a more catholic persuasion seek to give a sacrificial emphasis to the elements and the action of the eucharist itself. In 'Almighty Father, Lord most high' Vincent Coles notes that:

> What on the cross he offered up
> Is here our sacrifice indeed.

A more directly sacrificial interpretation of the eucharistic elements is expressed in James Quinn's translation of a hymn by Thomas Aqunias:

> Jesus in form of bread and wine
> His loving sacrifice displays,

and similar imagery occurs in the second verse of Josiah Conder's 'Bread of heaven, on thee we feed':

> Vine of heaven, the blood supplies
> This blest cup of sacrifice.

Writers of a more consciously Protestant and evangelical persuasion have tended to use sacrificial language in communion hymns to stress the total efficacy and self-sufficiency of Jesus' atoning death. Thus John MacLeod's 'In love, from love, thou camest forth, O Lord' speaks of 'the one, pure, perfect, filial sacrifice' and Charles Wesley conveys a similar sense of the self-sufficiency of Jesus' sacrifice in his eucharistic hymn, 'O God of our forefathers, hear';

> With solemn faith we offer up,
> And spread before thy glorious eyes
> That only ground of all our hope
> That all-sufficient sacrifice,
> Which brings thy grace on sinners down,
> And perfects all our souls in one.

Controversy surrounding the application of the word 'sacrifice' to the eucharist has contributed so much to the scandal of division in Christ's Church through the centuries that one might have thought it best if it was quietly dropped from current discussions of the subject and contemporary liturgical texts. Some voices have indeed been raised to this effect but they are in a small minority. The general view among both theologians and liturgists is, in fact, that if anything the concept and language of sacrifice needs to be more central in our thinking about the meaning of the Eucharist and in the orders used for its celebration. Kenneth Stevenson, one of the Church of England's leading contemporary liturgists, has argued that 'sacrifice, so far from being an outdated way of understanding the Eucharist, lies at the very heart of what we are doing at the Lord's Table'.[11] Significantly, this is not just a view being expressed in Anglican and Roman Catholic circles, although it has received strong support from both those quarters as shown in recent statements from the Anglican Roman Catholic International Commission (ARCIC). It is increasingly also being articulated by those coming from a Reformed and more evangelical position: witness Colin Gunton's proposal that 'we shall begin a reshaping of the conceptuality of communion by a return to the metaphor or sacrifice'.[12]

I believe that by focusing anew on sacrifice, not in metaphorical terms but as the actual power which energises both God and his creation, we can find a shared and truly ecumenical understanding of the Eucharist as the central action of Christian worship. Fundamental to this understanding is the point to which I have returned again and again throughout this book: that all sacrifice has its source and origin in God. Seen in this perspective, the Eucharist is first and foremost the action of a sacrificing God. It is not primarily, as the churches have so often seemed to suggest, a sacrifice made by us to God nor a re-enactment by us of Christ's sacrifice to God. Therein lies the great heresy of propitiation. Of course there is a reciprocity of giving and offering in the Eucharist but the initial movement is from God to us and not vice versa. It expresses here and now what the Cross instantiated in history and what Christ's continuing high priesthood manifests eternally – the perpetual sacrifice of God who gives himself unsparingly to his creatures through his Son.

Seen in this way, the Eucharist has a dynamic character. First it involves us in receiving and acknowledging God's sacrifice, then we participate in it through Christ and finally we respond to it with out own sacrifice. The great weakness with all eucharistic liturgies as they are at present is that they largely fail to incorporate this first and fundamental stage of acknowledging God's sacrifice and so have a largely static character. They still lean towards the heresy that sacrifice, including the sacrifice of the Eucharist, is primarily something that we do to God and betray an essentially propitiatory position.

This point has been very well made by Nicol Blount, an Anglican layman with long experience in the Bristol diocese, in a privately published pamphlet which deserves a wider circulation, 'The Eucharist – not a static concept'. Its starting point is a profound sense of thanksgiving and praise for the gifts of a sacrificing God:

> All God's gifts – pleasures – freedom, whether they are found in nature, from or through our fellow man – near or far, are our Creator's continual sacrifice of himself to us. They 'become' this reality when we recognise/comprehend/appreciate that all things come from God and we then accept him cupped in our hand with awe, joy and thanksgiving.[13]

Mr Blount finds fault with contemporary eucharistic liturgies, and specifically with those in the Alternative Service Book of the Church of England, for failing to make enough of this aspect of sacrifice. He notes, for example, that 'there is impertinent insistence on making our offerings of praise and money before we accept God's gift of himself'.[14] He goes on to outline his objections to the ASB order for communion in more detail:

> There is a disproportionate emphasis on man's sacrificing and offering to God before and during the Eucharistic prayer. Precedence should be given to the receiving of

God's sacrifice of himself to man with thanksgiving.
Opportunity to explore and give thanks for 'all the blessings of this life' is lacking in the Eucharistic prayer....
The giving of God's self to be shared by mankind is not
apparent.... The notion of propitiation is perpetuated ...
God's sacrifice of himself to us in and through others is not
apparent.[15]

I think this is a very valid objection to virtually all contemporary eucharistic liturgies. It takes us back to the words of P.
T. Forsyth that I quoted near the beginning of this book (see
pp. 11–12). Our communion services do, indeed, display that
pagan strain he identified as having penetrated so deep into
Christian thought which conceives that 'it is God's one royal
work to accept sacrifice, and man's one saving duty to offer
it'. In our concern to be always at the centre of things and to
be ever actors rather than recipients, we have departed far
from the practices of the early Church and forgotten the original meaning of Eucharist which is, of course, thanksgiving.
We have come dangerously close to turning a sacrifice of
praise, in which the focus is on what God does for us, into a
man-made ritual in which the focus is on what we do to God.

I suspect that this development has less to do with medieval
Catholic notions of the sacrifice of the mass and other propitiatory notions that have crept into Christian worship over
the centuries than with a fundamental human unease about
being in a situation of passivity and receptiveness. We come
back to the importance of Vanstone's 'stature of waiting' and
of relating the circumstances of Christ's passion to our own
lives. We are back, too, to the importance of seeing the Son's
death on the Cross primarily as a revelation of the Father's
self-giving nature and therefore as a sacrifice which was
directed towards us rather than towards God. Nicol Blount is
surely right to say that here again our eucharistic liturgies
present the direction of this sacrifice the wrong way round
and that this is one of the main reasons why there has been so
much controversy over what exactly we do when we remember it. 'If Christ's sacrifice on Calvary can be regarded, not as

Christ's atoning sacrifice to God, but as the ultimate demonstration of God's continual sacrifice of himself to his creation from the beginning, the perennial problems with an understanding of the anamnesis do not arise – God gives himself now, and giving thanks, we can remember to discern and accept him at the Eucharist.'[16]

There are no references to God's sacrifice that I am aware of in any of the eucharistic liturgies presently in use by the mainstream churches. There are, indeed, few enough references to Christ's sacrifice and those that do occur tend to overstress its once-for-all nature and relate its purpose narrowly and exclusively to dealing with sin. These two features are conspicuously present in the Rite A Order for Holy Communion in the ASB. In the first eucharistic prayer the president says, 'We celebrate with this bread and this cup his one perfect sacrifice'. The third prayer speaks of Christ's 'perfect sacrifice made once for the sins of all men' and the fourth talks of him 'offering once for all his sacrifice of himself'.[17] I profoundly hope that those responsible for future reworkings of the eucharistic liturgy will feel able to put more stress on both the revelatory and the on-going aspects of Christ's sacrifice and so convey the truth that it is much more than a remedy for sin and is rather indicative and declaratory of the essential and eternal character of God.

With this starting point established, the Eucharist can have a much more dynamic character. Having first acknowledged and received God's sacrifice, his people then participate in it through sharing in Christ. In the sacrament of communion we are not imitating or repeating Christ's sacrifice but nor are we just acknowledging and recalling it. In the words of the ARCIC statement on the Eucharist, 'we enter into the movement of his self-offering'.[18] This is, of course, how Jesus himself put it to his disciples: 'The cup that I drink you will drink, and with the baptism with which I am baptised you will be baptised' (Mark 10:39). Communion, like baptism, is a sharing in Christ's death and resurrection. It is much more than a mere memorial of these events. As I have already suggested, when Jesus broke bread and passed round the cup of wine at the last supper and told his disciples, 'Do this in remembrance of me', he was surely thinking of 'remember' as the opposite of dismember rather than as the opposite of forget. What he asked of them, and what he asks of all of us who come to his holy table, is not that we simply recall his sacrifice but rather that we engage in the infinitely costly and painful task of remembering his shattered, broken body. That body incorporates our fragile and troubled world, the Church with its divisions and prejudices and ourselves in all our weakness.

This corporate and participatory dimenion needs to be more firmly embedded in modern eucharistic liturgies. We come to the communion table as members of the body of which Christ is the head, or as the Book of Common Prayer so beautifully puts it, as 'very members incorporate of the mystical body of thy Son which is the blessed company of all faithful people'. We come too as broken people to share and partake in elements which are also broken, the wine made by bruising and crushing the grape and the bread produced by pounding and milling the grains of wheat that have grown from the corn buried in the earth. The body on which we feed is likewise broken, the blood which we drink is spilt and poured out. There are strong echoes here of primal sacrifcal ritual with its purpose of bringing life out of death, wholeness out of brokenness and order out of chaos through the dark mysterious power of the shedding of blood and the surrender of that which is precious and valuable. We are reminded of the Hindu conception of the temple as a sacred space in which all that has been scattered and dismembered is brought back together again (see p. 70). We are reminded too that the one who is the founder of the feast, the celebrant and high priest, the head of the body of which we are members is also himself the suffering servant, the sacrificial victim and the wounded healer. What we share in when we receive communion has elements of tragedy as well as triumph. We are drawn into the fellowship of suffering as well as to the sure and certain hope of resurrection.

As well as stressing its corporate dimension, we need to

make more of the cosmic aspect of the Eucharist. The Lima Liturgy, drawn up by Max Thurian, a brother at Taizé for the 1982 plenary session of the Faith and Order Commission of the World Council of Chuches, is surely right in its affirmation that 'the eucharist is the great sacrifice of praise by which the Church speaks on behalf of the whole creation'.[19] We come back here to the point made by Nugent Hicks in his book *The Fullness of Sacrifice* (see p. 207): in celebrating the Eucharist, the Church is not simply offering up the sacrifice of praise of those who are communicating, nor even of the whole Christian community. It is also offering up the sacrifices (and I would add the suffering) of the whole world, conscious and unconscious, Christian and non-Christian alike.

Every true moral effort, every acknowledged failure, is equally part of the process of the full sacrifice of which the Eucharist is the symbol and the expression. By some the effort is made in a Christian consciousness already clear; and, for them, their part in the eucharistic approach is also clear. But there are many for whom the goal to which they are moving has not yet stamped itself in the recognised form of the Cross of Christ. It may be to them nothing more explicit than a general idea of self-denial and self-discipline. The Church can make its approach along the first steps of sacrifice on their behalf, as it can make its offering also to include the unconscious offering and self-dedication of many who could not find for themselves Christian words for the Christian things they are doing.[20]

The Lima liturgy's reference to the Church speaking on behalf of the rest of creation also reminds us of the priestly role which we have as humans with respect to the other creatures in the world. It may well be that the so-called dumb animals and the apparently insentient plants do in fact offer up their own sacrifice of praise to their creator. Indeed, the Hebrew prophets and psalmists suggest as much when they speak of the trees of the field clapping their hands and the mountains skipping like rams. Human beings, however, have a special consciousness of and relationship with God and are perhaps appointed by him to be the high priests of creation, offering up the praise and thanksgiving as well as the groaning and travail of the whole cosmos. Certainly that is how George Herbert saw it:

> Of all creatures both in sea and land
> Only to man thou hast made known thy ways,
> And put the pen alone into his hand,
> And made him secretary of thy praise.
>
> Beasts fain would sing; birds ditty to their notes;
> Trees would be tuning on their native lute
> To thy renown: but all their hands and throats
> Are brought to Man, while they are lame and mute.
>
> Man is the world's High Priest; he doth present
> The sacrifice for all: while they below
> Unto thy service mutter an assent,
> Such as springs use that fall, and winds that blow.[21]

Herbert's vision is clouded by the besetting human sin of anthropocentrism. I suspect that if the truth be known the 'ditties' of the birds may represent a purer and more spontaneous sacrifice of praise to their maker than our own somewhat grudging and hesitant efforts. Perhaps the anonymous author of a ninth-century Irish poem was nearer the mark when he wrote:

> Only a fool would fail
> To praise God in his might,
> When the tiny mindless birds
> Praise him in their flight.[22]

This cosmic dimension of the Eucharist is important because it helps us to keep in mind the essential sacramentality of the universe, to find the sacred in the material and the spiritual in the physical. It also reminds us that we are put into the world not to dominate or exploit it but rather to offer it up to God. This was the conviction that inspired the great Mass over the world which Teilhard de Chardin celebrated in the Chinese desert in 1923. If we are to save our planet we badly need to recover this sacramental perspective and with it the sacrificial understanding that it is through restraint, limitation and giving up that things are made holy.

We cannot altogether escape from the echoes of primal and pre-Christian rites that the Eucharist evokes. Nor should we. At the heart of primal religion, as we have seen, was an understanding of sacrifice as communion. It was on the sacrificial altar that time and eternity met and human beings encountered the gods as the ascending odour of fresh blood and burnt flesh mingled with the descending fragrance of divine approbation. This primal metaphysical encounter between earth and heaven also takes place at the Christian communion table. The great difference is that now God has come down to earth and it is his Son, at once the sacrificial victim and the eternal high priest, that we meet there. Once again, we are brought back to the key feature of the Christian understanding of sacrifice over and against the pagan view. The initiative lies firmly with God. The sacrifice is his through Christ and it is his real presence that we encounter when we partake of the Eucharist.

> We need not now go up to heaven
> To bring the long-sought Saviour down;
> Thou art to all already given,
> Thou dost e'en now thy banquet crown:
> To every faithful soul appear,
> And show thy real presence here.[23]

> Here, O my Lord, I see thee face to face;
> Here would I touch and handle things unseen,
> Here grasp with firmer hand the eternal grace,
> And all my weariness upon thee lean.[24]

The understanding that Christ is somehow present in the

Eucharist is fundamental to Christian belief, however this presence is conceived. It seems to me that this understanding is only possible if we hold to a view of his eternal and continuing priesthood. Through participation in the Eucharist we unite ourselves with the ongoing sacrifice of Christ. For Charles Gore the glory of the Eucharist lay in the fact that 'God has united the offerings of the church to the ever-living sacrifice of the great High Priest in the heavenly sanctuary'.[25] The same point is made in one of Charles Wesley's great eucharistic hymns:

> With him, the Corner-stone,
> The living stones conjoin;
> Christ and his Church are one,
> One body and one vine;
> For us he uses al his powers,
> And all he has, or is, is ours.[26]

This theme is strong in Eastern Orthodox theology where there is a clear understanding that in the Eucharist 'we are raised above our human, earthly plane to contemplate the perpetual self-offering of the Lamb of God. . . . He suffered once on earth and He offers continually His death to the Father on the heavenly altar. . . . Our Eucharist is the true representation of His true and continuous sacrifice, once for all time offered on the earth – on Golgotha – and perpetually presented to the Father on our behalf in Eternity'.[27] We badly need to recover this concept in contemporary Western Christianity and express it in our eucharistic liturgies. Its focus on the eternal and perpetual offering of Christ cuts through the bitter and sterile arguments that have raged for so long over the one-for-all sufficiency of the sacrifice on Calvary and its representation or renactment in the Eucharist. It is the eternal, sacrificial activity of the resurrected and ascended Christ, and through him of God, with which the Eucharist connects and links his body on earth. There is no sense of repeating the unique historical sacrifice on Calvary. Once again, one of Charles Wesley's eucharistic hymns which is particularly replete with sacrificial imagery makes this plain:

> Thou Lamb that sufferedst on the tree,
> And in that dreadful mystery
>   Still offerest up thyself to God,
> We cast us on thy sacrifice,
> Wrapped in the sacred smoke arise,
>   And covered with the atoning blood
>
> For us he ever intercedes,
> His heaven-descending passion pleads
>   Presenting us before the throne;
> We want no sacrifice beside,
> By that great Offering sanctified,
>   One with our Head, for ever one.[28]

Perhaps the finest poetic expression of this theme is to be found in the eucharistic hymn written in 1873 by William Bright:

> And now, O Father, mindful of the love
>   That bought us, once for all, on Calvary's tree,
> And having with us him that pleads above,
>   We here present, we here spread forth to thee
> That only offering perfect in thine eyes,
> The one true, pure, immortal sacrifice.

I find it very significant, and also very moving, that this hymn should have provided the basis for the deep agreement on the doctrine of eucharistic sacrifice that existed between two of the greatest theological minds in twentieth-century Scotland. Donald Mackinnon, an Anglo-Catholic, and Thomas Torrance, a staunchly Reformed Presbyterian, might not be expected to find common ground on a subject that has provoked so much bitter disagreement since the Reformation. They did so, however, on the basis of a shared appreciation of Bright's hymn and a conviction that, in the words of Torrance, 'the eucharistic rite does not halt with participation in the body and blood of Christ (as in Western liturgies), but reaches into the self-offering of the risen and ascended Christ in his high-priestly intercession before the face of the Father'.[29]

So far as I know, there is only one contemporary Western eucharistic liturgy which makes explicit reference to the ongoing sacrifice of Christ. The great thanksgiving prayer in both the first and third orders for Holy Communion in the Church of Scotland's new Book of Common Order contains the phrase (which is also found in earlier books), 'Remembering his work and passion, and pleading his eternal sacrifice, we follow his example and obey his command'.[30] It would be good to see an acknowledgement of this dimension of Christ's sacrifice, which is surely so vital to a proper understanding of the meaning and significance of the Eucharist, in the communion services of other churches. Better still would be a wider acknowledgement of the perpetual sacrificial activity of God. Then the Eucharist would embody the truth so clearly stated by Paul Fiddes:

> We are responding not only to one past act, but to the way that God goes on offering himself into human lives, constantly entering the pain and predicament of human experience. He calls us into a partnership of sacrifice, into a friendship which makes all life festivity, without ignoring its pain and sorrow.[31]

This call into the partnership of sacrifice leads us to the third and final stage of the Eucharist. After acknowledging and receiving God's sacrifice and uniting ourselves with the eternal sacrifice of Christ comes our own sacrificial offering of ourselves in response. There is, of course, an intimate connection between these three activities. They follow one another both naturally and necessarily as F. D. Maurice points out:

> Must not the presentation of the one real perfect Sacrifice to the Father, the continual thanksgiving for that sacrifice, be the central act of all worship to God – of all fellowship

among men? Must not the offering of the worshipper's soul and body as living sacrifices to God be the necessary fruit and accompaniment of this act, that which gives meaning to all the greatest and meanest services – to the most transcendent and the commonest acts of life?[32]

It has to be said that in expressing this third and final movement in the dynamic of the Eucharist almost all contemporary liturgies and orders serve us well. Most still closely follow the beautiful language of the first post-communion prayer in the Book of Common Prayer which is, of course, itself closely modelled on the words of Romans 12: 1: 'Here we offer and present unto thee, O Lord, ourselves, our souls and bodies to be a reasonable, holy, and lively sacrifice unto thee'. This formula is preserved, albeit in sadly truncated form, in the post-communion prayer in the Rite A Order for Holy Communion in the ASB: 'We offer you our souls and bodies to be a living sacrifice' and in the Church of Wales' 1984 Order for Holy Eucharist in modern language: 'We offer ourselves to you as a living sacrifice'.[33] The 1982 Liturgy of the Scottish Episcopal Church has a rather fuller version which is incorporated into the great thanksgiving: 'Made one with him, we offer you these gifts and with them ourselves, a single, holy, living sacrifice'.[34] The Church of Scotland's new Book of Common Order also puts its prayer of offering at the end of the great thanksgiving: 'Here we offer and present to you our very selves, to be a living sacrifice, dedicated and fit for your acceptance'.[35] For me one of the finest modern liturgical expressions of this part of the eucharistic offering, which also manages in the space of a short prayer to include the notion of the sacrifice of praise and thanksgiving and at least to hint at our participation in the eternal sacrifice of Christ, is to be found in the communion service of the American United Methodist Church:

> In remembrance of all your mighty acts
> in Jesus Christ,
> we ask you to accept this our sacrifice

of praise and thanksgiving
which we offer
in union with Christ's sacrifice for us
as a living and holy
surrender of ourselves.[36]

It is easy enough to offer ourselves in church on Sunday morning as a living and holy sacrifice: living this prayer out in practice through the week is a different matter. The difficulty does not lie in discerning what is involved but in carrying it out. It means a lifestyle which is based on the principles of limitation, restraint and surrender, holding back and giving rather than taking. The fact that this is precisely the kind of lifestyle to which we are all being called with an increasing sense of urgency by a growing body of scientists, 'alternative' economists and other experts concerned about our ability to sustain ourselves in the future does not make it any more palatable to us now. Costly and painful sacrifice characterizes the principles which pundits and prophets identify as crucial to the future survival and well-being of both our species and our planet: sustainability, integration, interdependence, holism, co-operation and community. Put forward on television chat shows and in the pages of Sunday supplements these buzz-words excite our imaginations. Once we realise their sacrificial implications, however, we shrink away from them in the spirit of Augustine's celebrated prayer, 'Give me chastity and continency – but not yet!'

How can Christians fulfil Jesus' calling to adopt a sacrificial lifestyle? The lesson of history is surely that this is best done through some kind of communal commitment. In our own times the idea of the Church as a body of people living modestly has inspired groups like the Life Style movement with its motto 'live more simply that all of us may simply live'. It was founded by Horace Dammers, an Anglican clergyman, after a Christian conference held in Birmingham in 1972 on the principle that 'living more simply, more frugally and thriftily, symbolises an inner transformation that liberates us for action'.[37] Those involved in the movement pledge themselves to restraint and limitation in their own personal consumption as well as to charitable giving and political action for peace and justice. A similarly disciplined and sacrificial approach characterizes the membership of the Iona Community and is also to be found in the burgeoning house church movement. With its strong similarities to the lifestyle of the first Christians as recorded in the Acts of the Apostles, it surely offers a model for the Church as a whole.

If the Church is to be a genuinely sacrificial community it must live and work in a spirit of brokenness and surrender and have as its role model the figure of the suffering servant rather than that of the triumphant king. This is not something that most churches find at all easy. We are happier being active and triumphalist than passive and sacrificial. We prefer launching appeals for new buildings to agonizing over what it means to be wounded healers and debating how we can extend the Sunday School roll or the new communicants class to working out the implications of our vocation as Christians to be broken that new life may come. With all its self-obsession, pomposity and complacency, the Church all too often presents an image which is in almost total opposition to the teaching of its founder. In the words of a contemporary critic, 'The world has no trouble believing in a man who sacrifically gave his life for others. What it cannot stomach are self-righteous, self-centred men who make a fortune out of preaching about a man who gave his life for others'.[38] This is a very valid criticism. Unless the Church as Christ's body itself more clearly bears the marks of suffering and the scars of sacrifice, it is hard to see how anyone will take its message seriously. It is only on the basis of practising Christ's sacrificial gospel that the Church can preach it with any authority.

Perhaps it is a consciousness of its own shortcomings in this regard that has made the contemporary Church so hesitant about preaching sacrifice. I suspect, however, that the lack of sermons on this subject has more do to with prevailing cultural values. Churches no less than other institutions have been profoundly affected by the self-centred 'me-too-ism' of the late twentieth century. Steve Chalke, the prominent evangelical campaigner and commentator who has called on the contemporary Church to adopt a more sacrificial lifestyle, has observed that 'in the United States, and increasingly in the United Kingdom, the Christian book market is flooded by hedonistic titles with themes such as "me and my quiet time", "me and my walk with the Lord", "me and my prayer life", "me and inner healing", "me and the gifts of the spirit" '.[39] Particularly, though by no means exclusively, in the newer evangelical churches and fellowships the accent seems to be much more on individual self-fulfilment through personal salvation and the 'feel-good' factor that follows from this than on Christ's uncomfortable but persistent call to a life of surrender, renunciation and self-giving. To quote Chalke again, 'The biblical concept of laying down our lives for others seems far removed from so much of what we now call "church". Perhaps we have emphasised the fun, fulfilment and fellowship aspects of Christianity to the detriment of the concept of sacrificial love'.[40]

At present many Christians do seem to be rather hesitant about preaching the power and importance of sacrifice. It is a theme that rarely appears in the religious press or in the texts of sermons and addresses by leading figures in the main churches. This is in marked contrast to the strong interest in and positive enthusiasm for the subject displayed by a number of prominent columnists in the 'secular' press.[41] Indeed, it is increasingly such pundits who are raising important moral and metaphysical questions and filling a vacuum which has perhaps been created by the churches' self-consciousness about appearing to preach or to raise 'difficult' religious issues.

It is true that some church leaders have been prompted to make strong statements on the need for sacrifice by the seriousness of the environmental crisis. A recent example is Pope John Paul II's message for World Peace Day 1991:

Modern society will find no solution to the ecological problem unless it takes a serious look at its life style. In many parts of the world society is given to instant gratification and consumerism while remaining indifferent to the damage which these cause. . . . Simplicity, moderation and discipline, as well as a spirit of sacrifice, must become a part of everyday life, lest all suffer the negative consequences of the careless habits of a few.[42]

This kind of utterance, however, is too broad and general in scope to have any real effect on people. There is a need to address and commend much more specific instances of sacrificial behaviour. Sticking to the environmental issue, for example, the Church could be actively supporting and encouraging those of its members, and those in the wider community, who are giving up commuting to work in their cars and turning to public transport in an effort to ease traffic congestion and curb the emission of poisonous gases. As I write this I have in front of me a newspaper cutting reporting that George Hazel, the transportation director of Lothian Regional Council, has decided to give up the parking space in the centre of Edinburgh that he gets as a perk of his job and travel to work by public transport: 'It is not going to be easy and I won't enjoy it', he is quoted as saying in an article which uses the word 'sacrifice' three times, 'but in all conscience I can't get in my car and drive to work when I am the head of a department that is urging everyone else to use public transport'.[43]

Significant gestures of this kind – and I suspect they may be becoming more common than we think – should be affirmed and supported by the churches as models of sacrificial behaviour. The recently formed Movement for Christian Democracy has already taken a commendable lead in seeking to raise the profile of concepts such as duty and responsibility in a political culture which is dominated by notions of freedom and rights. The churches as a whole could do more in this area, pointing, for example, to the widespread support that still exists in our increasingly privatized and fragmented society for public services and the idea of the common good and impressing on politicians of all parties the consistent finding of opinion polls that a majority of people would be prepared to pay higher taxes to maintain and improve education, health and welfare services.

All these arguments and campaigns can be greatly strengthened by being set in a global and cosmic context and related to an overarching ethical and philosophical framework. It is here that the churches have a special and distinctive role. We could do with recovering F. D. Maurice's conviction that 'the church exists to tell the world of its true Centre, of the law of mutual sacrifice by which its parts are bound together'.[44] The task for the churches now is to work out and proclaim a coherent, contemporary creed which acknowledges sacrifice as the supreme universal principle, the engine that makes the world go round and the power at the very heart of the Godhead. In more technically theological and specifically Christological terms, we want a new holistic theory of atonement which interprets the Cross in terms of sacrifice eternally begetting sacrifice and life continually coming out of death. As we have already seen, such a creed is in keeping with some of the major strands in late twentieth-century theology – patripassianism, process thought and the rediscovery of natural theology. It is strongly supported by recent discoveries in the physical and biological sciences. While distinctively Christian, it is also consonant with the growing consensus that is emerging between the world's great religions as a result of the interfaith movement. That consensus is exemplified in the life and teaching of Bede Griffiths, a Benedictine monk who spent much of his life in an Indian *ashram* and combined Christian spirituality with Vedic philosophy. When he died in 1993 an old friend commented, 'his message was one of wholeness, of surrender, of the transcending of separateness – both in terms of the ego, and of the rigid fundamentalism still inherent in so many faiths'.[45]

But if preaching a radical theology of sacrifice of the kind that I have outlined would bring the Church in line with many significant contemporary religious and intellectual movements, it would also involve taking a prophetic stance against most modern cultural and social values. Specifically it means confronting what the American writer Christopher

Lasch has described as 'the culture of narcissism' which dominates our age. As he points out, diminishing expectations, fear of the future and the end of optimism have had the effect of turning society in on itself (we are back to Luther's definition of sin as a state of being *incurvatus in se*) and making people more narrowly selfish and concerned simply with their own individual self-improvement. These values are encouraged by a shoal of popular magazines and television programmes which constantly invite us to ponder whether our relationships, sex lives, careers and homes are as satisfying, exciting or stimulating as they should be. As Professor Alan Torrance has observed, the poor reader or viewer finds himself drawn into a malignant process of self-analysis and introspection.

> Compelled by the fear that true self-fulfilment may irretrievably be slipping away from him in an all-too-fleeting lifespan he examines himself in order to discover whether he really is finding contentment in his life and relationships. Such questioning implies not only that self-fulfilment is, or at least ought to be, one's prime aim in life but also, rather more subtly, that the first step towards self-fulfilment lies in concerning oneself with it in such a way that introspective self-analysis serves as one's guide. As a result one can easily be caught up in a regressive, self-perpetuating 'attitude' of self-scrutiny. This whole process is initiated by a self-concern cultivated by popular journalism and advertising whose purpose in a competitive world is the fabrication of needs which only the proferred article or product can begin to satisfy.[46]

The religious creed of this new 'culture of narcissism' is to be found in the so-called New Age movement. One word constantly recurs in its list of goals and beliefs. It is about *self*-discovery, *self*-actualization, *self*-realization and *self*-transformation. Its key rituals and techniques include self-rebirthing, defined as 'getting to know and love your self' and channelling, in which messages from the spirit world are directed for individual consumption and self-improvement. A perceptive analysis of the diverse cults and groups that go to make up the movement in *Time* magazine commented: 'Somehow, the New Agers believe, there must be some secret and mysterious shortcut or alternative path to happiness and health. And nobody ever really dies'.[47] There is a widespread belief in reincarnation with the stress being on the self coming back again and again. It is significant that in so far as the New Age has a god, it is conceived of as a 'univesal transcendent Self' with whom we must get in tune.

Conscious adherence to New Age religion may not have spread far beyond the confines of California or Findhorn but its assumptions and values have penetrated deeply throughout Western society. We feel that life can be instantly and continually enjoyable and fulfilling. We are less and less ready to bear and put up with pain, misfortune, boredom and drudgery. We see health, wealth and happiness as rights rather than gifts and do our best to close our minds to the reality of suffering and death as though by not thinking about them they will disappear. In the words of Jürgen Moltmann, 'to be painlessly happy, and to conquer every form of suffering, is part of the dream of modern society'.[48]

Nothing could be further from the reality of a world which is animated and kept going by the power of sacrifice. Preaching this power, which is centred for Christians on the sacrificial process continuously at work at the heart of the Trinitarian Godhead and supremely realized in the Cross of Christ, puts the Church at odds with the whole thrust of modern culture. It means that there can be no synthesis of Christianity and New Age religion. Nor can the churches subscribe to the greast heresy of post-modernism and offer their wares in a 'pick and mix' selection so that individuals can build up their own self-tailored package of beliefs and rituals, taking on what seems appealing and discarding what they do not like. The message that we have to preach is one that most people do not particularly want to hear. It is about accepting and bearing pain and misfortune, facing the reality of death and finding it in the source of new being, thinking of life in terms of gifts rather than rights, being prepared to surrender, let go, limit desires and postpone wants, seeing beyond immediate self-gratification, acknowledging the existence of the other and feeling humble and dependent in the face of a power infinitely greater and more holy than that of the self.

One can see just how far the preaching of sacrifice would jar with the prevailing wisdom of our age by considering that ubiquitous four-letter word which still has considerable currency in both religious and secular parlance. I have long felt that the kernel of Christ's teaching, and the essence of Christian discipleship, can be summed up in the opening words of the Beatles' famous song, 'All you need is love'. The trouble is, of course, that the word 'love' has all sorts of different meanings. In the hugely influential world of pop music and television soaps it is a highly sexually charged and erotic commodity, often associated with possession, gratification and feelings of exclusivity and jealousy. Advertisers and marketing men portray it either as a perpetually sunny state of romance which is never clouded by doubts, troubles or disillusionment or as a self-directed want which can be instantly gratified. For most of us, as a result, love has connotations of having or possessing something or somebody. This is, of course, the antithesis of love as it was preached and practised by Christ and as it is understood in all the world's great religions. As Eberhard Jüngel has observed, 'In love there is no "having" which does not have its source in surrendering'.[49]

Christian love is costly, painful and endlessly self-giving. In a word it is sacrificial. In the words of Rowan Williams, 'the most clear and enduring mark of Christian identity is not (as has become fashionable in some quarters to suppose) a benevolence towards all and a generalized wish for their welfare, but an entirely costly *disponibilité*, availability in service which gives no room to the superficial interests of the ego'.[50] This kind of love is, of course, immensely difficult to practise. It drains our time, our spirits and our energies as well as our wallets. Steve Chalke has rightly observed that 'to love sacrificially is always inconvenient – it can't be scheduled in our diaries or neatly budgeted into our salaries. It forces us to change our plans, give up our privacy and our financial security. It often calls for us to part with whatever is most precious to us for the sake of others'.[51] It is hardly surprising that this kind of love is not one that we feel we need, particularly when we are living in a society which subscribes to a creed of maximum personal pleasure with minimum cost and pain. Other cultures have a rather different approach. In the Chinese language, for example, one is required to say love and pain in almost the same breath and the two concepts are indissolubly linked in the expression *thun-ai* (pain-love).[52] Contemporary Western societies, by contrast, have done their best to rid the word 'love' of any difficulty or costly connotations. The result, to quote Steve Chalke again, is that 'the Bible's concept of sacrificial love is a difficult one for us to grasp because our culture seems incapable of understanding that true personal fulfilment never comes as a result of self-gratification; it only comes through sacrifice'.[53]

Given the huge extent of this cultural gap, we come back to the question I posed earlier in this chapter: is there any point in trying to preach sacrifice in all its tragic starkness today? Isn't it all too negative and self-denying to make any contact with where people are now? Won't it simply further marginalize the churches and encourage the view that they are full of puritanical killjoys obsessed with death and giving things up? Yet if we are utterly convinced of the centrality and power of sacrifice in the world (and as Christians – or, indeed, as Jews or Hindus – we surely must be) then we cannot but preach it. The fact that our society has lost both the sense of and the taste for it should be a spur rather than a deterrent to our efforts.

As we have already noted, moreover, the mood of society is changing. The task of convincing our generation that sacrifice is the only route to the things that ultimately matter may not be as difficult as it might at first seem. It is not as though people are very happy with the results of the prevailing culture of unrestrained self-gratification. Virtually every social or psychological indicator one cares to take points to growing alienation and dissatisfaction in contemporary Western society. Levels of crime, divorce, drug dependency and depressive illness are all on the increase. It is more and more widely acknowledged that there is a direct connection between these indices of social and personal dislocation and the self-centred consumerist values which have been so dominant over the last thirty years or so. We may not yet be ready to change our ways as radically as we should but such is the depth of the malaise that affects our social, political and cultural institutions that we are at least, and at last, prepared to listen to hard and unpalatable truths about what has gone wrong and how we can begin to put things right. Dr Jonathan Sacks, the Chief Rabbi, has been less frightened than most leaders of the Christian community in Britain to call for a return to sacrificial values. This has not caused him to be dismissed as an out of touch fuddy-duddy. Indeed, when he declared in a television programme in September 1994 that the future survival of the family depended on 'one of the hardest things to attain – a love that involves discipline, effort and sacrifice' he struck a deep chord with many viewers and was widely praised in the media.

There are other more subtle aspects to our understanding of the contemporary malaise which are also conducive to a new appreciation of the healing power of sacrifice. We are increasingly aware of the phenomenon, long known to psychologists, of the tyranny of the self and the wholly illusory nature of freedom and licence. The growing number of lives wrecked by addiction, depression and utter boredom testify all too clearly to the truth that a lack of restraint and limitation can make us prisoners of ourselves and our brooding egos. In this context, when people are drowning and suffocating in their self-centredness, Jesus' words about the need to lose ourselves if we are to find ourselves take on a new meaning and relevance. So does the whole Christian paradox that it is in surrender and service to God that we find our true freedom and fulfilment.

The more we surrender our lives to God, the more true we become to ourselves. This may seem like a contradiction. If

I stop concentrating on myself, then surely I will lose out? In fact, we find that the reverse is true. As we give up concentrating on ourselves, our lives begin to reflect more clearly what it means to be human, as God intended us to be. Our lives become richer and more free as we give ourselves to God and to others. Relinquishing the self leads to maturity of the self in God.[54]

It should not just be by latching on to negative feelings about the failings of modern culture and society that we seek to convince our contemporaries of the power of sacrifice, however. As we have seen, it is an essentially positive force, creative, enabling, liberating and literally life-giving – the engine of evolution and the mechanism through which death is continually transfigured and transformed into life. The Church must accentuate this positive aspect and this means preaching the benefits of temperance, self-restraint, limitation and surrender and showing the essentially destructive quality of indulgence, excess, domination and exploitation. There is already, of course, a growing awareness of the truth of this message in respect of the environmental crisis but it needs to be extended to other areas of life. Sacrifice, as we have already observed, is intimately bound up with the bringing of order and harmony out of chaos in both the physical and the spiritual world. One of the clearest illustrations of its creative power, which could well be more widely expressed and celebrated by the Church, is in the whole realm of art. We could do with hearing and thinking more of the sacrifice that goes into the making of a symphony, a painting or a poem in terms of the artist's self-giving, limitation and surrender to convention and form. Indeed, we should also be celebrating the sacrifice that goes into the creation of a home-made casserole or fruit pie and which eschews the easy instant appeal of the supermarket freezer cabinet and the microwave.

Then there is the spiritual power of sacrificial love which even in our jaundiced and brutalized culture of compassion fatigue and video nasties can still move and inspire us. Arnold Toynbee was surely right when he identified Christianity's fundamental tenet as 'a belief that self-sacrificing love is both the best and the most powerful of all the spiritual influences that are known to us'.[55] In an age which is profoundly suspicious of heroes and hero worship and which finds most of the 'good and the great' to have feet of clay or skeletons in the cupboard, figures like Mother Teresa of Calcutta and Gordon Wilson, the Irish senator whose daughter died in the Enniskillen bomb blast, are almost universally admired for their selfless dedication to others. Dare I suggest that we need to tell more such stories of sacrificial lives both from our own times and from the past? I know that this sounds very old-fashioned, but I cannot help feeling that we have lost something very valuable by largely abandoning the practice which for so long prevailed in both Sunday Schools and weekday school history lessons of bringing children up on the heroic stories of martyrs and missionaries, saints and reformers. These stories taught helpful lessons and imparted important values. Our present reluctance to label anyone a hero, while having its good points, has not served our young very well when they are constantly presented with idols and role models from the world of pop music and television. In my experience, children now confuse heroism with celebrity and, hardly surprisingly, look up to those whose pictures adorn their magazines and favourite television programmes. Perhaps the time has come for us to introduce them to real heroes, past and present, and tell their stories of selflessness and sacrifice.

This is just part of what should be a wider agenda for the churches in the coming century. We need to restore and rebuild the metaphysical imagination that has collapsed in the self-centred relativism of post-modern culture. Sacrifice is only one of many values that look outwards beyond the self which have been victims of the shift from the objective to the subjective, from customs and traditions to impulses and whims, from structures and institutions to feelings and emotions, and from obligation and duty to rights and choice. In his fascinating book, *Understanding the Present: Science and the Soul of Modern Man* (1992), Bryan Appleyard has blamed the rise of the scientific worldview for creating our present culture of narcissism. By progressively eroding all external sources of values, most notably God, science has turned us in on ourselves and made the self and its relationships the moral centre of our lives.

The scientific world view has denied us an external anchor for our values. It seems to have made everything either controllable by our problem-solving ingenuity or understandable by our analytic and experimental powers. *Out there*, we seem to have no role; but *in here*, in the refuge of the self, we can find something to do, we can find values.... Science implicitly denies the self its place in the world and its source of values. So the self resorts, finally, to a pagan art devoted to its own cultivation and worship.... Narcissism is the result of having only one agreed truth system, science, which depends for its effectiveness on its refusal to tell us anything positive about ourselves or our place in the world and yet still becoming, in our imaginations, The Truth.[56]

Whatever its cause, the loss of the metaphysical imagination is at the root of much of the reductionism and brutalism of contemporary culture. It has also depleted the stock of transcendent values that enabled previous generations to cope with misfortune and to relate what happens in the world to higher purposes and wider themes. In the important task that now faces us of building up these values again. Christians will have the help of those of other faiths. We will also be able to draw on the significant shift in outlook which is taking place within the scientific community and showing itself in the tendency among physicists and astronomers in particular to express their discoveries about the world in terms of awe, wonder and mystery rather than in equations and formulae. Many agnostics and humanists will also welcome the restoration of overarching values which promote a sense of corporateness and interdependence in our increasingly fragmented and fragile world. Central among them must surely be that amalgam of mutual self-giving and respect for others, self-limitation, restraint and understanding of the mysterious interconnection between giving up and making holy which is summed up and concentrated in the metaphysical principle of sacrifice.

It is here that we come to what is perhaps the most important and certainly the most distinctive role for the Church. It is not enough for it to strive to be itself a sacrificial community and to preach the power of sacrifice. Alongside this practical and prophetic witness lie important priestly and pastoral responsibilities. Millions of people lead sacrificial lives, consciously and unconsciously, surrendering and giving up what is precious to them for the sake of others. Countless acts of sacrifice are committed every day. Millions more endure suffering, most of it unwanted and forced upon them. It is the Church's task to offer up all of this sacrifice and suffering to God that it may be transfigured through the medium of the Christ who was himself a passive victim before he rose triumphant from the grave.

In taking on this priestly role, the Church also has a pastoral responsibility to reassure people that sacrifice is not just something for saints and spiritual super-heroes. Rather it is a gift that God in his mercy and wisdom has made available to us all. We fulfil his purposes, and also conform ourselves with the rest of his creation, by playing our part in the great Divine economy of sacrifice, however uncertainly or imperfectly. To live sacrificially is to beat in time with the rhythm of life.

I think we may be helped back towards a sense of the naturalness of sacrifice, and also perhaps towards a greater acceptance of misfortune and things not going our way, by turning again to the sacred scriptures of Hinduism. In the *Upanishads* the moral, natural and social order which is brought about as a result of sacrifice (*Rṭa*) is presented as something that has to be accepted whatever it brings. Existence is ordered on the basis of the samsonic round and one's yogic path has to be fashioned accordingly. The *Bhagavad Gita* portrays sacrifice as the God-given principle which makes the world go round, promotes supreme good and happiness and brings humans into harmony with the gods:

Thus spoke the Lord of Creation when he made both man and sacrifice: 'By sacrifice thou shalt multiply and obtain all thy desires. By sacrifice thou shalt honour the gods and the gods will then love thee. And thus in harmony with them shalt thou attain the supreme good'.

Sacred action is described in the Vedas and these come from the Eternal, and therefore is the Eternal ever present in a sacrifice. Thus was the Wheel of the Law set in motion, and that man lives indeed in vain who in a sinful life of pleasures helps not in its revolutions.[57]

There are no propitiatory connotations in this view of sacrifice. Among Krishna's last words to Arjuna in the *Bhagavad Gita* is a reminder that 'works of sacrifice, gift and self-harmony ... should indeed be performed ... but these works should be done in the freedom of a pure offering, and without expectation of a reward'.[58] Indeed, Krishna goes so far as to say that 'when work is done with selfish desire, or feeling it is an effort, or thinking it is a sacrifice, then the work is impure'.[59] Sacrifice, in other words, should be an almost automatic, involuntary expression of one's conformity with the basic rhythm of life and the law which governs the universe rather than a self-conscious work. The *Rig Veda* attributes the widespread sense of guilt felt by so many people to their inability ever to say in any situation, 'There is nothing I can do about this'. The remedy for this state is to be found in the provision of sacrifice which is an ever open option. Always one can sacrifice. The oblation is provided in the ordered world. Agni is perpetually available as mediator and priest. Purusa may at any time be offered as the fractured all and the cosmos thus recreated and renewed. Human beings stand in the midst of potentiality. In the *Upanishads* this latent power is internalized and brought to its conclusion. Sacrifice becomes the dearly bought and all-consuming fire which finally burns up all alienation and leaves a total interpenetration of the human and divine identity as multiplicity, division and infinity finally rush back into the body of God.

There is much in this metaphysical presentation of the power of sacrifice that accords with the teaching of the Jewish and Christian scriptures. Indeed, I think it can help us in the contemporary Church to return to the roots of our own faith and recover elements that we have long neglected and even lost. We too have a tradition of seeing sacrifice as the God-given principle of order and reconciliation which is also provided as the remedy for human *angst* and alienation. It has its origins in that key verse of the story of the *Akedah*: 'God will provide himself a lamb for a burnt offering' (Genesis 22: 8). Here is the whole doctrine of providence first expressed, significantly, in the context of sacrifice. The theme is echoed in John Keble's morning hymn:

> New treasures still, of countless price,
> God will provide for sacrifice.[60]

Like Hinduism, Christianity has a profound sense of the cosmic power of sacrifice to redeem, perfect and renew all creation and unite it with its creator. For Christians, of course, this power is both manifested and actualized through the perpetual availability and mediation of Jesus Christ who is both sacrificial victim and sacrificing priest. It was supremely and uniquely instanced on the Cross, the inescapable and decisive historical sacrifice which is emphatically neither substitutionary nor propitiatory, nor yet just representative or exemplary, but inclusive, participatory and incorporative. We do not simply observe Jesus' crucifixion and resurrection as a demonstration of the mysterious truth that life comes out of death. We experience and share both its Godforsaken agony and its transforming power.

Christ's death was not a straight substitute for the death of sinful men; rather in his death, all men may die and rise again. By identification with Christ through faith, mankind is restored to perfect worship of God and complete self-offering to God in a life of proper obedience. This is why there is such a close relation between the atoning death of

Christ and the imitation of him which Christians called their sacrifice; this is why he is involved as priest in the offering of the spiritual sacrifices of perfected humanity. They in Christ, and Christ in them, offer the sacrifice.[61]

So we cast ourselves on God in our helplessness and dependence, giving him back all that he has given us, surrendering our pride and self-will as well as our pain and suffering and offering everything through Christ.

> All that we have we bring to thee,
> Yet all is nought when all is done,
> Save that in it love can see
> The sacrifice of thy dear Son.[62]

The sacrifice of Christ was not finished and completed on the Cross. Still less was it an unfortunate emergency rescue operation which had to be mounted by God to deal with the unforeseen consequences of human sin. It is the ongoing and eternal offering of the Lamb slain from the foundation of the world which reveals the endlessly self-giving character of God and points to the tragic yet triumphant mystery of life through death which is at the heart of all being. In the words of John Moses, 'the sacrifice of suffering love continues its silent work of redemption. Atonement is the travail of the ages. It is made explicit in Gethsemane and Calvary; but the sacrifice of God is continually offered in the passion of the Holy Spirit, transforming the world into the image of the Son of God'.[63]

And what is our role in this great continuing cosmic process? How do we help the revolutions of the wheel of sacrifice which keeps the world turning by constantly creating and recreating, building and destroying, transfiguring and making earthly things holy? It is by conforming ourselves to Christ, living according to his teaching, remembering his dismembered body and drinking his spilt blood, letting him live in us that we may dwell in him and so share in the eternal sacrifice of God's Son, which is both the heart of the Church and the living centre of the world. This will be a painful and costly process which will not end until we reach death, that last earthly act and oblation which seals our sacrifice and marks the beginning of new creation and eternal life:

> Ready for all thy perfect will,
> My acts of faith and love repeat,
> Till death thy endless mercies seal,
> And make my sacrifice complete.[64]

It would be fitting to end on this note of finality and completion. But while Charles Wesley's words may, indeed, be true at the individual level, we cannot be sure that our own sacrifices are, in fact, completed by death. What we do know is that God's great work of sacrifice through Christ does, in fact, go on. Risen, ascended and glorified, Jesus continues his work of 'reconciling to himself all things, whether on earth or in heaven, making peace by the blood of his cross' (Colossians 1: 20). The great purpose of sacrifice, as we have seen, is to lead things to their end. When the ultimate destiny of all is to be fulfilled, and the whole of creation perfected and gathered up in one final oblation and restored to its source and resting place in the eternal life of God, we do not know. All that we can do is to join John Wesley, who changed the last line of his brother's great hymn to give it a less individualistic and a more cosmic dimension, and pray that Christ will in the fullness of time and under God's unfailing providence 'make the sacrifice complete'.[65]

Notes

(The place of publication for works cited is London,
unless otherwise stated.)

Introduction The love that dares not speak its name: the riddle of sacrifice

1 F. Young, *Sacrifice and the Death of Christ* (SPCK, 1975), p. 3.
2 Quoted in the *Church Times*, 26 February 1983.
3 *The Times Magazine*, 29 May 1993, p. 13.
4 R. Osmond, *Changing Perspectives: Christian Culture and Morals in England Today* (Darton, Longman & Todd, 1993).
5 E. Masure, *The Christian Sacrifice* (Burns, Oates & Washboune, 1944), p. 41.
6 *Chambers Dictionary of Beliefs and Religions* (1992), p. 451.
7 J. Calvin, *Institutes of the Christian Religion*, II.xvi.2.
8 See M. McNeill, *The Silver Bough* (William MacLellan: Glasgow, 1957), p. 23. In his *Lectures on the Religion of the Semites* in 1889 William Robertson Smith based the institution of sacrifice on a communal meal in which the gods and worshippers together ate the sacred flesh of a 'theanthropic animal'. This totemic interpretation of the origin of sacrifice has been challenged by E. O. James, *Sacrifice and Sacrament* (Thames & Hudson, 1962).
9 P. T. Forsyth, *God the Holy Father* (new edn, New Creation Publications: Sydney, 1977), pp. 43–4.
10 L. W. Grensted, *A Short History of the Doctrine of the Atonement* (Manchester University Press: Manchester, 1920), p. 209. See the interesting discussion of the ecumenical implications of sacrifice in I. U. Dalferth's contribution to *Sacrifice and Redemption: Durham Essays in Theology*, S. W. Sykes (ed.) (Cambridge University Press: Cambridge, 1991), pp. 300–2.
11 D. Cupitt, *The World to Come* (SCM, 1982), p. 92.
12 A. Gnanadason, *No Longer a Secret: The Church and Violence Against Women* (World Council of Churches, Geneva, 1993), p. 50.

13   A. Carr, *Transforming Grace: Christian Tradition and Women's Experience* (Harper Collins: New York, 1988), p. 174; C. Hayward, *The Redemption of God: A Theology of Mutual Relation* (University Press of America: Washington, 1982), p. 69.

14   Gnanadason, *op. cit.*, pp. 49–50.

15   J. Carlson Brown and R. Parker, *Christianity, Patriarchy and Abuse: A Feminist Critique* (New York, 1989), quoted in *ibid.*, p. 51.

16   D. Hampson, *Theology and Feminism* (Basil Blackwell: Oxford, 1990), p. 140.

17   J. M. Soskice, 'Blood and defilement' (paper delivered to the 1994 conference of the Society for the Study of Theology, Westminster College, Oxford), f. 16.

18   *Ibid.*, f. 16.

19   *Ibid.*, f. 12.

20   F. Capra, *The Turning Point* (Flamingo, 1982), p. 306.

21   J. Moses, *The Sacrifice of God: A Holistic View of Atonement* (Canterbury Press: Norwich, 1992), p. 168.

22   These lines precede the song 'You are sixteen, going on seventeen' (though not in the film version of the musical from which they are unaccountably missing). Those who are offended at such a source as this being cited in a work of academic theology might care to reflect on Dennis Potter's observation that 'cheap songs contain something of the Psalms of David'.

23   *Daily Telegraph*, 5 October 1987, p. 4.

24   G. Matheson, *Moments on the Mount* (Nisbet & Co., 1884), p. 213.

25   P. Rodger, 'What's the point of Lent?', *Life and Work*, March 1994, p. 13.

26   Quoted in M. E. C. Bourdillon, *Sacrifice* (Academic Press, 1980), p. 30. F. C. N. Hicks, *The Fullness of Sacrifice* (SPCK, 1946), p. 24 makes the point that 'cost is the essential of sacrifice'. The same author also asserts (p. 177) that 'life, its recovery, uplifting and communication – is the ruling conception of sacrifice'.

27   *Church Times*, 9 October 1992.

28   J. S. Whale, *Victor and Victim: The Christian Doctrine of Redemption* (Cambridge University Press: Cambridge: 1960), p. 42.

29   *Scotsman*, 30 August 1993.

30   *New Statesman and Society*, 9 April 1993, p. 17.

31   *Scotsman*, 21 April 1994, 7 June 1994.

32   *Church Times*, 30 July 1993.

33   J. Daley, *The Times*, 11 November 1993, p. 18.

34   Quoted in Bourdillon, *op. cit.*, p. 29.

35   *A Simple Church Dictionary* (Mowbray & Co., 1924), p. 26.

36   A. Bloom, *God and Man* (Darton, Longman & Todd, 1971), p. 68.

37   O. Quick, *Doctrines of the Creed* (Nisbet & Co., 1937), pp. 219–20.

38   Moses, *op. cit.*, p. 80.

39   Cyril Richardson, 'The eucharistic sacrifice', *Anglican Theological Review*, January 1950, pp. 57–8.

40   Masure, *op. cit.*, p. 41.

41 William James, *The Varieties of Religious Experience* (Penguin, 1985), p. 303.
42 F. W. Dillistone, *The Christian Understanding of Atonement* (SCM, 1984), p. 411.

1 The pelican, the lamb and the burning bush: the relevance of sacrifice

1 P. Fiddes, *Past Event and Present Salvation: The Christian Idea of Atonement* (Darton, Longman & Todd, 1989), p. 187.
2 Dillistone, *op. cit.*, p. 41.
3 J. Moltmann, *The Trinity and the Kingdom of God* (SCM, 1981), p. 32.
4 P. Fiddes, *The Creative Suffering of God* (Oxford, 1988), pp. 1, 29.
5 C. Gunton, *The Actuality of Atonement* (T. & T. Clark: Edinburgh, 1988), p. 197.
6 Moses, *op. cit.*, pp. 23–4.
7 *Ibid.*, p. 56.
8 *Ibid.*, p. 159.
9 *Ibid.*, pp. 161–2
10 *Ibid.*, p. 178.
11 *Ibid.*, p. 161.
12 It is only fair to note that Daly himself expresses some uneasiness about the term 'spiritualization' as applied to the Christian approach to sacrifice. He concedes that some terms associated with it, such as 'dematerializing' can be positively misleading and points out: 'Spiritualization does not mean a radical dematerialization of sacrifice which would be at odds with the incarnational theology which we have found to be essential to the views of Paul, Barnabas, Irenaeus, the two Clements and Origen', R. J. Daly, *Christian Sacrifice: The Judaeo-Christian Background Before Origen* (Catholic University of America Press: Washington, 1978), p. 4.
13 R. J. Daly, *The Origins of the Christian Doctrine of Sacrifice* (Darton, Longman & Todd, 1978), p. v.
14 *The Friend*, 27 April 1990, p. 534.
15 G. Ashby, *Sacrifice: Its Nature and Purpose* (SCM, 1988), p. 102.
16 R. Gill, 'Beyond self-interest' (typescript of the 1993 Winton Lecture delivered at King Alfred's College, Winchester), f. 17.
17 Moses, *op. cit.*, p. 81.
18 Dillistone, *op. cit.*, p. 399; Moses, *op. cit.*, p. 3.
19 L. C. Martin (ed.), *The Poems of Richard Crawshaw* (Oxford, 1957), p. 293.
20 *Ibid.*, p. 296.
21 A. Loisy, *Essai historique sur le sacrifice* (Paris, 1920), p. 22.
22 M. Wilson, *The Rural Spirit* (Collins, 1990), p. 181.
23 G. H. Sabine (ed.), *The Collected Works of Gerard Winstanley* (Cornell University Press, 1941), p. 113.

2 Osiris, Purusa and Zimsum: creation as sacrifice

1 Hicks, *The Fullness of Sacrifice, op. cit.*, p. 33.
2 H. Hubert and M. Mauss, *Sacrifice: Its Nature and Function* (University of Chicago Press: Chicago, 1964), p. 81.
3 R. A. Downie, *James Goerge Frazer: The Portrait of a Scholar* (Watts, 1940), p. 28.
4 J. G. Frazer, *The Golden Bough* (abridged edn, Macmillan, 1987), pp. 372–3.
5 J. Gwyn Griffiths, *The Origins of Osiris and His Cult* (Studies in the History of Religion, Vol. XV, E. J. Brill: Leiden, 1980), pp. 159–63.
6 Frazer, *op. cit.*, pp. 381, 382.
7 W. Robertson Smith, *Lectures on the Religion of the Semites* (3rd edn, A. & C. Black, 1927); E. Durkheim, *Elementary Forms of Religious Life* (Allen & Unwin, 1915).
8 On this see J. Campbell, *The Hero with a Thousand Faces* (Paladin, 1988), especially pp. 93, 143.
9 L. S. Thornton, *Revelation and the Modern World* (A. & C. Black, 1950), p. 279.
10 *Rig Veda*, 10.81; 10.82.
11 K. Sivaraman, (ed.), *Hindu Spirituality: Vedas through Vedantas* (SCM, 1989), p. 12.
12 *Rig Veda*, 10.90, verses 6–14. I have used the translation in F. Edgerton, *Beginnings of Indian Philosophy* (Allen & Unwin, 1965), pp. 67–8.
13 R. C. Zaehner, *Hinduism* (Oxford University Press: Oxford, 1962), p. 44.
14 *Rig Veda*, 10.90.16; 1.164.50.
15 *Rig Veda*, 10.51.
16 Zaehner, *op. cit.*, p. 45. See also the comments of Eliade quoted in A. W. Dillistone, *The Christian Understanding of Atonement, op. cit.*, p. 65 and of Charles Eliot in *Hinduism and Buddhism. A Historical Sketch* (1921), Vol. 1, p. 67. For Dillistone, sacrifice in Hindu thought is simply 'the power that makes the world go round' (*Christianity and Symbolism*, SCM, 1985, p. 224).
17 *Rig Veda*, 10.190. I have here used the translation of W. D. O'Flaherty (Penguin, 1981), p. 34.
18 *Bhagavad Gita*, 3. 10–16. The translation is that of J. Mascaro (Penguin, 1962), p. 57.
19 *Brihadaranyaka Upanishad*, 1.1. The translation is that of R. C. Zaehner, *Concordant Discord* (Oxford University Press: Oxford, 1970), p. 68.
20 M. Eliade, *The Myth of Eternal Return* (Princeton University Press: Princeton N.J., 1971), p. 78.
21 *Ibid.*, p. 88.
22 Romans 6: 4; Colossians 2: 12.
23 W. Dyrness, *Themes in Old Testament Theology* (Inter-Varsity Press, 1979), p. 65.
24 C. Westermann, *Genesis 1–11: A Commentary* (SPCK, 984), p. 106.
25 Justin Martyr, *Apology*, 10.2.

26 P. Fiddes, *Past Event and Present Salvation, op. cit.,* pp. 21–2.
27 Masure, *The Christian Sacrifice, op. cit.,* p. 79.
28 Gunton, *The Actuality of Atonement, op. cit.,* p. 118.
29 Quoted in I. Prigogine and I. Stengers, *Order out of Chaos* (Heinemann, 1984), p. 313.
30 A. Peacocke, *Science and the Theology of Creation* (paper delivered to the Society for the Study of Theology Conference on creation, St Andrews, 1990), f. 11.
31 J. V. Taylor, *The Christlike God* (SCM, 1992), p. 197.
32 B. Brassnett, *The Suffering of the Impassible God* (SPCK, 1928), p. 11.
33 'Why did God not make a better job of it?', *Church Times,* 3 December 1993, p. 10.
34 Moses, *The Sacrifice of God, op. cit.,* p. 45.
35 L. Blue, *Blue Heaven* (Coronet, 1987), p. 27.
36 A. Green (ed.), *Jewish Spirituality: From the Sixteenth Century to the Present* (Routledge & Kegan Paul, 1987), p. 65.
37 J. Moltmann, *God in Creation* (SCM, 1985), p. 88. Moltmann's thoughts on *zimsum* are to be found on pages 86–93 of this book. See also the section on God's self-limitation in his *The Trinity and the Kingdom of God, op. cit.,* pp. 108–11.
38 P. T. Forsyth, *The Person and Place of Jesus Christ* (Independent Press, 1909), p. 308.
39 Letter in *Alpha* magazine, November 1993, p. 5.
40 Moltmann, *God in Creation, op. cit.,* p. 88.
41 Quoted in Dillistone, *The Christian Understanding of Atonement, op. cit.,* p. 33.
42 *Ibid.,* p. 72.
43 N. Berdiaev, *Freedom and the Spirit* (Bles, 1935), p. 179.
44 See E. A. S. Butterworth, *The Tree at the Navel of the World* (Walter de Gruyter: Berlin, 1970).
45 Quoted in Dillistone, *op. cit.,* p. 73.
46 *Ibid.,* p. 74.
47 *Ibid.,* p. 75.

3 **The sacrifice of God is a broken spirit: sacrifice in the Old Testament**

1 W. James, *The Varieties of Religious Experience, op. cit.,* 1985), p. 462; Daly, *Origins of the Christian Doctrine of Sacrifice, op. cit.,* p. 8; Young, *Sacrifice and the Death of Christ, op. cit.,* p. 35; E. Hulmes, 'The semantics of sacrifice' in Sykes (ed.), *Sacrifice and Redemption: Durham Essays in Theology, op. cit.,* pp. 265–71.
2 Eliade, *The Myth of the Eternal Return, op. cit.,* p. 108–10.
3 H. Maccoby, *The Secret Executioner* (Thames & Hudson, 1982), pp. 74–86.
4 *Ibid.,* p. 10.
5 M. Barth, 'Was Christ's death a sacrifice?', *Scottish Journal of Theology Occasional Papers,* No. 9 (1961), p. 18.

6 *Ibid.*, p. 26.
7 R. Daly, *Christian Sacrifice: The Judaeo-Christian Background Before Origen* (Catholic University of America Press, 1978), p. 86.
8 Dyrness, *Themes in Old Testament Theology, op. cit.*, p. 157.
9 *Mundaka Upanishad*, 1.2,10 and 11 as quoted in S. Radhakrishan, *The Principal Upanishads* (Allen & Unwin, 1953), pp. 677–8.
10 'The story of the sacrifice' in Max Müller (ed.), *Sacred Books of the Buddhists* (Henry Frowde, 1895), Vol. I. pp. 93–104.
11 M. Ali, *The Holy Qur-an* (Ahmadiyya Anjuman-i-Ishaat-i-Islaam, Lahore, 1917), pp. 670–1.
12 Gunton, *op. cit.*, p. 124.
13 A. Heschel, *The Prophets* (Harper & Row, 1962), p. 226.
14 O. Kaiser, *Isaiah 1–12: a commentary* (SCM, 1983), p. 259.
15 *Ibid.*, p. 261.
16 G. Ashby, *Sacrifice: Its Nature and Purpose* (SCM, 1988), p. 126.
17 *Ibid.*

4 The cult and the Cross: sacrifice in the New Testament

1 E. Hoskyns and F. Davey, *Crucifixion-Resurrection* (SPCK, 1981), pp. 92–3.
2 Daly, *The Origins of the Christian Doctrine of Sacrifice, op. cit.*, p. vi; Gunton, *The Actuality of Atonement, op. cit.*, p. 123; Moses, *The Sacrifice of God, op. cit.*, p. 122.
3 S. W. Sykes, 'Outline of a theology of sacrifice' in Sykes (ed.), *Sacrifice and Redemption: Durham Essays in Theology, op. cit.*, p. 287.
4 Hicks, *The Fullness of Sacrifice, op. cit.*, pp. 240, 346.
5 E. O. James, *Sacrifice and Sacrament* (Thames & Hudson, 1962), pp. 54–5.
6 James, *The Varieties of Religious Experience, op. cit.*, p. 462.
7 H. Maccoby, *The Sacred Executioner* (Thames & Hudson, 1982), p. 105.
8 M. Hengel, *The Atonement* (SCM, 1981), pp. 4ff.
9 Maccoby, *op. cit.*, p. 99.
10 Hicks, *op. cit.*, p. 197.
11 Dillistone, *The Christian Understanding of Atonement, op. cit.*, p. 315.
12 Hengel, *op. cit.*, p. 60.
13 V. Taylor, *Jesus and His Sacrifice* (Macmillan, 1951), p. 48.
14 *Summa Theologiae*, III, q. 48, art. 3.
15 Masure, *The Christian Sacrifice, op. cit.*, p. 263.
16 J. F. McHugh, 'The Sacrifice of the Mass at the Council of Trent' in Sykes (ed.), *op. cit.*, p. 180; I. U. Dalferth, 'Christ died for us: reflections on the sacrificial language of salvation' in *ibid.*, p. 306.
17 Gunton, *op. cit.*, p. 124.
18 W. H. Vanstone, *The Stature of Waiting* (Darton, Longman & Todd, 1982), pp. 17–33; 101–15.
19 R. Bultmann, *The Gospel of John* (SCM, 1971); J. T. Forestell, *The Word of the Cross: Salvation as Revelation in the Fourth Gospel*

(Analecta Biblica 57, 1974); B. Grigsby, 'The Cross as an expiatory sacrifice in the Fourth Gospel', *Journal for the Study of the New Testament* 15 (1982), pp. 51–86.

20   W. Temple, *Readings in St John's Gospel* (Macmillan, 1959), p. 169.

21   I. Watts, 'Join all the glorious names' (verse 7); 'Not all the blood of beasts' (verses 1 and 2).

22   James, *op. cit.*, p. 119.

23   William Milligan, *The Resurrection of Our Lord* (Macmillan, 1884), pp. 140, 141.

24   D. Baillie, *God was in Christ* (2nd edn, Faber, 1955), p. 195.

25   There is an interesting discussion of German contributions to this debate in J. G. Dunn, 'Paul's understanding of the death of Jesus' in Sykes (ed.), *op. cit.*, p. 41.

26   H. Maccoby, *The Mythmaker: Paul and the Invention of Christianity* (Weidenfeld & Nicolson, 1986), pp. 101, 102, 196; Hengel, *op. cit.*, pp. 34–9.

27   Irving is quoted approvingly in Gunton, *op. cit.*, p. 133.

28   A. M. Ramsey, *From Gore to Temple. The Development of Anglican Theology between 'Lux Mundi' and the Second World War* (Longman, 1960), p. 30.

29   M. Barth, 'Was Christ's death a sacrifice?', *Scottish Journal of Theology Occasional Papers* No. 9 (1961), p. 52.

30   *New Jerusalem Bible* (Standard edn, Darton, Longman & Todd, 1985), p. 1947.

31.   C. F. D. Moule, *The Sacrifice of Christ* (Hodder & Stoughton, 1956), p. 35.

32   F. Young, *Sacrificial Ideas in Greek Christian Writers* (Philadelphia Patristic Foundation, Cambridge Mass., 1979), p. 236.

33   A. R. George, *Communion with God in the New Testament* (Epworth Press, 1953), p. 184.

34   Temple, *op. cit.*, p. 169.

35   L. Brunschvicg (ed.), *Pensées de Pascal* (Paris, 1934), p. 553.

36   Quoted in J. Moltmann, *The Trinity and the Kingdom of God* (SCM, 1981), p. 227.

37   Fiddes, *The Creative Suffering of God*, *op. cit.*, p. 3.

38   J. Behm, 'Sacrifice' in *Theological Dictionary of the New Testament* (Eerdmans, Grand Rapids, 1966), III, 185.

39   Masure, *op. cit.*, p. 41.

40   Fiddes, *Past Event and Present Salvation*, *op. cit.*, pp. 24, 29.

41   Taylor, *op. cit.*, p. 298.

42   Daly, *Christian Sacrifice: The Judaeo-Christian Background before Origen*, *op. cit.*, p. 252.

43   Barth, *op. cit.*, p. 54.

44   *Ibid.*, p. 51.

45   Moses, *The Sacrifice of God*, *op. cit.*, p. 201. On the extent to which the sacrifice of Jesus reveals the character of God see also Gunton, *op. cit.*, p. 201.

46   Moule, *op. cit.*, p. 46. It is worth noting that the Greek verb ιλασκεσ-θαι which is sometimes rendered as 'propitiate' in English translations

always has 'sin' rather than 'God' as its object when it is used in the New Testament.

47 J. Donne, *Sermon on Christmas Day*, 1626, quoted in Moses, *op. cit.*, p. 93.

48 S. Weil, *First and Last Notebooks* (Oxford, 1970), p. 213.

49 P. Tillich, *Systematic Theology* (Nisbet & Co., 1957), II, p. 203.

50 H. W. Bartsch (ed.), *Kerygma and Myth* (SPCK, 1960), p. 42.

51 R. Daly, *The Origins of the Christian Doctrine of Sacrifice*, *op. cit.*, p. 83.

5 Martyrs and mystics: images of sacrifice from Irenaeus to St John of the Cross

1 R. Lane Fox, *Pagans and Christians* (Viking, 1986), p. 444.

2 Quoted in Daly, *Christian Sacrifice*, *op. cit.*, p. 353.

3 Young, *Sacrifice and the Death of Christ*, *op. cit.*, p. 90. The key works on this subject are Young, *The Use of Sacrificial Ideas in Greek Christian Writers from the New Testament to St John Chrysostom*, *op. cit.*, and Daly, *Christian Sacrifice: The Judaeo-Christian Background before Origen*, *op. cit.*

4 Quoted in Young, *Sacrifice and the Death of Christ*, *op. cit.*, p. 58.

5 Quoted in Daly, *Christian Sacrifice*, *op. cit.*, p. 394.

6 *Ibid.*, p. 398.

7 *Ibid.*, p. 340.

8 Moltmann, *The Trinity and the Kingdom of God*, *op. cit.*, pp. 23–5.

9 Quoted in Young, *Sacrifice and the Death of Christ*, *op. cit.*, p. 78.

10 *Ibid.*, p. 60.

11 J. Stevenson (ed.), *A New Eusebius* (SPCK, 1963), p. 45.

12 *Ibid.*, p. 18.

13 *Ibid.*, p. 22.

14 *Ibid.*, p. 22.

15 Quoted in Daly, *Christian Sacrifice*, *op. cit.*, p. 381.

16 J. Witheridge, 'Martyrs' seed for the Church', *The Times*, 14 February 1987.

17 T. S. Eliot, *The Complete Poems and Plays* (Faber, 1969), p. 261.

18 Witheridge, *art. cit.*

19 T. Merton, *The Wisdom of the Desert* (Sheldon Press, 1982), pp. 7–8.

20 S. Davies, 'Light in darkness – the relevance of Celtic spirituality today' (unpublished paper), f. 4.

21 *De Civitate Dei*, 10.6. The translation is that of P. Schaff (ed.), *St Augustine's City of God* (Eerdmans Publishing Co.: Grand Rapids, Michigan, 1972), p. 184.

22 S. W. Sykes, 'Outline of a theology of sacrifice' in Sykes (ed.), *Sacrifice and Redemption. Durham Essays in Theology*, *op. cit.*, p. 291. Sykes' very interesting observations on St. Augustine's theology of sacrifice are on pp. 290–2.

23 *De Civitate Dei*, 10.6.

24 This is the altered version of Francis Bland Tucker's translation of

Abelard's hymn which appears in *The Church Hymnary* (Oxford University Press: Oxford, 1973), p. 347.

25 G. Warwick (ed.), *Revelations of Divine Love* (Methuen, 1958), p. 150.

26 *Ibid.*, pp. 40–1.

27 *Ibid.*, pp. 150, 47–8, 63–4.

28 Quoted by S. Hardman Moore, 'Sacrifice in Puritan typology' in Sykes (ed.), *op. cit.*, p. 185.

29 *Ibid.*, p. 188.

30 *Ibid.*, p. 189.

31 'The Cross', lines 1–4 from H. J. C. Grierson (ed.), *The Poems of John Donne* (Oxford University Press: Oxford, 1929), p. 302.

32 'The Cross', lines 17–24 from *ibid.*, p. 303.

33 'Good Friday, 1613', lines 9–18 from *ibid.*, p. 307.

34 'The Sacrifice', lines 205–7 from C. A. Partridge (ed.), *The English Poems of George Herbert* (Dent, 1974), p. 54.

35 'The Banquet', lines 25–30 (spelling modernized) from *ibid.*, p. 186.

36 Quoted in G. Rowell, 'Reasons of the Sacred Heart', *The Times*, 11 June 1994.

37 E. Stein, *The Science of the Cross* (Burns & Oates, 1960), p. 212.

38 N. Cummins, *Freedom to Rejoice: Understanding St John of the Cross* (Harper Collins, 1991), p. 10.

39 Stein, *op. cit.*, p. 209.

40 *Ibid.*, p. 210.

6 The grand law of the universe: sacrifice in Victorian and Edwardian thought

1 H. Bushnell, *God in Christ* (John Chapman, 1850), p. 216.

2 H. Bushnell, *The Vicarious Sacrifice* (Alexander Strachan, 1866), p. 64. In his book *The Impassibility of God. A Survey of Christian Thought* (Cambridge, 1926), J. K. Mozley identified this statement as the earliest example of the patripassian theology which identified the Cross with the eternal nature of the Godhead.

3 *Ibid.*, pp. 387–8.

4 N. Gorodetzky, *The Humiliated Christ in Modern Russian Thought* (SPCK, 1938), p. 11.

5 *Ibid.*, p. 56.

6 *Ibid.*, pp. 121–2.

7 *Ibid.*, pp. 171–2.

8 Quoted in Dillistone, *The Christian Understanding of the Atonement*, *op. cit.*, p. 249.

9 *Sermons by the Revd. F. W. Robertson preached at Brighton*, 1st series (Kegan Paul, 1902), p. 138.

10 *Ibid.*, pp. 138–9.

11 *Ibid.*, p. 139.

12 *Ibid.*, p. 142.

13 *Sermons by the Revd. F. W. Robertson preached at Brighton*, 3rd series (Kegan Paul, 1902), p. 100.

14 *Ibid.*, p. 100.
15 *Ibid.*, p. 100.
16 *Ibid.*, p. 100.
17 *Ibid.*, p. 102.
18 F. D. Maurice, *The Doctrine of Sacrifice Deduced from the Scriptures* (Macmillan, Cambridge, 1854), p. xlvi.
19 *Ibid.*, p. xlviii.
20 *Ibid.*, p. xlvii.
21 *Ibid.*, p. 15.
22 *Ibid.*, pp. 43–4.
23 *Ibid.*, p. 65.
24 *Ibid.*, p. 66.
25 *Ibid.*, p. 101.
26 *Ibid.*, p. 102.
27 *Ibid.*, p. 224.
28 *Ibid.*, p. 109.
29 F. D. Maurice, *The Epistles of St John* (Macmillan, Cambridge, 1857), p. 208.
30 Maurice, *The Doctrine of Sacrifice, op. cit.*, p. 226.
31 *Ibid.*, p. 106.
32 Maurice, *The Epistles of St John, op. cit.*, p. 208.
33 Maurice, *The Doctrine of Sacrifice, op. cit.*, p. 230.
34 *Ibid.*, p. 322.
35 Letter to Sara Coleridge quoted in F. M. McClain, *Maurice, Man and Moralist* (SPCK, 1972), p. 73.
36 Letter to Sara Coleridge quoted in *ibid.*, p. 81.
37 F. D. Maurice, *The Conflict of Good and Evil in Our Day* (Smith, Elder & Co., 1865), p. 164.
38. F. D. Maurice, *Social Morality* (Macmillan: Cambridge, 2nd edn, 1872), p. 234.
39 F. D. Maurice 'Sermons preached in Lincoln's Inn Chapel' (new edn, 1891), ii, p. 27.
40 A. R. Vidler, *F. D. Maurice and Company* (SCM, 1966), p. 194.
41 Letter to T. J. Ormerod in A. P. Stanley (ed.), *The Life and Correspondence of Thomas Arnold* (3rd edn, 1844), II, p. 262.
42 *The Saints' Tragedy*, Act IV, Scene 3, in *The Works of Charles Kingsley* (Macmillan, 1879), I, p. 130.
43 N. Vance, *The Sinews of the Spirit* (Cambridge, 1985), p. 150.
44 H. Newbolt, *Collected Poems, 1897–1907* (Nelson, n.d.), p. 129.
45 M. Richter, *The Politics of Conscience. T. H. Green and His Age* (Weidenfeld & Nicolson, 1964), p. 101.
46 *Ibid.*, p. 35.
47 *Ibid.*, p. 131.
48 *Ibid.*, p. 132.
49 *Ibid.*, p. 127.
50 C. Gore, *Belief in Christ* (John Murray, 1922), p. 522.
51 C. Gore, *The Body of Christ* (John Murray, 1901), p. 252.
52 R. W. Moberley, *Ministerial Priesthood* (1897), p. 246.
53 M. Ramsey, *From Gore to Temple* (Longmans, 1960), p. 45.

54 H. Scott Holland, *Logic and Life* (Rivingtons, 1882), p. 83.
55 *Ibid.*, p. 84.
56 *Ibid.*, p. 88.
57 *Ibid.*, p. 89.
58 *Ibid.*, pp. 95–6.
59 *Ibid.*, p. 98.
60 *Ibid.*, pp. 107–8.
61 *Ibid.*, p. 114.
62 *Ibid.*, p. 114.
63 P. T. Forsyth, *The Person and Place of Jesus Christ* (Hodder & Stoughton, 1909), p. 271.
64 *Ibid.*, p. 311.
65 P. T. Forsyth, *The Work of Christ* (Hodder & Stoughton, 1910), p. viii.
66 P. T. Forsyth, *Marriage: Its Ethic and Religion* (Hodder & Stoughton, 1912), p. 34.
67 W. Milligan, *The Ascension and Heavenly Priesthood of Our Lord* (Macmillan, 1892), pp. 144–5. It is interesting to note that another earlier and more unorthodox Scottish churchman, Edward Irving, also held a high doctrine of the eternal priesthood of Christ which is discussed approvingly by Colin Gunton in *The Actuality of Atonement*.
68 *Ibid.*, p. 142.
69 *Ibid.*, pp. 310, 309.
70 G. Matheson, *Studies in the Portrait of Christ* (Hodder & Stoughton, 1901), pp. 71, 73.
71 *Ibid.*, p. 75.
72 G. Matheson, *Can the Old Faith Live with the New?* (Blackwood: Edinburgh 1885), p. 391.
73 I. C. Bradley, *O Love that wilt not let me go* (Collins/Fount, 1990), p. 75.
74 D. Macmillan, *The Life of George Matheson* (Hodder & Stoughton, 1910), p. 128.
75 Bradley, *op cit.*, pp. 96–7.
76 Matheson, *Can the Old Faith Live with the New?*, *op. cit.*, p. 9.
77 *Ibid.*, pp. 249–50.
78 C. Birch and J. Cobb, *The Liberation of Life. From the Cell to the Community* (Cambridge, 1981), pp. 120–1.
79 G. Matheson, *Can the Old Faith Live with the New?*, *op. cit.*, p. 244.
80 *Ibid.*, pp. 244–5.
81 *Ibid.*, pp. 250–1.
82 *Ibid.*, p. 385.
83 Bradley, *op cit.*, pp. 39–40.
84 *Ibid.*, p. 40.
85 *Ibid.*, p. 98.
86 *Ibid.*, p. 172.
87 D. H. S. Nicholson (ed.), *The Oxford Book of Mystical Verse* (Oxford: Oxford University Press, 1917), p. 538.
88 P. Murray (ed.), *The Deer's Cry. A Treasury of Irish Religious Verse* (Four Courts Press: Dublin, 1986), p. 195.

89 Quoted in review of John Pollock's biography of Gordon by Alan Wilkinson in the *Church Times*, 14 January 1994, p. 12.

90 R. Kipling, 'God of our fathers, known of old', verse 2.

91 B. F. Westcott, *Lessons from Work* (Macmillan, 1901), pp. 281, 381.

92 *Ibid.*, p. 395.

93 'The Children's Song' from R. Kipling, *Puck of Pook's Hill* (Macmillan, 1917 edn), p. 305.

94 'For all we have and are', verse 4, in *Rudyard Kipling's Verse 1885–1918* (Hodder & Stoughton, n.d.), p. 37.

95 A. Wilkinson, *The Church of England and the First World War* (SPCK, 1978), p. 29.

96 *Ibid.*, p. 19.

97 *Ibid.*, p. 188.

98 *Ibid.*, p. 189.

99 The frequent recourse to sacrificial imagery among those involved in the 1916 rising is the subject of an interesting article by Sheridan Gilley, 'Pearse's sacrifice: Christ and Cuchulain crucified and risen in the Easter Rising, 1916' in S. W. Sykes (ed.), *Sacrifice and Redemption* (Cambridge, 1991), pp. 219–34.

100 A. Wilkinson, *op. cit.*, p. 258.

101 L. Macdonald, *1914–1918. Voices and Images of the Great War* (Penguin, 1991), p. 111.

102 A. Wilkinson, *op. cit.*, p. 190.

103 *Ibid.*, p. 138.

104 *Ibid.*, p. 190.

105 *Ibid.*, p. 188.

106 *Ibid.*, p. 191.

107 I. Bradley, *The Penguin Book of Hymns* (Viking, 1989), p. 192.

108 *Ibid.*, p. 193.

109 H. Montefiore, 'The uses of patriotism', *Church Times*, 17 June 1994.

7 **Sharing in God's suffering: sacrificial theology in the twentieth century**

1 *Daily Mirror*, 20 November 1918.

2 A. Wilkinson, *The Church of England and the First World War*, *op. cit.*, p. 172.

3 Moltmann, *The Trinity and the Kingdom of God*, *op. cit.*, pp. 31–4.

4 Quoted in W. Temple, *Readings in St John's Gospel* (Macmillan, 1959), p. 385.

5 L. W. Grensted, *A Short History of the Doctrine of Atonement* (Manchester, 1920), p. 189.

6 I. U. Dalferth, 'Christ died for us: reflections on the sacrificial language of salvation' in Sykes (ed.), *Sacrifice and Redemption*, *op. cit.*, p. 301.

7 Hicks, *The Fullness of Sacrifice*, *op. cit.*, pp. 337–8.

8 *Ibid.*, p. 348.

9 *Ibid.*, p. 350.

10 Berdiaev, *Freedom and the Spirit*, *op. cit.*, p. 177.

11 W. Temple, *Christus Veritas* (Macmillan, 1924), pp. 203–6, 272–3.

12 *Ibid.*, p. 270.

13 *Ibid.*, p. 234.

14 *Ibid.*, p. 221.

15 *Ibid.*, pp. 238–9.

16 W. Temple, *Thoughts in War-Time* (Macmillan, 1940), pp. 26–7.

17 The subject of William Temple's theology of sacrifice and the transformation which it underwent is dealt with admirably in Alan Suggate's essay, 'The concept of sacrifice in Anglican social ethics', in Sykes (ed.), *Sacrifice and Redemption, op. cit.*, pp. 235–46. I have made considerable use of this essay in my own remarks on the subject.

18 E. Powell, *Reflections of a Statesman* (Bellew Publishing, 1991), pp. 19, 52.

19 D. Bonhoeffer, *Letters and Papers from Prison* (SCM, 1967), p. 197.

20 *Ibid.*, p. 196.

21 *Ibid.*, p. 198.

22 *Ibid.*, pp. 201–2.

23 J. A. Phillips, *The Form of Christ in the World. A Study of Bonhoeffer's Christology* (Collins, 1967), pp. 239–40.

24 D. T. McFarland, *Simone Weil* (Frederick Ungar, New York, 1983), p. 136.

25 Quoted in A. L. Loades, 'Eucharistic Sacrifice and Simone Weil' in Sykes (ed.), *Sacrifice and Redemption, op. cit.*, pp. 248, 258.

26 R. Niebuhr, *The Nature and Destiny of Man* (Nisbet & Co., 1943), p. 116.

27 D. Baillie, *God was in Christ* (Faber, 1948), p. 198.

28 U. Simon, *A Theology of Auschwitz* (SPCK, 1967), pp. 83–4.

29 *Ibid.*, p. 88.

30 *Ibid.*, p. 86.

31 J. G. Williams, *The Bible, Violence and the Sacred* (Harper, San Francisco, 1992), p. 211.

32 Review of *A Study of History* in *The Times Literary Supplement*, 22 October 1954.

33 A Toynbee, *Experiences* (Oxford, 1969), p. 135.

34 J. Moltmann, *The Future of Creation* (SCM, 1979), p. 72.

35 J. Moltmann, *The Trinity and the Kingdom of God, op. cit.*, p.32.

36 *Ibid.*, p. 119.

37 J. Moltmann, *The Way of Jesus Christ* (SCM, 1990), p. 175.

38 J. Sobrino, *Christology at the Crossroads: A Latin American Approach* (SCM, 1978), p. 227.

39 K. Rahner, *Foundations of the Christian Faith* (Darton, Longman & Todd, 1978), p. 217.

40 J. V. Taylor, *The Christlike God* (SCM, 1993), p. 123.

41 Choruses from 'The Rock', VI, in *The Complete Poems and Plays of T. S. Eliot* (Faber, 1969), p. 159.

42 The Dry Salvages, V, in *ibid.*, pp. 189–90.

43 Euros Bowen's poems can be found in Welsh and English in *Euros Bowen: Priest-Poet* edited by Cynthia and Saunders Davies (Church in Wales Publications, Penarth, 1993). Alan Llwyd's 'Rebirth' is in *A*

Welsh Pilgrim's Manual edited by Brendan O'Malley (Gomer, Llandysul, 1989), p. 132.

44 'Sea Cycle' in *Leth-Cheud Bliadhna (Contemporary Poems in Gaelic and English)* (Gairm, Glasgow, 1978), p. 26.

45 'Carol' in *The Deer's Cry* edited by Patrick Murray (Four Courts Press, Dublin, 1986), p. 254.

46 'The sun at midnight rising red' in *ibid.*, p. 195.

47 G. Mackay Brown, *Magnus* (Hogarth Press, 1973), p. 166.

48 *Ibid.*, pp. 168–70.

49 *Ibid.*, p. 170.

8 Unselfish genes and suicidal cells: towards a new natural theology of sacrifice

1 L. Wolpert, 'Religious thinking does not produce knowledge', *The Times*, 10 April 1993, p. 14.

2 W. Paley, *Natural Theology, or Evidence of the Existence and Attributes of the Deity* (R. Faulder, 1802), p. 490.

3 J. Bowker, *Problems of Suffering in the Religions of the World* (Cambridge, 1975), p. 200.

4 R. Dawkins, *The Selfish Gene* (new edn, Oxford University Press: Oxford, 1989), p. 7.

5 V. C. Wynne-Edwards, *Evolution through Group Selection* (Blackwell Scientific Publications: Oxford, 1986), p. ix.

6 *Ibid.*, p. ix.

7 F. Lake, *The Kingdom of the Octopus* (Jarrolds, 1957), p. 116.

8 Dawkins, *op. cit.*, p. 7.

9 *Ibid.*, p. 111.

10 *Ibid.*, p. 7.

11 *Ibid.*, p. 66.

12 See, for example, Paul Davies and John Gribbin, *The Matter Myth* (Penguin, 1992), especially pp. 6–7.

13 P. Slater (ed.), *Collins Encyclopaedia of Animal Behaviour* (Collins, 1986), p. 112.

14 C. J. Barnard, *Animal Behaviour: Ecology and Evolution* (Croom Helm, 1983), p. 120.

15 E. J. Ambrose, *The Mirror of Creation* (Scottish Academic Press, Edinburgh, 1990), p. 216.

16 D. McFarland (ed.), *The Oxford Companion to Animal Behaviour* (Oxford University Press: Oxford, 1981), p. 15.

17 G. Matheson, *Can the Old Faith Live with the New?*, *op. cit.*, p. 244.

18 Dawkins, *op. cit.*, p. 60.

19 Ruth McKernan, 'Death is our best friend for life', in *The Independent*, 17 May 1993.

20 V. Wynne-Edwards, 'A Rationale for group selection' in *The Journal of Theoretical Biology*, Vol. 162, No. 1, 7 May 1993, p. 1.

21 BBC 2 Horizon programme, 'Death Wish'.

22 Quoted in C. F. Evans, *Resurrection and the New Testament* (SCM, 1970), p. 169.
23 W. Kunneth, *The Theology of the Resurrection* (Scm, 1965), p. 154.
24 J. Moses, *The Sacrifice of God, op. cit.*, p. 168.
25 A. Peacocke, unpublished paper on 'Science and the theology of creation', *op. cit.*, p. 12.
26 J. Bowker, *Problems of Suffering in the Religions of the World* (Cambridge, 1975), p. 201.

9 Sin, suffering and salvation

1 N. Berdiaev, *Freedom and the Spirit, op. cit.*, p. 158.
2 F. D. Maurice, *The Doctrine of Sacrifice, op. cit.*, p. 119.
3 G. Kendrick, 'Lord, the light of your love is shining'.
4 Prayer of Reinhold Neibuhr.
5 Prayer of Ignatius Loyola.
6 Prayer attributed to St Francis of Assisi.
7 E. Norman, 'Cost of humility', meditation in *The Daily Telegraph*, 2 July 1994.
8 Quoted in Sykes (ed.), *Sacrifice and Redemption, op. cit.*, p. 212.
9 Quoted in Young, *The Use of Sacrificial Ideas in Greek Christian Writers from the New Testament to John Chrysostom, op. cit.*, p. 67.
10 Quoted in J. Bowker, *Problems of Suffering in Religion of the World* (Cambridge, 1975), p. 37.
11 S. Cassidy, *Sharing the Darkness: the Spirituality of Caring* (Darton, Longman & Todd, 1988), p. 163.
12 J. V. Taylor, *The Christlike God* (SCM, 1993), p. 196.
13 *Ibid.*, p. 205.
14 Quoted in A. Wylie, 'One man's faith put charity above money', *The Independent*, 8 August 1992, p. 13.
15 D. Robinson, 'Dying young', *The Scotsman Weekend*, 26 September 1992, p. 14.
16 *The Sunday Telegraph*, Review Section, 19 September 1993, p. 5.
17 R. Llewellyn, *Prayer and Contemplation* (SLG Press, Fairacres: Oxford, 1980), p. 18.
18 D. Young, *F. D. Maurice and Unitarianism* (Oxford University Press: Oxford, 1992), p. 180.
19 W. H. Vanstone, *The Stature of Waiting* (Darton, Longman & Todd, 1982), p. 105.
20 *Ibid.*, p. 115.
21 Quoted in A. Gnanadason, *No Longer a Secret: The Church and Violence Against Women, op. cit.*, p. 51.
22 *Ibid.*, p. 51.
23 O. Quick, *Doctrine of the Creed* (Nisbet & Co., 1937), p. 197.
24 C. Westermann, *Praise and Lament in the Psalms* (T. & T. Clark: Edinburgh, 1981), p. 275.
25 J. Moltmann, *The Crucified God, op. cit.*, p. 252.
26 P. Fiddes, *Past Event and Present Salvation, op. cit.*, p. 208.

27 T. Witlivet, *A Place in the Sun* (SCM, 1985), p. 153.

28 C. S. Song, *The Tears of Lady Meng* (World Council of Churches, Geneva, 1981), pp. 40, 43.

29 This is the translation of the *Stabat Mater* which appears in the *New English Hymnal* (Oxford, 1986). It is by various hands.

30 'Drop, drop, slow tears' by Phineas Fletcher (1582–1650).

31 This is the version of 'O come and mourn with me awhile' which appears in the third edition of the *Church Hymnary* (Oxford University Press: Oxford, 1973). It is an altered version of the original by F. W. Faber.

32 I owe this reference to a talk given by Fr Gilbert Màrkus in a day conference on Celtic Christianity at New College, Edinburgh, in November 1993.

33 T. Merton, *The Wisdom of the Desert* (Sheldon Press, 1974), p. 18.

34 Fiddes, *op. cit.*, p. 212.

35 J. V. Taylor, *A Matter of Life and Death* (SCM, 1986), p. 67.

36 T. Merton, The New Man (Burns & Oates, 1962), pp. 2–3.

37 W. H. Draper's translation of St Francis' *Canticle of the Sun* as found in *Hymns Ancient and Modern Revised* (Hymns Ancient and Modern, Norwich, 1984).

38 Quick, *op. cit.*, p. 213.

39 Introit written by the author for St Leonard's Church, St Andrews.

10 Making the sacrifice complete

1 R. Jeffery, *Anima Christi: Reflections on Praying with Christ* (Darton, Longman & Todd, 1994), p. 59.

2 *The Scotsman*, 26 August 1994.

3 Sykes, 'Outline of a theology of sacrifice' in Sykes (ed.), *Sacrifice and Redemption, op. cit.*, p. 282.

4 Quoted in A. M. Allchin, *The Dynamic of Tradition* (Darton, Longman & Todd, 1981), p. 67.

5 A. M. Allchin, *Praise Above All: Discovering the Welsh Tradition* (University of Wales Press, Cardiff, 1991), p. 6.

6 Gunton, *The Actuality of Atonement, op. cit.*, pp. 200–1.

7 D. Forrester, *Encounter with God* (T. & T. Clark, Edinburgh, 1983), p. 5.

8 *A Shorter Alternative Service Book* (Central Board of Finance of the Church of England, 1980), pp. 132, 134, 138.

9 *Book of Common Order of the Church of Scotland* (St Andrew Press: Edinburgh, 1994), pp. 130, 152.

10 *The Holy Eucharist in Modern Language* (Church in Wales Publications, 1994), p. 8.

11 Quoted in N. Blount, *The Eucharist – Not a Static Concept* (Nicol Blount, Filton, Bristol, 1992), p. 42.

12 Gunton, *op. cit.*, p. 196.

13 Blount, *op. cit.*, p. 10.

14 *Ibid.*, p. 11.

15 *Ibid.*, p. 17.
16 *Ibid.*, pp. 28–9.
17 *A Shorter Alternative Service Book*, pp. 132, 137, 140.
18 Anglican and Roman Catholic International Commission, *The Three Agreed Statements* (CTS & SPCK, 1978), p. 10.
19 Quoted in K. Stevenson, 'Eucharistic sacrifice – an insoluble liturgical problem?', *Scottish Journal of Theology* Vol. 42, No. 4 (1989), p. 479.
20 Hicks, *The Fullness of Sacrifice, op. cit.*, p. 350.
21 G. Herbert, 'Providence II', quoted in I. C. Bradley, *God is Green* (Darton, Longman & Todd, 1990), p. 103.
22 Translation by Brendan Kennelly. Quoted in I. C. Bradley, *The Celtic Way* (Darton, Longman & Todd, 1993), p. 57.
23 C. Wesley, 'Victim Divine, thy grace we claim' (verse 5) quoted in H. A. Hodges & A. M. Allchin, *A Rapture of Praise: Hymns of John and Charles Wesley* (Hodder & Stoughton, 1966), p. 151.
24 H. Bonar, 'Here, O my Lord, I see thee face to face' in *The Church Hymnary*' (3rd edn, Oxford, 1973), No. 573.
25 C. Gore, *The Body of Christ* (John Murray, 1901), p. 252.
26 C. Wesley, 'See where our great High-Priest' (verse 2), quoted in *A Rapture of Praise*, p. 153.
27 Professor Nikolai Arseniev quoted in D. Baillie, *God was in Christ* (Faber, 1961), pp. 196–7.
28 C. Wesley, 'Thou lamb that sufferedst on the tree' (verses 1 and 4), quoted in *A Rapture of Praise*, pp. 151–2.
29 T. Torrance, Obituary of Professor Donald Mackinnon, *Church Times*, 18 March 1994.
30 *Book of Common Order*, pp. 134, 162.
31 Fiddes, *Past Event and Present Salvation, op. cit.*, p. 78.
32 F. D. Maurice, *The Epistle to the Hebrews* (Macmillan, Cambridge, 1846), pp. 95–6.
33 *A Shorter ASB*, p. 145; *The Holy Eucharist in Modern Language*, p. 10.
34 *The Scottish Liturgy* (Representative Council of the Scottish Episcopal Church, Edinburgh, 1982), pp. 8–9.
35 *Book of Common Order*, p. 134.
36 Quoted in Stevenson, *art. cit.*, p. 476.
37 Life Style Movement pamphlet produced in December 1984.
38 S. Chalke, 'Jesus the Leader – Sacrificial Love' in *Alpha*, December 1993, p. 32.
39 *Ibid.*
40 *Ibid.*
41 See, for example, Janet Daley's column in *The Times* on 11 November 1993 quoted on p. 22, Clifford Longley's 'Sacred and Profane' columns in *The Daily Telegraph* on 22 April, 16 September 1994 and Joyce McMillan's 'Commentary' in *Scotland on Sunday* on 13 February, 25 September 1994.
42 Quoted in *Theology in Green*, No. 3, July 1992, p. 25.
43 J. Watson, 'City planners who do not practise what they preach', *Scotland on Sunday*, 25 September 1994, p. 8.

44   Maurice, 'Sermons preached in Lincoln's Inn Chapel', *op. cit.*, Vol. 1, p. 251.

45   Obituary of Dom Bede Griffiths by David Lorimer, *Church Times*, 28 May 1993, p. 6.

46   A. Torrance, 'The self-relation, narcissism and the gospel of grace' in *Scottish Journal of Theology*, Vol. 40, No. 4 (1987), p. 482.

47   *Time* magazine, 7 December 1987, quoted in J. Drane, *What is the New Age Saying to the Church?* (Marshall Pickering, 1991), p. 64.

48   J. Moltmann, *The Way of Jesus Christ* (SCM, 1990), p. 151.

49   E. Jungel, *Gott als Geheimnis der Welt* (Tubingen, 1977), p. 437.

50   R. Williams, *The Wound of Knowledge* (Darton, Longman & Todd, 1979), p. 12.

51   Chalke, *art. cit.*, p. 33.

52   C. S. Song, *Third Eye Theology* (Lutterworth Press, 1980), p. 67.

53   Chalke, *art. cit.*, p. 32.

54   J. Houston, 'Living in awe', *Alpha*, December 1993, p. 25.

55   A Toynbee, *Experiences* (Oxford, 1969), p. 135.

56   B. Appleyard, 'Science and spirit', *The Times Saturday Review*, 25 April 1992, pp. 12–14.

57   *Bhagavad Gita*, 3.10–11; 15–16. The translation is that of Juan Mascaro (Penguin, 1962), p. 57.

58   *Ibid.*, 18.5–6 (Penguin edn, p. 115).

59   *Ibid.*, 18.24 (Penguin edn, p. 117).

60   J. Keble, 'New every morning is the love' (verse 3).

61   Young, *The Use of Sacrificial Ideas in Greek Christian Writers from the New Testament to St John Chrysostom*, *op. cit.*, p. 299.

62   V. S. S. Coles, 'Almighty Father, Lord most High' (verse 3).

63   Moses, *The Sacrifice of God*, *op. cit.*, p. 179.

64   C. Wesley, 'O thou who camest from above' (verse 4 as it originally appeared in *Short Hymns on Selected Passages of Scripture*, published in 1762).

65   John Wesley's revision of 'O thou who camest from above' as it appeared in the 1782 edition of the Methodist Hymn Book.

Index